VENICE AND ITS ART

Venice; Panorama from San Giorgio

VENICE AND ITS ART

H. H. POWERS, Ph.D.

PRESIDENT BUREAU OF UNIVERSITY TRAVEL

New York
THE MACMILLAN COMPANY
1930

GARDEN CITY PRESS, INC.
Newton, Mass., U.S.A.

PREFACE

The present work is in a sense the continuation of an undertaking which began with the publication of the Art of Florence in 1912. It was intended from the beginning to cover briefly the art of the Italian Renaissance in two volumes, a plan now tardily realized after many and prolonged interruptions. The present volume differs from its predecessor in that more attention is given to the city itself, to its history as a key to the understanding of its art and to its own growth and physical transformation as a work of art in itself. This is in line with the growing feeling of the writer that art is an expression of the spiritual and cultural life of a people and that their history is the key to its interpretation.

The purpose of the book will be clear to those who are familiar with the earlier volume or with the author's work in the galleries of Europe. The book is not a record of personal research. No archives have been ransacked, no records discovered, no manuscripts edited or read. Information regarding the works here discussed is to be found in any good library. Nor has any attempt been made to make the list of works inclusive or to give all known facts regarding them. The works considered have been chosen as being representative of the artists in question and illustrative of the characteristics discussed.

The problem has been one of interpretation and presentation. We have Venice and the treasures of her great art. What is their significance to one who is interested, not in painting, but in art, in humanity, in human culture and civilization.

Nearly forty years in the art galleries of Europe spent in the inspiring task of assisting intelligent inquirers to answer these questions is the author's preparation for this work. Libraries have made but a secondary contribution, the studio none at all. But through prolonged opportunity acquaintance has seemed to ripen into something of understanding and the message of the masters has in some small part sounded clear. It is this message that he attempts to present in the following pages.

CONTENTS

Part I. Venice

Part II. Venetian Art

LIST OF ILLUSTRATIONS

PART I
VENICE

CHAPTER I

A glance at the map of Europe gives the impression that Italy is a natural unity. This impression is enhanced by the fact that just now the peninsula is printed in a single color which expresses the political accident of our time. Surrounded by the sea on all sides but one and fenced in on that side by a huge barrier, it seems predestined to a separate and unit existence. Such a unity it has at last attained but this unity is recent and probably transient. Politically and culturally Italy has usually been either divided or included in a larger whole. The tendency has always been to develop local centers of great individuality and persistence, and as these have acquired power to expand they have more often found their affinity and their opportunity outside of Italy than within it. Pisa, Genoa and Venice are examples of Empires ruled from Italy yet not essentially Italian. Rome indeed united the peninsula under her sway, but only because she established a world dominion in which Italy was included. But inclusion did not mean unity or community of feeling. It is doubtful whether the Cisalpine Gauls ever thought of themselves as a part of Italy or forgot that they were a part of greater Gaul. Roman rule, it is true, gave to these parts of Italy a common language and a degree of common culture. But these were given also to France and Spain. Neither in the one case nor in the other were the barriers which divided these peoples overcome or a permanent unity effected. With the dissolution of the imperial power

1

Italy was promptly resolved into the original component parts which went their separate ways, developing
distinct and even contrasted cultures and pursuing their
several aims with a ruthlessness unsoftened by a millen-
nium of imperial union. Gradually all semblance of
uniformity disappears. Different political systems, different codes of law, different economic interests, and different culture ideals differentiate more and more these
one-time members of a common family. This is the
more remarkable when we recall that the unifying administration of Rome had endured for a thousand years
to be followed through all the later centuries by the
unifying pressure of the all powerful Roman Church.

The apparent unity of Italy is an illusion. Italy is
neither so united in herself nor so separated from her
neighbors as the map seems to indicate. The peninsula
is divided by barriers, passable, to be sure, and that increasingly as civilization has become more resourceful,
but always an obstacle to communication and trade. It
is physically possible to cross the Apennines but for
the most part it is not economically practicable. It
formerly cost less to ship goods across the Mediterranean
than across the Apennines. Hence the peoples thus
separated had few dealings with each other and saw
each other but seldom. Differences were encouraged
and sympathies stifled by this isolation.

On the other hand the sea is not a barrier between
civilized peoples unless they will it and make it so. Of
all forms of transport the sea affords the easiest and the
cheapest. Hence peoples that have access to the sea
find their neighbors over-seas and their enemies over the
mountains behind them. They may not love either the
one or the other but it is the former that they will know,
it is from them that they will learn, and it is their culture
that they will appropriate and blend with their own.

If therefore our map is to express the significant facts we must redraw it in a very extraordinary and bizarre fashion. The coast line, so sharply defined and so emphasized by the contrast of Italian color with the ocean's blue, we must pretty much efface even at the risk that the colors will "run" and the blue be tinted by the hue of the adjacent terra firma. On the other hand the mountains and other barriers that nature has interposed between peoples must be drawn in with heavy lines to indicate their obstruction to intercourse between them. With our map thus reconstructed in imagination we shall be better able to understand the stubborn persistence of these separate units which have traveled such different ways toward power and glory.

It is with one of these units and indeed with the most distinctive and considerable of them that we now have to deal. Seeking its location upon the map we are struck by the mighty mountain wall which, starting in the neighborhood of Vienna, sweeps westward in a broadening mass for some five hundred miles, then suddenly turns southward and again swerves abruptly to the east just in time to avoid falling into the sea at Genoa, and under the name of the Apennines meanders in an irregular southeasterly course back to the Adriatic. Doubling thus back upon itself it encloses a vast flatiron shaped plain which was once a bay or arm of the sea. The rainfall upon these mountains on either side, once far heavier than now, is the source of a dozen or more rivers which, even in these tamer geologic days, in the season of rains and melting snows are raging torrents which tear out bridges and are with difficulty kept within the huge levees that have been built in recent centuries to restrain their violence. Thus confined, these active builders of the plain carry their burden of gravel and silt over ever lengthening courses into the sea. There the current ceases and the silt is dropped to be distributed by the prevailing winds and sea currents in long reefs or dunes along the coast.

Thus the bridging of the Adriatic goes on, slowly, it may seem, as we are wont to measure things, but rapidly as compared with like processes elsewhere. Ravenna, a seaport in the days of Augustus, is now six miles inland; Adria, another ancient seaport, is now nearly fourteen miles inland. On an average the coastline is advancing about three miles in a thousand years or about fifteen feet a year. Were the progress a systematic and orderly one the change in a lifetime would be distinctly visible.

But the process is anything but systematic and orderly. Coastlines remain fixed for decades while broad areas of sea are slowly growing shallower and changing from lagoon to marsh. The rivers obstruct their own channels and cut new ones through the mud they have deposited. They lay out reclamation projects, too, which seem too ambitious and build new barriers against the sea without cleaning up their work behind. Lagoons and mud flats and marshes remain as witnesses to their unfinished work. Such marshes are found around Milan and even out as far as Turin. In the east where the work is still in progress, immense areas of lagoon or shallow water alternating with mud flats at low tide constitute a sort of no-man's-land, something that is not quite either land or sea. Gradually little clumps of grass or other vegetation appear on the unsightly mud and their mingled growth and gathered dust slowly raise them above the few inches of tidal water and thus the amphibious ooze gives birth to land. All this may be observed, if not in the immediate vicinity of Venice where all has been toilsomely artificialized, at least in the unfettered lagoons to the north and to the south.

As has been noted, however, the sea is more or less on

the defensive against the action of the rivers. The prevailing winds from the east beat back the silt and the sea current that moves slowly southward along the western shore strings it out in long sandy barriers, natural breakwaters that stretch almost unbroken for fifty miles along the shore, the highest and driest land of all. Sheltered behind these lies the broad expanse of the lagoons, half marsh, half lake, sprinkled with low lying islands, small and large, and furrowed by devious river channels hidden beneath the shimmering surface. It was at once the safest and the most unattractive of all human habitations.

We have no record or relic of the earliest habitation in the lagoons. We know that the Veneti, a people who come from the other side of the Adriatic, inhabited the adjacent mainland where they maintained themselves against the attacks of the invading Gauls and other enemies until all fell under the sway of Rome and became Romans in due course like the other Italian peoples. When the Pax Romana was fully established and the gateways of the north were held by the imperial legions northern Italy awoke to new life and great cities sprang up like magic almost rivaling in wealth and culture the great capital itself. Such were Mediolanum, the modern Milan, Bononia (Bologna) and Verona. But the greatest and richest of all was Patavium (Padua) which lay within the territory of the Veneti. This was the northern Rome.

So long as these conditions lasted there was little temptation to settle on the mud flats of the lagoon. Yet it is probable that even then they were inhabited by a harmless fisher folk whose primitive life was scarce touched by the culture of the mainland and who found in the security of the lagoons and the absence of the tax gatherer a compensation for their isolation.

Between them and the city dwellers of Patavium the gulf must have been wide and deep. Primitive savagery still exists within a day's march of our modern cities. How much more so in this earlier day and guarded by the sheltering lagoon.

But the Pax Romana failed from off the earth. The barbarian broke the cordon of the legions and his hosts poured through the opened gateways upon devoted Italy to settle his long score with regnant civilization. The great cities of the north lay helpless in his path. The inhabitants fled before the storm to whatever refuge seemed to promise safety. To the cities of the eastern plain the choice could not be doubtful. The lagoon with its primitive savagery had little to tempt the city dweller but it offered in fullest measure the one thing needful. Armies might march and countermarch, storming the walled cities and even penetrating the mountain fastnesses but no army could cross this morass. The triremes and the galleys, too, must stop short of these deceptive shallows where even a skiff would ground. Only to those who knew the devious and submerged channels kept fitfully open by the capricious rivers were these island homes accessible.

Hence this sudden pilgrimage of polished urbanites from the great eastern cities to the scattered fisher settlements of the lagoon. It is a subject that appeals to the imagination. What were the sentiments of these humble folk toward their unbidden guests? What of the demand upon the accommodations of their mud huts? Upon the resources of their commissariat? What luck did the city lawyer or merchant have as he tried his hand at deep sea fishing or strove to rear a mud dwelling for himself and pen in its uncertain ground with stakes and twisted osiers? What of the pampered girl accustomed to her perfumed bath and the services of coiffeur and dressing maid and who now had to shift for herself and share menial duties and exchange her luxurious couch for a resting place on the hard earth floor? It is needless to inquire about the aged, the infirm, the woman with child. Not a few, there must have been, who had occasion to envy those who fell by the sword.

And to all this inevitable misery was added the equally inevitable friction between the refugees and their unwilling hosts, a friction which can be traced for centuries in the history of the great community which had this inauspicious beginning. Whatever may have been the attitude of the lagoon dwellers at the outset toward these refugees who were fleeing from imminent destruction they must speedily have found them a burden. Though coming as suppliants they were Romans accustomed to command and not too considerate of those whose interests conflicted with their own. If there were cases where the alternative to starvation was forcible appropriation we can hardly doubt as to their choice. These early years have left no record, but when somewhat later the curtain is lifted there is an unmistakable rift between patrician and plebeian in which we can hardly fail to recognize these two elements so unwillingly united upon the islands of the lagoons.

It is important that we should impress upon our minds both the fact and the character of this forced migration. It was little enough that these refugees carried with them. Slaves were scattered and chattels abandoned and jewels lost. But whatever they took or left they were Romans and they carried with them the spirit and the gathered wisdom of Rome to the founding of a new empire. We shall hardly account for the great things that follow unless we bear in mind this great beginning. It is no accident that Venice was modern while the rest of the world was mediæval, that she was a republic while her

neighbors were despotisms, that she developed central
authority while other nations dragged out the helpless
existence of feudalism. Venice was founded by Romans
while they were founded by Vandals and Lombards and
Goths. Though not a little beholden to Roman tradition, the nations that struggled into existence under
barbarian leadership had to pass through an apprenticeship which Venice was spared. In Venice alone the
continuity of Roman development, though profoundly
modified by peculiar conditions, was unbroken. Was
Venice ever mediæval?

The first settlements in the lagoons were not permanent. The refugees at first sought temporary shelter
expecting to return to their homes when the barbarian
withdrew, as in the earlier instances he did. Then for
the most part the refugees returned, though doubtless
some remained from necessity or choice. Then there
was a new invasion and a new exodus, doubtless with
additions to the permanent colony of the lagoons and
some amelioration of conditions. The barbarians in
their turn were making permanent contributions to the
population of the mainland and lessening by so much
the temptation of the refugees to return. Finally after
more than a century of this intermittent misery came a
last invasion more barbarous and more permanent than
before, and the refugees fled to the lagoons to remain.

It is a curious fact that in all these migrations the
cities of the mainland maintained their identity. There
was no indiscriminate mingling in the lagoons nor did
the colonists unite in a single settlement. In general
each city chose its own island refuge where it maintained
the traditions as well as the jealousies of the mainland.
As the cities revived under barbarian rule the island
colonies not infrequently based claims of their own on
former jurisdictions or privileges of their parent cities.

All in all, occasions of discord were plentiful and the strong rule of Rome, if potentially present, was at first in abeyance. For a time they sought control in a council representing the twelve principal settlements by as many councillors. This merely voiced the discords without suppressing them and at last resort was had to a single head, the Doge, who for the next eleven hundred years embodied or symbolized the power of a united state.

But this union did not at once result in a single consolidated community. The Venice that we know was not the state; it was not even its capital nor did it bear its name. It was a minor member of the twelve scattered communities that it was later to dominate and ultimately to absorb. A visit to Torcello, an island now given over to market gardens but which once had a population of twenty thousand as its splendid deserted church attests, is an instructive reminder to the traveler of what has taken place in the lagoons. In the factional struggle between patricians and plebeians already referred to, each party had its stronghold in one of the twelve settlements. Since neither party would tolerate the possession of the seat of government by the other a neutral settlement was chosen, Malamocco, out on the sandy breakwater where one of the rivers, putting through, offered a convenient entrance for shipping. And here our Venice might have grown up with the waves of the blue Adriatic dashing against its seawalls if Charlemagne had not sought to add the lagoons to his Italian dominions. Warned of an impending sea attack the government and its valuables were removed from the outlying and exposed Malamocco to the group of islands known as Rivo Alto, "high bank," (later, Rialto) which, though less convenient and less favored than others, could not be attacked either by land or sea.

Between these low lying islands two rivers wended their sluggish way in shallow channels later to be lined with warehouses and palaces. At last were laid the foundations of Venice.

The security of Venice was soon doubly assured by an acquisition of priceless importance which it is difficult for us to appreciate. Some Venetian merchants who happened to be in Alexandria when the Moslems were demolishing the church in which rested the bones of Saint Mark appropriated the precious relics and bore them in triumph to Venice where they were received with indescribable rejoicing and a new church built to receive them. The future of Venice was now assured. It is true that these relics were acquired by methods to which a really ethical evangelist might be expected to take exception. They were taken without the consent of their owners to whom they were as sacred as to the Christians. Moreover relics of this kind were objects of commerce in which Venetians dealt extensively then and later, and the bones of an evangelist were rated with crown jewels. But the theft of Christian relics from Moslem owners would hardly have troubled a mediæval conscience. The theft was successfully perpetrated and the relics were smuggled out packed in pork which the vigilant Moslem officials refused to investigate. These antecedents in no way lessened the efficacy of the relics to the men of that time. Relics, it would seem, have no choice but to exert their potency in favor of those who possess them, no matter how acquired. As this conviction was entertained both by possessors and would-be marauders, the relics did in fact protect the Venetians. A truly pious thief — and most thieves were of this class — would think twice before molesting aught that had been committed to the protection of Saint Mark. How it was that stolen relics should protect those who stole them from the depredations of other thieves is one of those gratuitous inquiries which the modern mind injects to its own embarrassment into the placid mentality of a vanished age.

Meanwhile other momentous things had been happening with results of the utmost importance which we are quite too much inclined to take for granted. We have seen that the different lagoon settlements remembered their parent cities and were inclined to assert their claims on occasion. In like manner these cities remembered them and asserted their claims to them even after their own character had quite changed. Patavium in particular, now a Lombard capital, claimed as of ancient right, jurisdiction over the valley of the Brenta to its mouth, a claim anciently reasonable and valid. But the Brenta was one of the rivers which flowed in submerged channel between the islands of Rivo Alto. Hence Patavium claimed jurisdiction over Venice, and the patricians who, it will be remembered, represented the Roman refugees, at first favored this claim, for as yet the struggling community had no thought of being other than a part of that great Roman world which it was the wish of all to restore and maintain. But Patavium and all else on the mainland had ceased to be Roman. A barbarian sat on the throne of Caesar and although he might use the old insignia the change was patent to all. Meanwhile another power with clearer title claimed allegiance in the name of Rome. The Eastern Empire, still intact and flourishing, claimed the Roman heritage and sought to wrest Italy from the barbarian. The brief result of this effort was the Exarchate of Ravenna where for a few decades the exotic art of the east maintained a splendid oasis in the midst of the barbarian desert.

In this enterprise the Eastern Empire sought and

obtained the aid of Venice and laid claim to her allegiance. And since the Patricians favored the claims of
the mainland, the Plebeians favored the claims of Constantinople and they won. There is reason to suspect,
however, that the Venetians were already beginning to
entertain the heretical idea of independence. It may
seem strange to speak of this as heretical. It is, as we
all know, the orthodoxy of our day. It is the almost
universal assumption of modern thought that all human
aggregates which show a certain distinctness, territorial,
racial, or what not, "are, and of right ought to be, free
and independent states." Many facts, to be sure, mili-
tate against this assumption. The existing world lends
itself but poorly to division into independent states. No
existing state is ideally constituted for independent existence and no theoretical division would satisfy even its
author. Moreover when we have completed our division
there is a demand for subdivision and so on indefinitely.
But no matter what the difficulties or how numerous our
failures, we never falter in our belief that in independence
and "self-determination" we are to find our much desired
harmony and welfare.

The men of an earlier day thought very differently.
Long accustomed to Roman rule they had found in it
all the peace and prosperity they knew. The basic assumption underlying all thought was that only world
rule could bring world peace. Nay, more. That world
rule, however inoperative in their day, existed still.
It might be in abeyance but it could not perish. Somewhere was the crown and purple of Caesar and somewhere was one who was entitled to wear them. When
the Pope crowned Charlemagne Emperor of the Holy
Roman Empire he was merely acting on this universal
idea. He was recalling the long absent Caesar and
restoring the longed for world dominion.

It was wholly natural, therefore, that dominion should be claimed in the name of Rome and that the Venetians should weigh rather than repudiate the claim. But from a very early date the modern and very different ideal was shaping itself in the Venetian mind. In acknowledging the sovereignty of Constantinople they were unconsciously influenced by the fact that Constantinople was weak and far away, and that her yoke would be a nominal one. Soon even this nominal allegiance was repudiated and a Venetian envoy could tell the emperor to his face: — "God who is our help and protector has saved us that we might dwell upon these waters. This second Venice which we have raised in the lagoons is our mighty habitation; no power of emperor or prince can touch us." Here is no vision of a returning Caesar or a unifying world empire. There would seem to be equally no thought of world dominion from this stronghold in the lagoons. The conception is one of independence, of impregnable aloofness. It announces the policy which Venice was to maintain so triumphantly for a thousand years. Venice was the first modern state.

It is significant that this independence was maintained, not merely against the overshadowing tradition of the Roman imperial power but against the living reality of the powerful Roman church. It is true that the church nowhere quite succeeded in asserting the authority that it claimed over all Christian potentates and peoples. Revolts were numerous even in states which, like Florence, fully recognized papal authority. But in nearly all Christian lands down to the time of the protestant reformation the Pope was at least represented by a church organization of his own creation. Bishops, archbishops, and cardinals were of his appointment. As such they were ministers of his will which was not infrequently asserted in effectual intervention in their affairs.

Not so in Venice. Venice was not protestant or schismatic. She championed no heresy, no reform in church government or ecclesiastical morals. A Venetian Savonarola is unthinkable. Nor were the Venetians indifferent or lacking in respect for religion. As judged by the standards of the time they were patterns of regularity and zeal. But they were independent. The Patriarch of Grado, one of the original twelve settlements which had dropped into convenient insignificance, was this recognized religious head. The patriarchate was completely dependent upon Venice for its maintenance and was correspondingly subservient. The relation to the papacy was one of outward deference but never of subjection. When Venice joined with the crusaders, the commands of the papal legate were politely disregarded and he was told that he might accompany the expedition as a crusader but not as a papal legate. The Pope condemned the campaign step by step and then acquiesced in the result. He could do nothing else.

Most astonishing of all was the complete assertion of the civil authority over ecclesiastics and ecclesiastical property. The patriarch was elected by the Grand Council precisely like the Doge. The parish priests, amazing to relate, were elected by the inhabitants of the parish much as in New England in the early days, the choice being not always unto edification. Church property was taxed on the same terms as any other. Ecclesiastics and monks, even if of noble birth, were excluded from civil office. Clerical offenses against the civil law were tried in civil, not in ecclesiastical, courts. Those who know how long and bitter was the struggle in western Europe to establish these principles will realize the amazingly modern character of Venetian national organization.

With all her independence, however, Venice never

allowed herself to appear at variance with the Pope. Papal sanction was prized for decisions in religious matters but never purchased by concession. It was the Pope who finally removed the patriarchate from Grado to Venice, it is needless to ask at whose instance. A papal envoy was received with regal honors. If a cardinal, the Doge went to meet him in his gilded barge and lifted his cap when they met, an honor otherwise shown only to kings. But the envoy not infrequently went away empty handed. Honor in plenty but never authority.

We are tempted to ask how Venice became independent of this all embracing papal authority. The answer is that this authority was slowly established and extended during the course of centuries. The Bishop of Rome, whatever the validity of his claims, did not always and altogether exercise supreme authority over the church. Only gradually and by statecraft of various kinds did he bring other bishoprics, patriarchates, and the like under his sway. This sway was not established in the lagoons until long after it was generally recognized elsewhere. Thanks to the powerful backing of Venice the patriarchate of sleepy little Grado retained its independence until it was finally absorbed by its all powerful protector. This patriarchate, once conquered by the mainland patriarchate of Aquileia, Venice came swiftly to the rescue and inflicted upon the aggressor an enduring and humiliating retribution.

But Venice was not only independent of Rome. She was equally careful to maintain her independence of Grado. The utter impotence of Grado was its chief recommendation. During the earlier centuries there was distinct advantage in having the patriarch at a safe distance and with no backer, instead of having him in the city itself. Not till the fifteenth century when

Venice was at the zenith of her power and the patriarch had thoroughly learned his place was it deemed wise to transfer the see to Venice and then only to a humble church in a detached island portion of the city. Not one traveler in a thousand ever threads his way to remote San Pietro di Castello which for three hundred and fifty years was the cathedral of Venice.

Meanwhile the gorgeous Saint Mark's had the technically inferior status of a simple church. But in compensation Saint Mark's had the unique status of official church of the Republic. Its ministering personnel was appointed by the Doge. It was here and not in the humble, out of the way cathedral that the Venetians met in times of peril or of state ceremonial. It was the Doge and not the bishop who here addressed them. It was in this gorgeous shrine and not in San Pietro di Castello that reposed the bones of Saint Mark. Judge where was the real headship of the church in Venice.

It is worth recalling in this connection that the single Venetian who distinguished himself in the field of letters and learned controversy, Fra Paolo Sarpi, an ecclesiastic, won fame as a defender of the civil power against the claims of the church. His thesis was but the instinct of every Venetian, just as later it became that of the Englishman. The supremacy of the state over the religious establishment is a modern thesis and one not yet altogether established. To the Venetian it was an axiom. Once again Venice was the first modern state.

In still another important particular Venice stands out in sharp distinction from other European powers and in a measure anticipates by many centuries the results of their toilsome evolution. In Europe generally the break-up of the Roman Empire was followed by feudalism. This was in theory a hierarchy of despotisms, each supreme in its sphere but subject to the will of a superior.

In practice it meant a weak or nominal central authority with unequal and primitive administration in local units. A feudal state was inherently incapable of sustained policy or effective assertion. There is hardly a nation in Europe today so small or so weak that it could not put forth a more effective effort than all Europe was able to do during the Crusades.

Slowly these loose aggregates were transformed into despotisms by the strengthening of the central power and the suppression of local prerogatives. Then in turn these despotisms were converted into constitutional or popular governments by wresting prerogatives from the despot and bestowing them upon the people or a representative class. This is still in progress and the outcome is not yet altogether predictable.

The outstanding fact in connection with Venice is that she omitted that tedious thousand years of feudalism. As a city state it did not fit her circumstances. We have noted the bickerings of the original settlements not yet overshadowed by any one of their number, and the final resort to a Doge or single head as a cure for dissension. The Doge held office for life but he was elected by the people and could not transmit his authority to his son. Of course he tried to do so and for a time he nearly succeeded in making the office hereditary. This would have made Venice a despotism, anticipating thus the next normal stage of development.

But even this stage Venice managed to pass over. The powerful merchant class of Venice expelled the Doge who seemed about to consummate the design, elected a successor from an untraditional line, required him to cooperate with councillors and in important matters to call a meeting of leading citizens for consultation. Venice thus cut out both feudalism and despotism and began at once the creation of popular government.

This calling of the principal citizens into counsel might amount to little or much according to the personalities involved. If the citizens were unenterprising and the meetings perfunctory it would soon become a dead letter. If they were vigilant and assertive they would soon absorb all real power and make the Doge their servant. The latter is what happened in Venice. The leading citizens were not military barons or landed proprietors but business men, probably the ablest that the world had ever seen. A French nobleman of the period would have counted it a deep disgrace to engage in commerce or even to superintend the cultivation of his estates. A Venetian Doge made it his boast that he had been a great merchant. We sometimes indulge our imagination as to what would happen if our own government were conducted by business men. That of Venice was so conducted and the result goes far to justify our most sanguine imaginings.

When it was settled that the chief citizens of Venice were to rule the state and that the Doge was to become their agent and representative the question naturally arose as to who and how many these citizens were to be. For a long time there seems to have been no restriction or definition of citizenship. There had been classes whom we have denominated patricians and plebeians, but if there was any distinction of political privilege it is not recorded. But as the responsibilities of government became greater and extensive dealings with foreign states were involved there was a legitimate distrust of the humbler citizenship. This was brought to a head by a rash declaration of war by the popular assembly which ended disastrously. Thereupon, the representatives of the great families drew up a list of those of their number who had had experience in the service of the state, constituted themselves a closed body, and assumed permanent direction of public affairs. Such was the origin of the Great Council whose vast hall of assembly is one of the attractions of Venice to the tourist. This council passed no laws and made no decisions. It was merely the collective legal citizenship of Venice and it met to elect the Doge, the senators, and other functionaries of government. There was of course opposition to this arrogation of authority on the part of self selected citizens but the opposition was bloodily and permanently repressed. The whole transaction is odious to our modern democratic philosophy. We are inclined to favor democracy as an end in itself. To the Venetians it was a means to an end. They had tried it and it had failed and they restricted it as they judged necessary. If we are tempted to judge them harshly we may well recall that they gave Venice security, prosperity, and peace and the most enlightened legislation in Christendom for six hundred years. During that period Venice had no revolution while England, the single European government which we may compare with hers in beneficence and stability, had two revolutions in a century. These families were chosen for ability proven in the service of the state and they maintained their standard through the years. They were business men and they acted on business principles. Election to public office was but promotion from the ranks based on a personal record of which the electors were perfectly competent judges.

All this had its reaction upon Venetian character. It produced a type — more uniform, perhaps, than that produced by other states — but unrivaled in ability and force in the world of affairs. The common impression that Venice produced no great men is the extreme of error. Venice might almost reply that she produced no other. If there are few outstanding figures, there are few who would not be outstanding in another city. The list is long of the Doges who matched and overmatched the greatest captains and the ablest diplomats of Europe in their day. The portraits of these men as they appear in the canvases of all the Venetian masters from Bellini to Veronese and Tintoretto form a gallery which has no parallel in masculine beauty and power. But the ideal was a practical one and the ability that was prized and bred was business ability. These men are not subtle or imaginative or poetical. They are little inclined toward the fanciful or the abstract. We look in vain for the philosopher, the scientist, the prophet, the poet, or the scholar. Venice has given us no Dante, no Petrarch, no Galileo, no Savonarola, no Macchiavelli. To the fine arts, it is true, she has made her splendid if somewhat specialized contribution. But after all, Titian is not Michelangelo and the brilliant series of Venetian painters with a single exception have impressed upon their magnificent works the stamp of mundane reality. That they have glorified it and made fact the peer of fancy is no whit to their discredit.

Thus Venice passed over both feudalism and despotism and achieved popular government centuries before other peoples. But it was popular government of a limited and peculiar type based upon a specialized citizenry which she selected and trained for her purpose. Such Plato had enjoined and such he might have approved, and found in six centuries of success the justification of his philosophy. Did Venice fall short of our achievement? Or did she perchance outdistance us too and anticipate conclusions toward which we are moving unawares?

CHAPTER II

Just when the settlements in the lagoons began their career as traders we cannot tell. Possibly the fisher folk made small beginnings before the great migrations. Surely the refugees, coming from great commercial cities and under the dire necessity of earning a living, cannot have been long in conceiving the idea of trading for gain. Their food had, in any case, to come from the mainland and something must be offered in exchange.

Their first specialty was salt which they could evaporate in their shallow waters, a commodity which men must have and which could not easily be gotten elsewhere. They soon held the monopoly of this lucrative traffic within an extensive territory. But the trade routes to the east had been known for centuries and the taste for oriental products acquired under happier conditions persisted in spite of general poverty and disorder. The trade routes were no longer safe and traffic had correspondingly diminished, but the result was to increase prices and therefore profits to those who successfully braved its dangers. It would have been strange indeed if our needy Roman exiles had not made the venture. Certain it is that within a hundred years of the last flight to the lagoons the Venetians were known widely as a trading community. Without following the development of Venetian commerce from its humble beginnings to its imperial days we may note its general character and the reason for its existence.

Venice, as we have seen, was situated at the mouth of a number of rivers which traverse the great, fertile plain that they have created. Only one of them is of impressive size and none of them have now the slightest commercial importance. But before the advent of railroads or even of tolerable highways all these rivers, from the least unto the greatest, were utilized for the transportation of commodities. All could be entered from the protected waters of the lagoon. This made the lagoon the natural distributing point for all northern Italy, still richer and more populous after all its calamities than any other equal area in Europe. A comparison with Genoa climbing up its mountain slope from the very edge of the sea reveals at once the advantage of Venice.

Beyond this local hinterland lay Europe to be reached over the mountain passes or by a long detour by sea. Venice did not at first control any of these passes which could be reached only by traversing the mainland. It was the necessity of keeping these routes open, as we shall see, which led Venice bit by bit to annex the mainland and thus to a military policy which was ultimately her undoing. But through these routes Venetian commerce reached central Europe more directly and cheaply than it could be reached in any other way. The great cities of Augsburg and Nuremberg owe their development and wealth in large measure to the far reaching commerce of Venice. By this route, too, commerce reached the Rhine and found access to a farther extensive territory. In the east a far larger and more productive territory was tributary to Alexandria, Constantinople, and other ports in Syria, Anatolia, and the Black Sea. This included not only the territories neighbor to these ports but distant China and India whose wares, transported over long caravan or sea routes, reached the Mediterranean at Alexandria or other port. These strange, exotic products had a fascination for the mediæval fancy which insured large profits for those who could provide them.

To link up the east and the west was the problem of commerce from the fifth to the fifteenth centuries. Among the many routes which were open to the merchant there were two which easily surpassed all others.

The first was the sea route from the Levant to Sicily and thence through the straits of Messina along the west coast of Italy to the north. This route was economical, though exposed to storms. It was the natural route for commerce with Sicily, southern and central Italy, France and western Europe generally. It made the fortunes of three great trading cities which succeeded and successively destroyed one another. During the brilliant Saracenic and Norman domination of Sicily the center of gravity was at Amalfi, where fifty thousand inhabitants occupied the narrow gorge which now seems crowded with a tenth that number. With the wane of the south the center moved to Pisa and later to Genoa where it seemed to find its natural seat.

The other route started as before from the Levantine ports but after passing the rocky promontories of Greece it turned north along the Ionian and Dalmatian coast to the head of the Adriatic. This route was relatively direct and much less exposed than the other, being lined with islands and long reaches of protected water which offered shelter to the mariner, though unfortunately to the pirate as well. Northern Italy and central and northern Europe as well as the shores of the Adriatic were naturally tributary to this route. It will be seen, therefore, that nature had created no monopoly in the carrying trade between east and west, but man was possessed with a determination to do so. It was not a question of cut-throat competition but of very literal throat cutting that characterized this early rivalry. The sword was freely grasped as a normal means to commercial supremacy and scruple seems to have been

entirely wanting. Pisa smote Amalfi and ruined her forever only to be smitten by Genoa in turn with the same
result. Genoa thus remained mistress of the western
route.

The task of Venice was different and in a sense simpler.
There was no Sicily to intercept trade on the way and
build up a southern rival nor was there a second lagoon
to rival her incomparable site. But pirates infested the
archipelagoes of the Adriatic and raided her commerce
as it passed. These pirates were not the homeless sea
rovers of romance. They were a powerful organization,
perhaps we may say a state, with a fortified capital, an
almost impregnable stronghold from which they dominated the traffic of the Adriatic as in a later day the
Barbary pirates dominated and preyed upon that of the
Mediterranean. Pirates like these do not waylay stray
ships and kill their crews and loot their cargoes. They
simply assume ownership of the waters under their
control and levy tribute on the ships that pass, sometimes
even commuting the charge for an annual payment by
the trading power involved. Thus the nations of Europe
paid to the Barbary pirates an annual tribute the amount
of which was fixed by agreement and proportioned to
the volume of their commerce until the American government put an end to it all a century since. What the
relations of Venice were to the pirates of the Adriatic
during the early centuries we do not know. They
probably passed through the various stages of raiding
and irregular levy down to organization and systematic
tribute as in the case of the Romans before them. But the
arrangement was unstable and the system was obviously
parasitic. Finally on Ascension Day in the year 1000
the Venetian fleet put forth under the great Doge,
Orseolo, defeated the pirates in a pitched battle, burned
their capital, and returned with their galleys loaded with

prisoners to stock the slave markets of Venice. Like
Pompey, who had previously performed an identical
exploit in the same waters, Orseolo was henceforth known
as "The Great."

There were two results of this victory, one spectacular
and the other of profound moment, which endured
through the life of the Republic. The first was the
famous pageant of the marriage of Venice to the Adriatic,
a pageant instituted to celebrate this victory and repeated annually thereafter on Ascension Day. On this
wonderful pageant succeeding generations lavished the
incomparable resources of Venetian splendor.

But the splendor of this pageant must not blind us
to the second and greater fact which this pageant was
designed to symbolize. Venice now owned the Adriatic.
It belonged to her as a bride belongs to her husband.
She may not be unqualifiedly his but she at least can
belong to no other. Thus in a very literal sense Venice
construed her claim. The modern rule of international
law which limits national control to a line three miles
from the shore was still far in the future. The pirates
owned the Adriatic and had collected pay for the privilege of using it. Venice had acquired their title by the
time-honored right of conquest. Those who used it
henceforth did so on her suffrance. Her claim was
confirmed and strengthened by the annexation of the
islands and the adjacent mainland with the ports which
she now made feeders to her commerce. Thus the pathway to the east was a good half in her keeping.

But once out of the Adriatic and beyond the sheltering
Ionian Islands she was at the mercy of both nature and
man. Here she met the competition of Pisa and Genoa,
the latter destined soon to be her relentless enemy and
to meet at the hands of Venice the fate that she had
meted out to her rivals. Of co-operation or of live and

let live there could be no question. It was war to the knife and *vae victis*. Venice had become Queen of the Adriatic. Could she become Queen of the Mediterranean? For the one crown was after all but an apanage of the other.

It was another hundred years before opportunity greatly beckoned. The occasion was the Crusades. The first appeal found the Venetians cold. They were less confident of the outcome than the feudal knights. They knew the Saracens better, and withal they had trading relations with them which they were unwilling needlessly to jeopardize. Not till Jerusalem was taken in 1099 did they see their way to join. If the east was to fall to the western powers, most decidedly Venice must be of the number. In the long war that followed Venice played an important and in general a brilliant part. With the incidents we need not deal but the results concern us deeply.

The first result was the establishment of Venetian posts or settlements of a new kind in the conquered seaports and islands throughout the east. These posts which were destined to play a very large role in the development of world commerce, a role not yet finished, were apparently a Venetian idea. Their character may be best understood by reference to Shanghai or Tientsin whose "concessions" are the lineal descendants of these commercial posts the organization of which was perfected by Venice in the twelfth century. The visitor to one of these Chinese cities finds himself in a handsome, well ordered European community. The streets are paved, lighted, and policed; business blocks with plate glass fronts and concrete sidewalks line the streets; banks, hotels, churches, and railway stations all remind him of his own land. But a single step beyond the well marked frontier takes him into a different world. The narrow crowded streets, the dragon signs, the joss houses, the creaking wheelbarrows pushed by half-naked coolies, and ere long the squalor and filth of the Orient arrest his attention. Farther acquaintance will but deepen the contrast. It would reveal in the concession an organized society in which he would be at home, a city council of his countrymen or his similars, hospitals and schools of familiar type, golf links and clubs like his own, and above all a government of laws enacted by his own people. In a word, he would find here a little oasis of his own civilization, and the briefest experience outside these limits would make it plain to him that only this could make possible his normal life and activity among these people. And such an oasis is possible only on condition that the foreign community be given control of the limited area in question. The granting of this control is the concession involved in the name.

Venice quickly discovered that if she was to have successful commercial relations with the Levant she must acquire in the various eastern ports concessions of this character. If her cultural demands were less than those of modern Europe the need of protection was more urgent. Above all she felt the need of regulating commercial transactions by an adequate body of law. For one of the noteworthy facts in the history of Venice was her early development of a body of commercial law essentially modern in character at a time when commercial law hardly existed in either adjacent territories or feudal Europe. That law has since been borrowed by all modern nations. Americans and Englishmen are familiar with the statement that the law under which they are living is based on the English common law. To this there is one important exception. The law of negotiable instruments which is virtually the law covering commercial transactions is based upon the law of

Venice, a law which she created and which was already well developed at the time of the Crusades. Therefore the policy was adopted in her co-operation with the Crusaders of demanding in every city captured the concession of a portion which was to be permanently under Venetian control. As her Crusader allies were not traders she was doubtless free to choose the most advantageous site. Whether the inhabitants were expelled or expropriated we are not told. The essential thing was that she should have under her own control and governed by her own laws a trading station where she could establish warehouses, docks, and a depot of naval supplies, not to mention the indispensable fortifications and garrison. These stations established all over the Levant, though insignificant in area, were a source of immense wealth and power. They developed by a natural evolution into the famous "capitulations" by which the western powers later secured the right for their citizens of living under their own law in all parts of the Turkish Empire. When Japan and China were later opened up to commerce with the west, both the concessions and the capitulations were imposed upon them by the more developed conquering powers. So great has been the development of this original Venetian idea.

There were features in these establishments which are hardly equaled today. Americans are proud of the standardization of which they have made so extensive an application and which they conceive to be their own invention. Venice made an application of it which was peculiarly her own. Venetian ships were largely owned by the state and were leased to the highest bidder. The ships for which Antonio waited so anxiously were probably not his own. These ships were built with standardized parts which were everywhere kept in stock. If a rudder or a mast was broken on the voyage there was a standardized duplicate at the next station ready to slip into place. Thus the magnificent Venetian organization minimized the risks and economized the labor of its citizens.

A second result of the Crusades was conflict with Genoa. Had it been only a question of the western market it is possible that they might have acquiesced in what seems a natural division of the field. But in the east there was no natural division and their interests were completely opposed. Genoa, of course, adopted the same policy of establishing commercial posts and there was little scruple on either side in the struggle for coveted sites. Minor clashes led to greater ones and finally to a desperate struggle which lasted more than half a century. The energy shown by both combatants is almost incredible. In the final and decisive phase of the war fortune long favored the Genoese whose fleet at last entered the lagoon and besieged Chioggia which defended the entrance. Then individual genius tipped the scale. The Genoese fleet was blockaded and starved into surrender, and peace was made on the conqueror's terms. Venice was Queen of the Mediterranean.

The third result of the Crusades, one interwoven with the preceding, was a rupture with Constantinople. It will be remembered that at an early day Venice had acknowledged the sovereignty of Constantinople. This was soon altogether ignored but never officially repudiated. But Constantinople, pressed by enemies on every side, had steadily declined while Venice had as steadily increased in wealth and power. The change did not make for cordiality. The Crusaders made the matter worse. Whatever the Emperor might think about recovering the Holy Sepulchre he was extremely averse to having it done by Latin Christians who would establish there a rival kingdom with consequences not to be foretold.

The Emperor had a pardonable skepticism as to the reign of brotherly love among Christians in the event of their military proximity. In his weakness he resorted to the old device of playing off rivals against each other, favoring the Genoese against the Venetians and vice versa as the balance of power seemed to require. They in turn used him as a pawn in their game. Extreme measures were occasionally adopted and produced their inevitable reaction. Thus in 1171 the Emperor, inspired by the Genoese, ordered all Venetian concessions in the empire canceled and their inhabitants to be imprisoned. The preposterousness of this decree may be gathered from the contemporary statement that the population of the Venetian quarter in Constantinople numbered two hundred thousand. The Venetians at once declared war but the campaign was ill prepared, mismanaged, and unsuccessful.* For a time they had to swallow their wrath and await their opportunity.

The opportunity came with the Fourth Crusade. The Crusaders bargained with Venice to transport them to Palestine. When the appointed day came the ships were ready but only a part of the Crusaders were there. The rest, faithless to their agreement, had withdrawn or taken another route. The Venetians waited long for them and their money but in vain. Business instinct suggested a compromise as an alternative to failure and loss. Would the Crusaders render a small service to the Republic in lieu of the missing money? Zara across the Adriatic had been lost and could be restored to its allegiance in passing. The Pope protested but the Venetians were unmoved and the Crusaders overcame their misgivings. Ultimately the great expedition sailed as a

---

*It was this war which was declared by a vote of the people and the mismanagement and failure of which led to the formation of the Grand Council and the limitation of the citizenship.

joint enterprise with the usual agreement about trading privileges and Venetian quarters in conquered cities.

Zara fell as expected and the Pope acquiesced and sought to resume direction of the enterprise. But now came a new temptation. The expedition was invited to restore to the Byzantine throne the rightful heir in return for huge promises and concessions. The Pope protested and threatened and there were renewed misgivings but the temptation was irresistible. Venice had her grievances and the promised reward was dazzling. The Emperor was restored to his throne and then did not — probably could not — keep his promises. The allies negotiated and waited, waited for months and at last lost patience. Then they stormed the city and looted it.

The result must have been a surprise to all concerned. The world has hardly yet recovered from its amazement. The defenders outnumbered the allies five to one, some say ten to one, and they were behind the strongest walls in the world. Only an exasperation which deprived the allies of all reason and prudence can explain the desperate adventure. Yet thanks to conditions which must connote the extreme of demoralization within the walls, the daring attempt succeeded, its spectacular character being heightened by the action of the ninety-year old blind Doge, Dandolo, in heading the party that scaled the walls. The indomitable energy of this grand old man won him a little later the honor of a tomb in Santa Sophia, the grandest church in Christendom.

The capture of Constantinople had little permanent result except to weaken the empire as a bulwark against the encroaching east and to hasten the catastrophe which Europe had most reason to fear. The Byzantine rule was soon restored with diminished splendor and resumed with quickened pace its progress toward inevitable dissolution. But to the men of that time it seemed as if the world had shifted on its axis. The west had triumphed over the east, the Latin church over the Greek, and the yawning chasm between the two had been bridged. Venice dreamed of a monopoly of world trade. The Pope, again reconciled by the event, dreamed of dominion over all Christendom. A Latin empire was established and administration, central and local, was organized on western lines. It was a serious essay in statesmanship and would deserve our serious notice if it had endured. But lacking permanence, it interests us chiefly in its relation to Venice.

It is needless to say that in this general readjustment in which Venice had so large a part the interests of Genoa were not sympathetically considered. The ruthless use which the Venetians made of their advantage was a match for the like ruthlessness of the Genoese a generation earlier and embittered the struggle which continued intermittently for nearly two hundred years with the result that we know. Aided by dissensions in the Genoese state such as happily Venice never knew, Venice became by the end of the fourteenth century the unchallenged mistress of the seas and unquestionably the richest and most powerful state in the world. That position she was to maintain seemingly for another century though a penetrating observer would have noted even then the seeds of decay. After 1500 the decline was clearly visible and went on at an accelerating rate, but it required three hundred years more to bring about dissolution.

The trouble with sea empires is that they cannot altogether forego dominion on land. In the readjustment above noted Venice had felt compelled to appropriate and garrison all the islands along her route to Constantinople as she had earlier felt it necessary to annex the islands and shores of the Adriatic. The great island of Crete, the Peloponnesus, and other parts on the mainland followed in due course and for identical reasons. Annexations on the Italian mainland had early been found necessary to insure food supply and access to the mountain passes. The trouble with all such advances is that there is no stopping place. This was particularly true on the Italian mainland where boundaries were necessarily arbitrary unless annexation were pushed to the mountain confines and the whole plain absorbed. This did not accord with Venetian tradition or Venetian interests, yet it was rather forced upon her. The states of northern Italy, Padua, Verona, Milan, etc., had become despotisms with aggressive programs of expansion. The ruling families were unfriendly to Venice whose stable, popular government was a mute condemnation of their own and whose power and wealth they envied and feared. Venice was inevitably drawn into the struggle and as inevitably extended her territories. It is noteworthy that these territories for the most part stayed by her to the end and parted from her, if at all, through no choice of their own. Venetian administration was unique in its day for business methods, impartiality, and adherence to law. The mainland adventure was on the whole a brilliant one and successful as judged by contemporary standards. But as judged by Venetian, that is, business standards, it was disastrous. Like all experiences of prolonged military adventure it was ruinously expensive and gave to Venice possessions which were almost as costly to hold as to win. The experience of Britain, risen to the pinnacle of wealth and power by identical means but compelled in the end to assume crushing responsibilities, will occur to all.

Yet it is not easy to see what else Venice could have done. The warning of her dying octogenarian Doge

against the growing jingo policy which was to prevail
under his successor is often cited as marking out the line
that she might better have chosen. It is an open question whether the choice was really open to her. If the
pacific policy enjoined by the sage could have been
effectually urged upon her quarrelsome neighbors Venice
might well have adopted it. Nay, she would surely have
done so. But her mood was not one of supine and sui-
cidal pacificism. She stood her ground and took the consequences, consequences that might have been different
in incident but not in essence.

More deadly was the unavoidable struggle with the
Turk. Venice, though unfailingly religious, had never
shown any scruple about trading with the infidel, Saracen
or Turk, somewhat to the scandal of feudal and fanatical
Europe. As the Turk gradually displaced the Greek
in the East the natural thing was to continue with the
new master the commercial relations so long maintained
with the old. This indeed was done, the conquerors
being eager for the wealth that commerce had brought
to their predecessors. But the Turk was not a trader
or a business man and he has never become such. On
the other hand he was the foremost militarist of the age
and was in the full tide of a brilliant military career.
Considerations of commercial advantage could not be
expected to stay his victorious advance. Hence another
intermittent struggle of two hundred years which ended
in the ruin of Venice and the permanent exhaustion of
the Turk. That this purely commercial state should
have been able to resist the greatest military power of
the age and permanently to stay its advances is one of
the marvels of history.

The wonder grows immeasurably, however, when we
learn that at the moment when the great struggle was
about to begin, the foundations of Venetian prosperity

had been undermined beyond remedy. It was in 1486, only a generation after the capture of Constantinople by the Turks, that a Portuguese navigator rounded the Cape of Good Hope and discovered the sea route to India and the far east. The long caravan routes, the Mediterranean voyage, Venetian profits, and mountain passes, all were now unnecessary. Exploitation of the new route began at once, Portugal being assured a monopoly by the Pope whose grievance against Venice was perennial. Venice was unable in any case to compete with Lisbon on this outside route. With her usual resourcefulness she shifted her emphasis from trade to manufacture. The crafts, it is needless to say, were not strangers to Venice. Though her location was less favorable to industry than to trade this disadvantage was offset by her stable government and traditional tolerance which made her the haven of refuge for exiles from the restless industrial cities of the mainland. While she thus acquired the specialties of her neighbors she had her own some of which, like glass blowing, were jealously guarded monopolies. Her fabrics, too, were unrivaled and were in wide demand. Every craft known to the age was represented in Venice and made its contribution to her resources in the days when commerce failed her. To this industrial activity which embraced the fine arts with the lesser crafts, stimulating them most in the days of marked decline and prudently exploiting their business possibilities, we must attribute in no small degree the amazing vitality of the stricken Republic.

But Venice was ground between the upper and the nether millstone. In the west the League of Cambrai headed by an empire-building Pope and including the chief powers of western Christendom overwhelmed her in an exhausting and savage war and appropriated her mainland territories at the moment when they were becoming her chief reliance. In the east the powerful Turkish Empire, then in full tide of expansion, let loose upon her its savage fury. When the long struggle was ended Venice was utterly ruined. Her treasury was burdened with a debt which anticipated those of our day. Her possessions were lost, her commerce destroyed, and her private fortunes dissipated. Nobles whose proud names were written in the golden book were pawning their treasures and renting their palaces; nay, there were scores of them who became utter paupers living on doles paid by the impoverished state. Then the golden book was opened to upstarts and even to foreigners who could pay to have their names inscribed in this most honored list of the world's nobilities. At last it went begging and men of substance were petitioned to accept the doubtful honor and the undoubted burden of manning the sinking ship of state. More melancholy than this decline of fortune was the inevitable decay of morals in public and private life. Graft was universal and wits were turned to mean expedients that had before been devoted to high adventure. Grave and reverend signors became pedlars of beads and displayed their trinkets where of old had gathered the procurators of the republic. The hurrying gondolas of merchant princes now idled around the paper lantern float of a mendicant singer and the Queen of the Adriatic danced in tatterdemalion garments for the amusement of a heedless world.

And, tragedy of tragedies, this heedless world assumes that this is the real, the true Venice. Venice is the amuser among the nations. The Grand Canal is a plaisance and its palaces a stage setting for vaudeville. What tragedy in this abasement of the City of Men!

It is a consolation to recall that the declining days of Venice were illumined by the noblest of her achievements.

From the time when Venice became Queen of the Adriatic to the time when Portugal usurped her crown, five glorious and prosperous centuries, her great mission in the art that she was to make supremely her own remained unaccomplished. In 1486 when the fateful route to the east was discovered, only a single great painter had reached maturity and even he had scarcely revealed his powers. Carpaccio was still a youth; Giorgione and Titian were children and Veronese and Tintoretto were still unborn. The mellow tones that glow from their immortal canvases are sunset hues soon to be lost in the deepening night. Like the plant which ceases growth in the season of flower and withers in the season of fruit, art the most enduring of human creations, set the crown upon Venetian achievement in the days of imperial decay.

CHAPTER III

We have traced in barest outline the history of imperial Venice with its far ranging commerce and its widespread dominion, all as the necessary background for the more intimate study of the city itself. This study to which we now turn is concerned with but a single aspect of the city's character, its relation to art. That art is revealed in the various fine arts with which we are familiar, architecture, painting, sculpture, mosaic, and perhaps even more in the technic arts, the art crafts, some of which, like lace and glass, have acquired world wide fame. But more significant than any or all of these is the city itself considered as a work of art. Its palace bordered canals, its open squares, its domes and campanili, form an artistic aggregate which has scarcely a rival on our planet. We shall consider later the achievements of Venice in the arts, notably in painting, the art which she made peculiarly her own. For the present we are concerned with the city as a work of art itself.

Our study will be to little purpose, however, unless we study things in their becoming, noticing how each suggests and in a sense creates its successor, also how each new manifestation of art reflects developments in other departments of life. Art is the subtlest and truest of all commentaries upon contemporary life and finds in this its chief significance. It must therefore be studied with constant consciousness of social and political development and in its historic setting.

The simple historic framework which our study requires is almost ideally furnished by Venetian history.

38

Beginning with the removal of the capital from exposed Malamocco to the mud banks of Rivo Alto the history of Venice lasts almost exactly a thousand years. This period is divided by epoch making events into four periods, the first three of two centuries each and the fourth of four centuries. These periods were marked by great differences of policy, of situation, and of artistic achievement. To enhance the symmetry and convenience of this arrangement the epoch making events above referred to happened in each case at or near the turn of the century. A brief enumeration of these events, most of them already familiar, will be worth while.

Venice becomes the capital of the lagoon settlements following the repulse of Charlemagne in 810.

Venice becomes Queen of the Adriatic as the result of the victory of Orseolo the Great over the pirates in the year 1000.

Venice captures Constantinople and destroys its prestige and culture leadership in 1204.

Venice begins her conquest of the mainland in 1399.

Venice loses her independence and terminates her career as a nation in 1797.

We shall do no violence to the essential truth of history if we eliminate these trifling discrepancies in an arrangement so nearly ideal and indulge our preference for even centuries. As thus perfected Venice requires us to memorize but five easy dates, 800, 1000, 1200, 1400, and 1800.

As has been noted, the intervals between these dates constitute sharply defined and characteristic periods in Venetian culture which we shall find it convenient to consider separately in the following chapters in their relation to Venetian art. These again we may usefully summarize.

800–1000, primitive Venice; the building of the new capital.

1000–1200, Byzantine Venice, the Crusades and Empire.

1200–1400, Gothic Venice; the aftermath of the Crusades.

1400–1800, Renaissance Venice; from sea to land dominion.

It is to the first of these periods that the present chapter is devoted. Its purpose is to recall, so far as may be, a Venice which, save for one important feature, has utterly passed away and to trace its rise from the humble settlement which had hitherto scarce merited notice.

The earlier aspect of the city is known only by inference. Living cities eat up their dead, and no city has been more living than Venice. The Venetians had nothing of that archaeological temper which now distorts and impedes the development of historic cities, blocking needed thoroughfares and pre-empting valuable sites to preserve a historic association, an architectural record, or even a fragment of shapeless brick work sanctified by mere antiquity. The unconcern with which the Venetian destroyed old Venice to make way for the new found its precedent in Athens and Rome during their creative age.

Nevertheless some data are available for the reconstruction of earlier Venice while the city as it stands is the work of seven or eight hundred years.

The primitive settlement which we may safely assume to have existed on this site has left no trace. Yet if we explore the lagoon in its unfrequented parts we shall even now come upon settlements which, we have reason to believe, preserve the type of two thousand years ago. Houses built of mud stiffened by stalks of wild cane (much as the modern worker in concrete reinforces his structure with steel rods) and roofed with thatch perpetuate the early tradition. A ditch or miniature canal dug in the mud accommodated the indispensable boat and the building lot as thus defined was strengthened and protected from the waste of the waves and the boatman's oar by stakes driven at frequent intervals and interlaced with osiers. When completed the whole looked like a big basket set in the water and filled with earth with a mud hut on top of it. These osier palisades which are now used only for gardens or minor, outlying settlements, were used as late as the fifteenth century in the very center of the city as old engravings attest. They find their place in heraldry and the manuscript illuminations of this region, a basket filled with earth and growing plants being the symbol of a garden.

There is every reason to believe that this earliest settlement was planless and irregular following the accidents of the location. The site, it must be remembered, was not an island but a large group of islands — sixty or seventy, we are told — all small and of the nature of mud banks. The early settlers had no option but to accommodate themselves to their peculiarities. The buildings, too, for the most part mud hovels, can hardly have been imposing. There were few if any buildings of a public or communal character. Differences in individual habitations doubtless existed, probably with the usual social connotations, but these differences can hardly have been impressive.

To such settlements came the fleeing Romans, dwellers in palaces and long accustomed to substantial architecture, public and private. So long as they regarded the lagoon as a temporary refuge from which they would return at the earliest opportunity they doubtless accommodated themselves pretty much to conditions as they found them. But when repeated visitations made return hopeless and exile became permanent they must have undertaken at the earliest practicable moment the construction of more suitable dwellings. Churches followed, for these exiles were Christians of long standing. We may assume, too, that other buildings faintly reflecting the civic establishment of the mainland now made their appearance. It would be interesting to know what this early building which we may now begin to call architecture was like. It is surmised that wood, then more easily obtained than now, was more extensively employed than upon the mainland, the difficulty of building with brick or stone on the soft mud bank being overcome but gradually and as the result of unfortunate experiences. It must be remembered that no building even of present day Venice rests upon bed rock and the method later adopted of building upon closely driven piles implied resources and mechanical appliances which were not at first available. Indeed there are buildings now standing in Venice which are without this pile foundation. This must have been true of all in the early Roman period. But in all this we are left to conjecture. The lagoon which preserves the primitive hut and the osier paling, its natural products, offers no modern counterpart for this intermediate period. The serious builder had no reason to perpetuate these transitional and imperfect styles. It is doubtful if they had any appreciable outward comeliness since even the church builders of this period sought beauty and architectural effect only in the interior. The settlement was still planless and haphazard.

To this straggling and ill-ordered community now came the honor of a call to the headship of the lagoon federation. Hardly was this distinction won when the acquisition of the bones of Saint Mark accentuated the boom which the city had already begun to experience. To meet the new requirements a radical program of reconstruction was deliberately undertaken and carried through with characteristic Venetian sagacity. The most fundamental undertaking and the only one which endures to this day was the systematic development of the island site. The layout of the new capital was not left to the caprice of nature. A commission was appointed by a far seeing Doge with power to study the situation and to take measures conformable to the requirements of a growing commercial community. New canals were dug where needed, useless ones filled up, old ones deepened, and the enclosed land raised by the mud thus removed. With but slight modifications at a later period this gave us the foundations of the Venice of today.

The construction of a residence and administrative headquarters for the Doge was begun at once and shortly afterward a church at first dedicated to Saint Theodore but destined soon to receive the bones and the name of an evangelist. These buildings, both long since destroyed, must have surpassed anything that the city had known up to this time. The confederation of the lagoons, already populous and now beginning to be wealthy, was flushed with victory and the new capital doubtless reflected its enthusiasm and its wealth. It would be of interest to know what they were like, but of the church at least we have no definite knowledge. It is believed by some to have been built of wood, though the considerable period spent in its construction would seem to indicate a more substantial architecture. Its general plan probably followed that of other churches built at this period as we know to have been the case with the church which replaced it after the great fire of 976. This church did not in the least resemble the Saint Mark's of our day. It is described as a Romanesque church without transepts, that is, rectangular in shape and with three apses or semicircular niches at the far end, a large one in the center and a small one on either side. This plan is represented in the church of Torcello originally built in the seventh century, rebuilt in the ninth and the eleventh, but with adherence to the original plan. Like the Torcello church the earlier Saint Mark's undoubtedly had an open timber roof and was devoid of either domes or spires.

It would interest us to know more of this church and in particular to know whence came its builders and what tradition governed their work. Was it of the east or of the west? We are often reminded that Venice is essentially oriental, that her cultural and aesthetic affinities are with Constantinople, not with Rome and the west. There is much of truth in this thesis but it is never the whole truth and it is very unequally true of different periods of Venetian history. It may be doubted whether at this time Venetian culture had acquired this historic orientation. Venice was Roman in origin and the mainland tradition brought by the refugees and maintained by their patrician sympathies had not yet spent itself when the city was called to the honor of heading the confederation of the lagoons. Intercourse with the east, though long since established, had not developed the proportions which later security and wealth made possible. It is farther to be remembered that Constantinople was at this time vastly larger, richer, and more splendid and that she had developed a style of church architecture which was far more difficult and costly than the fledgling capital of the lagoons could consider. Finally, there were ritualistic considerations which influenced church architecture. While Venice stood ecclesiastically somewhat between east and west her ritual affinities were on the whole with the western church and this tended to strengthen the western tradition.

For all these reasons Venice built her first monumental church in the simple and inexpensive style of the west, a style not only exemplified in nearby Torcello but made glorious in the great churches of Ravenna and other mainland cities. Constantinople with her peerless Santa Sophia awakened admiration rather than emulation. Another century was to pass before Venice could reach the momentous decision to reproduce one of these splendid churches in honor of the puissant Saint Mark.

Of the secondary features of this church we know nothing. Antique columns and capitals brought from some Roman temple, classical reliefs adapted to unintended uses, imported icons and gathered miscellany, of all this we may be quite sure. And along with this the carved designs of the wandering Byzantine artisan and perhaps the crude attempts of Lombard or Venetian, all interesting, revealing, but lost.

The new church and the Doge's castle were the conspicuous creations of the period but perhaps not the most important. Private building must have received an enormous stimulus as the new honor conferred upon the city brought additions to its population and affluence to its citizens. Probably private buildings of the period were still plain and not of a character to survive in a period of great opulence and luxury. Certainly few if any are here to satisfy our curiosity. But we are not left wholly in the dark as to their character. In certain important respects the architecture of primitive Venice was strangely unlike the Venice that we know. The houses, we are told were built with towers at the corners after the manner of castles, the towers being connected no doubt by a battlement along the top of the house after the manner so common in the older Italian cities. How far these were seriously intended it is difficult at this distance to determine. We are tempted to think of them as ornamental survivals, mere decorative motives derived from fortress construction and perhaps imported from the mainland. But there are other details which cannot be thus lightly explained. The entrance to the canals, we are told, was guarded by towers — a fact still commemorated by the name, *Canale Torisella*, "Canal of the Little Towers." Chains, too, were provided which could be stretched between these towers thus barring the entrance. The quays also, those parts of the city frontier which were not protected by buildings at the water's edge and where conceivably an enemy might effect a landing and rush the narrow streets, were shut off from the city behind by a wall with battlements and towers and ponderous gates precisely like the cities of the mainland. Finally the newly erected residence of the Doge was not at all the gracious palace that we know but a stern castle with huge towers at the corners and all the appurtenances of a fortress, a protection for the Doge against the turbulence of his subjects and a citadel for the city in more serious emergencies. It is difficult in the face of these facts to construe the towers and battlements of the householder as mere decorative features. It must be remembered that Venice was not yet mistress of the seas or even Queen of the Adriatic. Though victorious over the armies of Charlemagne, she was at the mercy of pirates who not only levied tribute upon her passing commerce but occasionally raided the lagoons themselves. Nor were they the only marauders that the householder of that age had to fear. Feuds and violence in personal and family relations were characteristic of the age and the security of our day, imperfect as we often esteem it, was a blessing unknown a thousand years ago.

Hence the Venetian like the Florentine made his house into a castle if his wealth permitted. Doubtless such houses were the exception, for security was then a luxury that few could afford. Possibly, too, the need diminished and the battlements became less frowning and the towers more decorative, perhaps were discarded altogether, by the more daring and progressive. Even so it must have been a strange Venice that met the gaze of the mediæval traveler. Imagine turreted castled fronts instead of marble palaces on the Grand Canal. Fancy the Doge's Palace and the broad quay before it all with towers and battlements like another Carcassonne set down in the sea. It baffles the imagination.

How long this continued we do not know. The need for it largely ceased in the year 1000 when Doge Orseolo destroyed the pirates. It was not simply that Venice had destroyed her arch enemy but she had learned the secret of her power. Like London, the unfortified capital of the modern sea empire, and Cnossus, its Cretan counterpart of four thousand years ago, the city of the lagoons now placed her defense in her navy and towers and chains became unnecessary. But cities are not rebuilt in a day and the castle houses of Venice long outlasted the conditions which created them. The old houses endured, and even those built later, if the Venetian builder was like others of his craft, were influenced by the old tradition. It is safe to say that for generations after Orseolo's victory they built houses with towers just because houses had always been built with towers. Certain it is that tower houses long continued in Venice. Petrarch lived in such a house in the fourteenth century, three hundred and fifty years after the great victory, and Carpaccio, whose pictures are a thinly veiled transcript of the Venice of his time, paints the familiar towers, though of a modified and ornamental sort, in this Venetian setting a hundred years later still.

That no trace of this castle architecture now remains

is due in part to the peculiar situation of Venice and in
part to the wealth and relentless progress of later generations to whose life of magnificent display these stern
structures were as unsuited as they were unnecessary.
In any other city this opulent class would have moved
outside the ancient limits leaving the earlier city as a
picturesque derelict to be first neglected and then preserved with artificial sanctity by the archaeologist and
the historian. In Venice this cult of the obsolete was
impossible. The eligible sites were few and located for
the most part along a single thoroughfare scarce two
miles in length. As the city changed from a crude,
frontier capital to a splendid metropolis of two hundred
thousand inhabitants, the richest community in the
world still confined within its narrow, inelastic limits, it
was not to be expected that these precious sites would be
relinquished at the behest of the antiquarian. And
besides, there was no antiquarian.

This destruction and replacement of the private
buildings of ninth century Venice is thus easily accounted
for, but the Venetians were quite too busy to leave us
records of detail. With regard to the new church and
the castle of the Doge they have been more explicit.
The church and palace, both much smaller than now
and of an entirely different character, perished by
fire in an insurrection in 976 after an existence of something more than a century and a half. The church,
though doubtless impressive and admired in its day, was
plain and originally served primarily as the private chapel
of the Doge with whose castle it was connected then as
now. It was replaced by a larger structure soon after
the fire of 976, a church still in the Romanesque style
and strongly reminiscent of the mainland, though the
work in part of Byzantine builders. Probably technical
difficulties rather than obstructive tradition in the now

eastward looking city prevented the adoption of the
more daring Byzantine style which governed the next
rebuilding a century later. We can form very little idea
of the appearance of this second Saint Mark's which
must also be accredited to this primitive period. Its
three apses and the absence of transepts suggests something like the church of Torcello, though probably smaller
and certainly without the later mosaic decorations of
the latter. It would seem to have borne no resemblance
to the present structure. The Doge's Palace was very
different. A small but powerful castle, its massive
walls and corner towers were not destroyed by the conflagration which gutted its interior. A portion of one
of the corner towers has survived all changes and is now
incorporated in the structure of Saint Mark's. The
castle was restored at the time, probably without material change of plan or character, to be burned again
and again restored and successively rebuilt with enlargement and embellishment until after the lapse of several
centuries it gave way to the magnificent structure of
today. It is suggestive to note the nature of the transformation which resulted from these changes. How little
does the modern palatial structure with its open arcades
and gracious balconies recall the fortress in which the
ruler of this earlier day defended himself from the turbulence of his untamed people! What has happened in
Venice that the mob who once stormed moat and draw-
bridge are later held in check by a lattice and the turn
of a burgher's key? Or again, compare it with the
strongholds in which the Visconti, the Sforza, the Scaligers or even the Popes held sway. Was it tyranny and
oppression that thus housed itself with gates unbarred?
But these halcyon days had not come yet and primitive
Venice was laying the foundations of an unforeseen
future to the accompaniment of insecurity and fear.

Our picture of primitive Venice would be seriously incomplete if we were to omit certain negative features some of which it would be pleasanter to ignore. There was not a particle of pavement in the city and the numerous streets or alleys which then as now were the ordinary approach to all the buildings in the city were by reason of their flatness and lack of natural drainage even more offensive than those of the hill towns of Italy and feudal Europe. The use of horses, then extensively employed in the city, and the careless habits of the inhabitants would have rendered futile the efforts of the street cleaner — if there had been a street cleaner. The canals, emptied twice a day by the tide and the obliging carriers of whatever was committed to them, were the salvation of the city and compensated for its lack of hillside slopes. On the other hand the unpaved squares were planted with trees and where not too frequented were grass grown much like the public square of Torcello today. Open spaces, both public and private, were more numerous than now and the austerity of early Venetian architecture would have been appreciably lessened if the palaces were embowered in trees.

Another peculiarity which would seem strange to a modern visitor was the use of the public squares, even the Square of Saint Mark, as markets where wares of every sort were exposed for sale in booths or under rude awnings. Such markets had existed in Italian cities from time immemorial and exist still. The visitor who, on a summer morning, enters the Piazza Erbe at Verona or the Piazza Garibaldi at Perugia will get an idea of Saint Mark's Square — then much smaller than now and traversed by a canal — as it existed almost to modern times. But he must not set up the vender's booths in the noble setting of today. Not only were the church and palace very different from those of today, but of all the stately buildings that now enclose the square not one was built for five centuries after the great victory. In their stead were irregular and commonplace buildings among which a stable and a butcher shop are of record as also a large tree to which the nobles tied their horses. An open, dirt square in front of an ungarnished, mediæval castle was the primitive square of Saint Mark. All this forms a rude and malodorous background to the Doge in his barge of state and the pageant of the wedding of the Adriatic. It is characteristic of the Middle Ages throughout Europe, squalor and pageant, pestilence stalking at noonday arrayed in cloth of gold.

Yet the picture changes even as we turn away. Alongside this uninviting square with its shambles, its stables, and its hucksters' booths, a new building is rising, a hospital, feeble alleviation of the pain which ignorance and callousness inflicted and men attributed to the wrath of God. The people, of course, put their trust in processions and relics and saints, but the hospital was built by Orseolo the Great.

CHAPTER IV

The period which we have now to consider is approximately that of the eleventh and twelfth centuries. It begins with Orseolo's great victory over the pirates in the year 1000 and ends with the capture of Constantinople in 1204. Of course these limits are somewhat arbitrary. Cultural epochs do not define themselves thus exactly. There is usually something of anticipation and something of holdover outside of the logical limits. So in this case. It is possible that some of the buildings which have come down to us from this period of Byzantine influence were built before the year 1000 or after 1204, but if so they were in a sense out of date. It is certain, too, that the most important of them all underwent periodic and almost continuous modification which it is now difficult to trace. Nevertheless these buildings properly belong to (and probably date from) the period in question, the true period of Byzantine ascendancy.

There were very obvious reasons for this ascendancy. In the first place the destruction of the pirates and the consequent control of the Adriatic by Venice released the pent up energies of Venice as the catch releases a spring. The impetus was enormous and the increase of commerce such as to excite the fear of Genoa and ultimately to incur her hostility. Following this came the Crusades with the founding of the Venetian commercial empire. All these advances eventually brought trouble and finally disaster, but not at once. The result during these two centuries was a rapid increase in wealth and civic pride and a more intimate contact with the East.

Constantinople was now as before the unquestioned center of art and culture, incomparably the most splendid of all earthly cities. The difference was that now Venice was rich enough to imitate her. There was no question of imitating anybody else. Rome was in ruins. Paris and London were uninteresting mediæval towns. When we recall that in the year 1000 not a single Gothic cathedral had been built and that the whole western world was in the chaos and gloom of the dark ages we can understand how inevitable was the leadership of Constantinople in all that pertained to art and culture. It is to be remembered that Constantinople was as yet untouched by the sacrilegious hand of either barbarian or Christian. Neither Crusader nor Turk had as yet "admired and destroyed" the treasures which fifteen consecutive centuries of Greek culture and imperial collecting had accumulated within her walls. In architecture she already had to her credit the grandest church ever yet erected by Christians, not to mention countless others, if lesser, yet akin. With such a city, to know was to admire, and, if one dared, to aspire, to imitate.

There was a further reason for this Byzantine ascendancy at this time. Constantinople which had been in its glory in the sixth century under Justinian had long rested on its laurels. From the middle of the sixth century to the middle of the eleventh her architects created nothing of a monumental character. But at the latter date there began a century of renewed activity which produced new architects and turned the Byzantine architecture from a dead tradition into a living reality. These architects and artisans of all the allied crafts eventually sought employment elsewhere and found it chiefly in Venice. The Byzantine architecture was thus transported, not in theory but in person, to the city of the lagoons.

A word is in order as to the terms, Byzantine and Romanesque, which we must use. Their etymology is clear but this does not quite give us their meaning. Byzantine refers to Byzantium (the later Constantinople being too long to take an adjective termination). Romanesque is derived from Roman and means — not Roman — but like the Roman, derived from the Roman. The two terms are thus distinct in origin and we naturally expect a definite distinction in meaning. But Constantinople was itself Roman and though it developed its Roman heritage in a way quite distinct from that of western Europe there was much in common between the two, quite enough in fact to introduce confusion into our terminology. Fortunately we do not need to go into the details of this technical discussion. A few fundamental principles will serve our purpose.

The distinctive principle of Roman architecture and of all its related forms is its use of the arch and of its derivatives, the vault and the dome. In this it differed radically from the Greek and the Egyptian, both of which used straight beams of wood or stone to bridge the spaces between columns, etc. The choice of the one or the other is largely a matter of materials. Peoples who do not have stone from which they can quarry great beams sufficient for their purpose adopt the arch which can be built with small stones or even with brick. Both Greeks and Egyptians were unusually favored in the matter of their materials. Hence their choice of the "post and lintel" architecture to which they adhered even after the more inexpensive arch had become quite familiar to them.

The arch if lengthened out becomes a vault, if whirled upon its axis it becomes a dome. In all these forms it was used by the Romans with great skill. Before the middle of the second century of our era they had built both vaults and domes of imposing dimensions. The dome of the Pantheon remains to this day one of the most marvelous and impressive of human constructions.

But both the vault and the dome in their simple form had serious limitations. The vault could be used only on a rectangular building, the dome only on a round one, and these only of limited size. The widest vault which the Romans ever built had a span of 116 feet, the dome of the Pantheon a diameter of 142 feet. These were probably the limits of practicable construction. But the Romans needed buildings much larger than this. Above all they needed buildings of more complex form. Suppose, for instance, they wanted a building the shape of a cross, how could they cover it? Not with domes, surely, for such a building furnished no circular supports. With the vault, however, they could at least make a start. It could be used both lengthwise and crosswise excepting only at the intersection where there were no walls on any side but only corner supports.

To meet this requirement the intersecting vault was devised. The lengthwise and crosswise vaults were extended until they intersected, the seams or lines of intersection being supported by arches carried diagonally from corner to corner across the central space. The pressure or thrust of the vaults thus came against these diagonal arches and they carried it down to the corner supports on which they rested.

Having learned thus to rest the vault on corner supports they could do anything with it. A simple vault could not be used on a colonnade for there would be no support for it between the columns, but an intersecting vault could be so used and by setting up long rows of columns acres of space could be covered with intersecting vaults, as in the Mosque of Cordova. The intersecting vault was enormously developed by the Romans and became the foundation of all the subsequent architecture of western Europe, attaining its dizziest heights of complexity and perhaps of beauty in the Gothic.

Meanwhile the dome had suffered eclipse. It was impossible to combine a lot of circles into a larger whole as could be done with a lot of squares. But about the time that the Empire moved its headquarters to Constantinople a way was discovered to put a dome onto a square. This was by the use of the pendentive, an ingenious structural support built into the upper corners of a square in such a way as to form a circle within it and make it support a dome. This accomplished and the four walls opened up by great arches substantially their whole width, squares could be grouped together and complex buildings covered with domes. This invention of course made a sensation and buildings covered with domes had a great run. The dome was in fact nothing like so adaptable to this purpose as the intersecting vault but it was new and the architects were fascinated with the problems presented. It must be admitted, too, that in their grandest creation, Santa Sophia, they produced a building which rivals and perhaps surpasses any Gothic cathedral ever built. Nor was this the only masterpiece of the architects of Justinian, one of the greatest builders in all history.

It so happened that this development of domed architecture came at a time when western Europe was utterly stagnant and creative activity was almost wholly confined to Constantinople and its sphere of influence. Hence it is known as Byzantine. In the east it ran its course and there alone it had vitality. When later it penetrated into southern France covering the long nave of the Latin churches with a row of domes as at Angoulême and at last challenged the Gothic it went down to prompt defeat. No device could make the dome as adaptable as the vault. The dome could be used at best only on squares. The vault could be used on rectangles, triangles, anything. The dome was heavy and required heavy supports thus encumbering the interior. No domed building of this sort has anything like the lightness and spaciousness of a Gothic cathedral. The dome, too, is far more expensive than the vault. But as against all these limitations a Byzantine cluster of domes produces a wonderful effect when seen from a distance, an effect which we associate with the dreamy East, unmindful of the fact that it all originated in the West.

The dome and the vault, therefore, furnish us the easiest of distinctions between Byzantine and Romanesque in cases where domes or vaults are used. But it will occur to the reader that these cases are the rarest exception. Witness the church considered in the preceding chapter which had a timber roof, or the palaces on the Grand Canal which are built in the way practiced everywhere with several stories separated by timber floors and ceilings and tile and timber roofs. Of all the buildings built in this period only one had domes and could thus claim to be structurally Byzantine. For the others we must fall back on such lesser features as the arched window and door openings (which are essentially the same in Byzantine and Romanesque) and finally upon differences of decorative detail. Here we are on much less certain ground and are dealing with more arbitrary and less constant characteristics, but the palaces too we must call Byzantine though it is certain that much is the work of Lombards and that in some cases the term, Romanesque, would be more accurate. It is a highly technical, and for us an unprofitable, task to disentangle these blended elements — to unscramble the architectural eggs.

The supreme monument of the period is Saint Mark's (Fig. 1) as we know it today. The original Saint Mark's, we have seen, was destroyed by fire in 976 and rebuilt along similar lines immediately thereafter. This second church was not burned but was deliberately pulled down to make way for a better one, a virtual copy in this

Fig. 1, Square and Church of Saint Mark

case of the Church of the Apostles in Constantinople. The reconstruction began in 1063 and the church was dedicated in or about 1085. Superficially, however, the church as dedicated bore little resemblance to the church as we know it. Structurally it was the same church that we see, but there was as yet little of the marble and mosaic which now completely cover it without and within. Most of this came later and by slow degrees. It is generally assumed that the church in this undecorated condition was quite unbeautiful. Those who, like Mr. Ruskin, base their plea for Saint Mark's chiefly on its color, claiming little for it on the score of proportion or line, are naturally of this opinion. But those who have visited the new Westminster Cathedral (not Westminster Abbey) built in the style of this period and as yet in the condition of undecorated brick (the mosaic decorations now in progress are spoiling it as rapidly as possible) will wish that they might have seen Saint Mark's in that condition. The majesty of that simple interior, unbroken by shafts or groins, is profoundly impressive. It is doubtful if Saint Mark's is the equal of this new creation but it is certain that in its present state we cannot tell. Whatever merit the marble and mosaic incrustation may have, it has the disadvantage of absorbing our attention and banishing all thought of the fundamentals of line and form.

The plan is essentially that of a Greek cross, a favorite with the Byzantine builders and in slightly modified form the rule in the later eastern church. Fundamentally this is represented by five squares on a checker board, four black ones grouped around one white. These arms, however, may be lengthened or shortened and even changed in shape, the essential being that they should remain equal. In the humble Greek churches of our day which are obliged to content themselves with a single dome the arms are usually shortened and reduced to large niches as in the little twelfth century church of Santa Fosca in Torcello which was built on this model. In Saint Mark's, however, the arms are lengthened, each of the four squares with its dome being removed a little from the central square by a short vault or powerful arch which is required to support the weight of the great dome on either side. There are also vaulted recesses on either side of the four arms in which are open galleries supported by colonnades. These galleries afford a closer but not altogether favorable view of the mosaics which from this level upward cover the entire interior of the church. These recesses and galleries and connecting vaults somewhat disguise the fundamental plan of the building as seen from within.

As seen from without the disguise is still more complete. In front and along one side of the foremost square which constitutes the nave is a vestibule or narthex which is covered with a row of little domes and is likewise encased in marble without and mosaic within. This long vestibule pretty nearly builds out the façade to the width of the transepts, completely concealing the plan of the Greek cross and giving the whole the appearance of a square. Above this vestibule is a gallery or second story which lifts it to the height of the building and presents in front a series of five great lunettes or semi-circular wall spaces crowned with huge, round arches corresponding to the five arched entrances below. All this is very Byzantine and corresponds closely to its Constantinople prototype the Church of the Apostles, a church later destroyed by the Turks but known to us by an intelligent and detailed description.

The structure once completed, the work of decoration began. This was decoration in a sense so fundamental as hardly to be distinguished from construction. The entire interior (Fig. 2) up to the gallery level was sheeted with marble in a manner favored by Romans and Byzantines but apparently not approved by the ancient Greeks. Colored and heavily veined marble was chosen and sawed into slabs. Two of these slabs turned opposite ways and placed side by side thus produced a symmetrical figure on the principle of folding a piece of paper through a fresh ink blot. Fortuitous symmetries of this sort do not rank high as art but the general effect of a room so covered may be rich. Not only wall surfaces but friezes, cornices, window frames, door jambs, and the like were thus applied to the brick surfaces.

Outside, the same incrustation was applied but here the process was more serious and approximated more nearly to the character of construction. Not only marble slabs but columns, capitals, and heavy architect-

Fig. 2, Saint Mark's, interior.

ural members in recessed portals and elsewhere formed parts of this very substantial addition. We must, however, exclude from our present inventory the little tabernacles, the stone tracery in the round-arched windows, and the fantastic, flame-like cresting on the great arches of the façade. These were added centuries later in the last days of the Gothic period. Last of all we may mention the mosaics which cover all the interior above the gallery line and fill the great tympana or lunettes of the façade. It is doubtful if any of these were added

in the period with which we are now concerned. The
oldest seem to be of the thirteenth century and it is
possible that the entire work was originally completed
in that century. But of these early mosaics all too few
remain. Many were replaced in the seventeenth century
by decadent pictorial compositions about as ill suited
to mosaic use as could well have been devised. By
rare good fortune, however, those in the interior have
preserved one essential feature of the original, the gold
background which dominates the entire interior and fills
it with a soft, lustrous glow which is profoundly impressive. The mosaics on the exterior suffered worse at the
vandal's hand. The gold background was sacrificed to
the usual color medley of picture, though even here the
choice was fortunate and blends harmoniously with the
marble in distant view. The original and far more
beautiful mosaics of the façade are admirably recorded in
Gentile Bellini's great painting in the Academy (Fig. 39,
page 190) which makes us realize how much we have lost.

One more fact is of vital importance to our understanding of this afterwork. The materials used were largely
finished materials taken from older buildings. Of the
hundreds of columns and capitals used upon the building
not one was made for Saint Mark's. The balustrade of
the gallery is formed of marble panels with reliefs in great
variety which have been trimmed, some of them most
pitifully, to fit them to their unintended place. On the
outside are figures in relief with upraised hands and
palms turned forward (Fig. 3). These are orantes or
praying figures, the upraised hands being the Greek
attitude of prayer, an attitude not used in the West at
this time. These, therefore, were almost certainly made
for the East and brought here for an unintended use. The
foreign character of these materials is emphasized by
the fact that some of these columns with their ornate

capitals are not built into the structure at all but merely stand in the vestibule alongside of others that are architecturally engaged. The inference is that these collectors of artistic junk became enamored of the costly marbles which they had collected and thought Saint Mark would like the supernumeraries even if no use were found for them.

Fig. 3, Orante or praying figure.

It would hardly be an exaggeration to say, therefore, that Saint Mark's is built of junk or second-hand materials originally executed for other buildings, not only the plan but the material being brought from the East. This inference is corroborated by definite record. We read that a law required all merchants trading with the East to bring back beautiful materials for the decoration of the church. How long this requirement continued we do not know but it is certain that the process of embellishment went on for centuries, indeed that it never quite ceased during the life of the Republic. Doubtless some of the decorations were executed on the spot as were certainly the mosaics, but both were in all probability the work of foreign artists. It is impossible at this distance to assign them with any certainty.

We cannot avoid the conclusion that the Venetians

with all their enterprise and their lively interest in things beautiful are as yet novices in art. They lavish upon their great shrine their wealth and their utmost devotion, but they are helpless both to plan and to execute. They are delighted to add, as the years go by, always another thing or two of beauty and of price, but with little thought or capacity to create an organic whole which should be more than the sum of its parts. This is devotion but it is not architecture. Let us admit, if we will, Mr. Ruskin's contention that the beauty of Saint Mark's lies in its color and that color effects at their best are only possible through incrustation. It does not follow that these results come by chance. If there is architecture in Saint Mark's it is in the original structure which later additions have not so much embellished as concealed. Doubtless incrustation was a part of the architect's plan and we may assume that if planfully carried out it would have produced a work of architecture, perhaps a masterpiece. As it is Saint Mark's is one of the most interesting churches in the world but interesting more as a museum than as a building. Its columns challenge attention for their variety rather than for their harmony. Its numerous capitals record well nigh the whole course of Byzantine development but they are arranged without sequence or congruity. Interesting, all this, but hardly beautiful in the same degree.

And yet in a building which records so many centuries of devotion the negatives are unwelcome and come tinged with reproach. Looked at in the right way and in proper historic perspective Saint Mark's is uniquely beautiful, so beautiful that we may well banish in its behalf the trouble making memories of our Gothic cathedrals that have taught us to look for beauty in another guise. Saint Mark's like so many of humanity's great

achievements, needs the saving grace of distance to efface
its incongruous details. The visitor who, coming from
his hotel on the Grand Canal, enters the Piazza at the
end opposite the church suddenly has his first view of
Saint Mark's. Happy if he realizes that this first view
is the best — better than all later views, even from this
same point — and prolongs it as much as possible. He
cannot yet see the miscellany of capitals, the superfluous
columns, and the various odds and ends which will soon
enough engage his attention. The too pictorial composition of the modern mosaics will not yet be apparent. He
will miss the towering majesty of the Gothic and the
simplicity and repose of the classic and had best forget
these things. But the symmetry of that rounded group
of domes and the soft opalescent colors of the façade
will not fail to impress him. And if he has seen the
polychrome façade of Siena and the blazing mosaic front
of Orvieto or of Saint Paul's Without the Walls in Rome,
he will realize how rare are such triumphs as the one
before him. Nor will he fail to note how much the
church owes to its setting, to its situation at the head of
the Square and to the long arcades which like marshaled
sentries line the regal approach. There are buildings
that are beautiful by reason of their details or parts.
Such a building is the Alhambra, architecturally insignificant but transcendent in its decorations. There are
buildings which are beautiful as wholes, regardless of
their details, perhaps even in spite of them. Such
buildings are the Parthenon and Santa Sophia. Finally
there are buildings that are beautiful neither in their
parts nor as wholes but as parts of a larger whole. Such
a building is Saint Mark's. The whole is the Square of
Saint Mark's in which the church takes its place as the
opal setting of a lady's ring.

This fact duly recognized and Saint Mark's appreciated in this its proper character, the visitor may seek a nearer acquaintance, beginning preferably with the interior. After the first stunning impression of the mosaics which demand his first attention and will not be denied, he will do well to think them away for a while and try to conceive the church in its own proper character. The Greek cross, it will be noticed, is surrounded on all sides by the galleries already noted which are covered by shallow vaults or very deep arches and a similar vault separates the side domes from the central dome. Thus each of the five domes is surrounded on four sides by these vaults or colossal arches, symmetry within symmetry. The conception is exceedingly fine, one worthy of the great architects of Constantinople with whom it originated. With all deference to Mr. Ruskin's insistence upon the merits of mosaic and marble incrustation we cannot allow the implied disparagement of the fundamental structure and concept of Saint Mark's.

Distinct from structure, yet intimately connected with it is the decoration in low relief which was executed on the spot, not brought from other buildings. Some of this is very beautiful in its combination of figure relief with conventionalized vine and geometrical designs, all in low relief and picked out with gold and color. It is noteworthy that the figure of Christ dominates every composition in contrast with the Virgin and others familiar to the mediæval repertory. Just what theological or other conclusions are to be drawn from this we will leave others to decide. More decorative, perhaps, and posssibly not without symbolic meaning are the conventionalized vines, stars, and other designs executed in the single plane characteristic of Byzantine relief and set off with color and gold. These are above all praise as individual decorations, though they are lacking in that organic unity necessary for a comprehensive scheme of decoration which stamps its character upon the building as a whole. Saint Mark's has ornaments worthy of Santa Sophia but Saint Mark's is not a Santa Sophia.

Closely related to this sculptured ornament and originally far surpassing it in importance are the mosaics, the closer examination of which we must reserve for a later chapter. Suffice it here to note that they have the merit which the other decoration lacks, that of embracing the church as a whole and completely dominating its interior while assuming perhaps the first place on the façade. There are better mosaics than those of Saint Mark's, but no other church that is so glorified by mosaic decoration.

Last and least in our study of Saint Mark's comes that collection of architectural miscellany which has been mentioned as giving the church something the character of a museum. Some of these things are but curiosities, mere oddities, not to be indulged unduly in their demands upon our attention. Such are the worthless prophyry statues, the so-called Four Emperors, that are built incongruously into a corner in the south façade. It may interest the antiquarian to learn whence they came and whom they misrepresent, but they tell us nothing about Saint Mark's and nothing about the Venetians except their magpie interest in showy trinkets at this time. Similarly with the square pillars of marble which stand isolated and useless nearby, and the functionless pillars in the vestibule near the inner door to which, in spite of learned opinion, we can assign no legitimate place in the structure of Saint Mark's. More legitimate but still rather feebly organic are the marble grills (Fig. 4) the numerous columns in both stories and on all fronts which support the varied capitals to which allusion has been made. Their interest, however, derives rather from their origin and their former use than from the part they play here. This museum study is a legitimate and valuable study if only we can bear in mind that it is not the study of Saint Mark's.

The building of Saint Mark's is so overshadowing an event in the history of this period that we are tempted to forget the few great houses which date from this

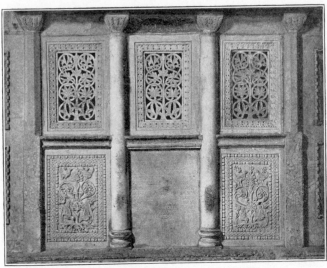

Fig. 4, Byzantine window grills and decorative panels used in the construction of a Tomb in St. Mark's.

period and which determine more or less permanently the character of Venetian palace architecture. The half dozen or less of these palaces that have survived are the representatives, no doubt, of a much larger number, the majority having succumbed gradually to decay and the ever recurring conflagrations of which Venice has been so often a victim. Even those now standing have not escaped unscathed. When Mr. Ruskin made his famous study in 1853 all were in extreme disrepair and devoted to ignoble uses. Walls were cracked, openings built up, and ornaments removed, defaced, or concealed under plaster. Since that time an era of reconstruction or restoration, more laudable in intent than in performance, has left its mark upon them. In their present condition they represent but imperfectly the architecture of the period. The essentials are there, however, and more easily appreciated in spruce reconstruction than in authentic dilapidation.

Structurally there was nothing remarkable about the Venetian palace. Packed in solid rows along the Canal, the façade is the only part of the exterior which calls for the architect's attention. Even when the side is exposed, as at the junction of a side canal, it seldom seems to have been thought worthy of decoration. The façade was the exclusive object of attention and that attention was correspondingly lavish.

In the period with which we are dealing and for centuries afterward the palace or house served a double purpose. The ground floor was devoted to business, and the business being ordinarily commerce, it was encumbered with bales of merchandise through which the family and their guests picked their way to the grand staircase in the inner court leading to the residence stories. It is recorded that one of the finest of Venetian palaces was burned as the result of an attempt to dry some bags of sugar by fires in braziers which were carelessly left burning over night. This intimate connection of business with home was significant and had its influence upon architecture.

The ordinary Venetian house is entered from the street, the back door opening on the canal. It is a surprise to many visitors to find that they can go to any place in Venice on foot and that the gondola takes them to a near by landing or to a back door entrance.

It is this that accounts in part for the unfavorable impression which the visitor to Venice sometimes receives. He insists upon going everywhere in a gondola which is

Fig. 5, Stairway of the Minelli Palace giving access to open loggias in each story.

like driving about a modern city all the way in back alleys. To the Venetian these canals are business conveniences devoted to every variety of commonplace traffic. The perverse assumption that Venice is a plaisance only prepares us for disillusionment.

But the Grand Canal is an exception to all this. Here the houses face the Canal and the main approach is by water. The houses are built out flush to the water's edge and are approached by a flight of steps rising from the water. The entrance opens into a broad passageway which leads to an interior court in which the stairway is not infrequently situated. This outdoor stairway, a beautiful architectural feature made possible by the mild climate of Venice, is exemplified in the famous Minelli stairway (Fig. 5), exceptional in its circular plan but representative in its elegance and architectural effectiveness. With the interior of these palaces we will not concern ourselves beyond noting that there was a predilection for large, stately apartments which both expressed and emphasized the Venetian tendency toward a formal and showy life and had not a little to do with the development of that grandiose style of painting so characteristic of Venice. Very few of these interiors, however, have come down to us unaltered. The later poverty of Venice converted most of them to humbler uses, always with a tendency to the subdivision of apartments and the rearrangement of the whole. So much for Venetian palaces in general.

The palaces of the Byzantine period are at once distinguished by their open arcades or galleries in both lower and middle stories. This is illustrated in the Loredan Palace (Fig. 6), pronounced by some the most beautiful on the Grand Canal, and in the Fondaco dei Turchi or Turk's Warehouse, for to such ignoble use did this once magnificent palace ultimately descend.

A second glance reveals the fact that these arcades are always divided into three parts, a center and two wings, the division being indicated by a pilaster or double column in contrast with the single columns of the arcade. As these palaces are now restored the lower arcade is converted in the wings into a pair of windows, but these windows are very large and their arches are identical with those of the arcade which thus seems to be continuous as the arcade of the middle story is in fact. The windows of the upper story in turn are grouped to form an arcade exactly corresponding to the central portion of those below. We have next to note that the arches, though always semi-circular at the top, are stilted or lifted on perpendicular supports considerably above the capitals on which they rest. The semi-circular arch, as we have seen, is characteristic of the Roman and all its immediate derivatives, both Byzantine and Romanesque, and we may add, of very much beside. But the stilted arch is much less common, and though not confined to the East is very characteristic of Byzantine architecture. It

Fig. 6, The Loredan Palace, a restored Byzantine Palace.

gives a peculiar appearance to the colonnade, considerably increasing the impression of height. In this respect we may perhaps regard it as the eastern counterpart of the Gothic pointed arch. Another characteristic common to all Byzantine palaces is the unequal spacing of the colonnade. The central opening is always noticeably wider than the others, but the inequalities do not end here. They are obviously intentional since they are alike on both sides. Efforts have been made to construe these inequalities as conforming to a subtle law of harmony something like that which prevails in the curves and proportions of the Parthenon. It can hardly be explained as mere caprice but this explanation seems rather recondite and baffling in the case of those who are so hopelessly removed from that intuitive perception of line and proportion which was the peculiar gift of the Greeks. It is simpler and more plausible to explain the wider central opening as a provision for the commercial requirements above noted. Other minor irregularities may be assigned to carelessness or accident.

Finally we have to note the ornamentation of these Byzantine palaces which is at once the most superficial and the most distinctive of their characteristics. The most noticeable of their ornaments and the one that is most nearly structural in its value is the peculiar dental which is almost invariably used as the enclosing moulding or border of the Byzantine arch. It is extensively employed on Saint Mark's where it may be observed at close range. Derived from the Greek dental but quite distinct from it, this is of Byzantine origin and may still be seen in Constantinople on buildings erected in this period. While distinctive it cannot be said to have special merit or appropriateness. Used as a moulding and in very small scale it quite loses its original dignity and meaning. It thus becomes a convenient ear mark

Fig. 7, Byzantine incrusted ornament from St. Mark's. The Byzantine dental is extensively employed.

by which we identify Byzantine architecture rather than
a serious decorative element.

More interesting is the incrusted ornament in which
these palaces abound (Fig. 7). Incrustation always
invites the insertion of ornament. It is here that our
palaces have suffered most from restoration. The
original ornament had fallen or had been removed from
these dilapidated buildings and used in later construction
as would not have been possible if it had been carved in
the solid stone of the structure itself. When the building
was restored it was easier — and we may add, better —
to restore with plain surfaces than to replace the missing
ornaments with modern work.

This ornament, usually in low relief with its raised
surfaces in a single plane, is inserted in bands, circles and
panels in great variety. A favorite panel form is that of
the Byzantine stilted arch which thus echoes, as good
ornament should, the structural forms with which it
is associated. The themes are religious, symbolical, or
purely ornamental, the line being very difficult to draw.
Animals devouring one another alternate with peacocks
symmetrically disposed and drinking out of a high cup,
the latter at times attaining to a decorative excellence
rarely equaled in human art. But beautiful as these
ornaments often are, it can hardly fail to strike the beholder that they are somewhat arbitrarily employed.
The practice of resting the square base line of the panels
upon the curved line of the adjacent arches is not felicitous. We have beautiful decorations but not beautiful
decoration. The elements are not yet united into a
harmonious, organic whole. How far this is due to defects inherent in the Byzantine style it is hard to say.
Certainly in masterpieces like Santa Sophia there is no
random or awkward distribution of ornament as we find
it here. We are tempted to see in this a Venetian rather

than a Byzantine characteristic. The Venetian was still a borrower rather than a creator and could not resist the attraction of pretty things. He finds his counterpart in the modern collector who too often fails to perceive that a room full of art is not necessarily an artistic room. In this he was encouraged by the essential superficiality of incrustation which is too much divorced from structure.

Again we must close our survey with a reminder of the things that are not. The city must have undergone a marked transformation during these two centuries when wealth was increasing by leaps and bounds and columned palaces were rising on the Grand Canal. There was doubtless much of that love of display which is so marked a characteristic of later Venice and we read of gilded barges and processions in cloth of gold. But Venice was still enclosed in her osier palings, the later brick and stone bordering of the canals being as yet undreamed. Pavements of brick recently introduced, were still limited to a few main streets. A noticeable change indeed had taken place when in 1176 the canal which traversed Saint Mark's Square was filled up and the church which occupied the center of the Square was pulled down and erected farther back where the rear arcade now stands. This doubled the size of the Square and made possible its later beauty and magnificence. But these were possibilities only. Neither the Doge's Palace nor the splendid arcades that now surround the Square were yet in existence. The Square was still but partly paved with brick. Horses were still tied to trees there and were stabled a few yards away. The butcher still displayed his wares to the passersby bound for Saint Mark's, and bakers occupied the site of the famous Library opposite the Doge's Palace. Stone cutters' yards covered a large part of the Square and furnished the chief reason for its extension. Most revolting of all a large public latrine unmitigated by modern sanitary and moral precautions was conspicuously present. These conditions, of course, could have been matched in any contemporary mediæval city, perhaps in ancient Rome or Athens.

Finally, the arts which were to make Venice immortal showed as yet no sign of their nobler beginning. This again was not peculiar to Venice. Even Florence and Pisa were slumbering yet, though destined soon to a glorious awakening.

CHAPTER V

The two centuries now under consideration were the most glorious in Venetian history. The capture of Constantinople in 1204 definitely established the ascendency of the west over the east and resulted in the establishment of Venetian trading stations in every strategic location in the eastern Mediterranean. Here Venetian ships were refitted and cargoes furnished. Here Venetian law was enforced and Venetian administration established. This administration was gradually extended until large territories like the Peloponnesus, the island of Crete, and others were brought under Venetian jurisdiction. Venice became an empire and found herself called upon to solve the problems of imperial organization and defense. A nation of merchants had to supply military engineers who could build fortresses and governors who could command armies and administer provinces. The merchant had to reach far back from the trading post and organize and stimulate production. In all this the Republic was notably successful. In contrast with the despotic governments of the period whose rulers seldom concerned themselves with industry or commerce except to fleece it by predatory exactions, Venice administered her provinces on business principles and through business men. Peace was maintained, taxes were uniform and surprisingly light, and caprice and arbitrary exaction well-nigh unknown.

This progress, however, was by no means unchallenged. The period opened with a fierce rivalry between Venice and Genoa, at that time fairly matched antagonists.

The position of Genoa, as we have seen, gave her the advantage in the trade with France and a large part of western Europe. Venice, on the other hand, was the natural purveyor for Germany and central Europe. The two merchant republics, however, never thought for a moment of accepting this natural division of territory and working harmoniously in a common cause. No such live-and-let-live policy characterized this age. Rivalry took the form of the fiercest and most uncompromising hostility which could end only in the destruction of one of the two contestants.

The result was a series of wars recurring at intervals throughout these two centuries and which, after bringing Venice to the brink of destruction, ended in her complete triumph in 1380. This victory was the more impressive because it followed hard upon a crushing defeat which gave Genoa complete control of the sea. The victorious Genoese admiral, realizing the difficulty of carrying Venice by storm in the shallows of her lagoons, thought to starve her out by blockading the harbor entrance. To avoid the storms of the Adriatic he anchored his fleet just inside the entrance at Chioggia. Then the Venetian admiral, discredited by his great defeat and imprisoned by his resentful countrymen but recognized as the most resourceful of their leaders, was asked to save the city. He saw at once the weakness of the Genoese position and having called the people together for a service of solemn consecration in Saint Mark's he called for volunteers and filling great barges with stone they sank them by night in the harbor entrance, blocking the exit. The Venetians now in their turn awaited the outcome. The Genoese fleet, imprisoned and helpless, soon exhausted its food supply and after vain negotiations with a relentless foe was compelled to surrender at discretion. This completed

the ruin of Genoa and left Venice supreme.   It is difficult to compare nations that are widely different in
situation and resources but it is hardly an exaggeration
to say that in the year 1400 Venice was the most powerful
as she was certainly the wealthiest, the best organized,
the best governed, and the most modern of all European
states.   Despite the cost of the long struggle with Genoa
and the interruption to her commerce which it from
time to time involved, the period was one of enormous
prosperity which has left its record in the shape of the
most splendid monuments, private and public, which the
city possesses.

We have noted that the influence of Constantinople
in the preceding period was due, not alone to her wealth
and to the monuments of her great past but to the
further fact that during a part of this period she enjoyed something of a renaissance and became not merely
the repository of art but its creative center.   This,
however, was short lived.   It was due to the energy of
a few exceptional individuals and was in opposition to
the general tendencies of the age.   The Byzantine
Empire was hopelessly corrupt and was approaching a
natural dissolution.   Only this can account for its
capture in 1204 by the Venetian and Crusader forces.
Although the city suffered frightfully at the hands of its
semi-barbarous captors, there was no injury which a
living and progressive people could not have repaired.
Compare the speedy and magnificent revival of Athens
after its destruction by Xerxes.   But Constantinople
was in the sere and yellow leaf and the disaster was
fatal.   There is no more monumental building, no
training of architects, no stimulus to art, until the Turks
four centuries later commission Christian architects to
rival the glories of Justinian.

This decadence and collapse of Byzantine culture

coincided with the almost incredible rise of the West. We are accustomed to speak of the futility of the Crusades and their poverty of result. It is doubtful if any organized movement in history ever accomplished so much. The result was of course not at all what was intended. The rescue of the Holy Sepulchre from the hand of the infidel was but briefly accomplished and was not worth the effort. The whole fabric of Latin Empire in the east went down like a house of cards. But if the Crusaders went back to Europe with little to show for their effort they went back different men. The inspiration derived from their brief successes expressed itself in the form of religious revival and constructive art on a scale unparalleled in any other age. To find a parallel for their revivals and their cathedrals we should have to combine the age of Wesley and the age of Pericles. It was near the close of this period that this movement in the west reached its zenith. Chartres Cathedral with its unrivaled windows was built by men exalted in spirit by the great revival which followed the brief success of the First Crusade. Coming from all directions in their ox carts, holding services of solemn consecration at each night's camping place, they drew near to this most famous shrine in France where the great temple rose under their consecrated hands. Even the stone was hauled by hand owing to the impossibility of sanctifying the oxen. Completed in 1190 it was soon burned down and again built ere the great revival had spent its force. Its second completion was in 1225. What wonder that it surpassed all other of man's dreams in stone. The Crusaders had found an empty sepulchre but it had for them life giving power. The Crusaders accomplished nothing. Go look at the cathedrals; go worship at Chartres.

It is noteworthy that western Europe, though drawing

its inspiration from the East, did not imitate the East in architecture or anything else. The Holy Land itself offered little that was worthy of imitation. Their contact with Constantinople had been slight. They, therefore, continued the development of their own magnificently creative architecture, whose unpretentious creations of the earlier day needed only the stimulus of the Saviour's Sepulchre to develop amazing possibilities. So at the beginning of the thirteenth century when Venice was wrecking the city whose leadership she had so unhesitatingly followed, Europe was building Chartres and a dozen more beside. Venice was still a borrower while Europe was at the flood tide of her creative period. But she could no longer borrow from Constantinople. Though still by far the most splendid city in the world, Constantinople had shot her bolt and was now ruined, discredited, dead. Politically and morally the city was an object of pity and contempt. It was psychologically impossible for Venice to turn to her for leadership at the moment when she was elated with victory. With rapidly expanding commerce and growing wealth, a building boom was inevitable. Complete originality was impossible. No adequate foundations for it had been laid. Yet with her culture in the ascending phase and her vast energy subject to an unparalleled stimulus mere imitation was out of the question; above all, imitation of a moribund and discredited rival. Inevitably Venice turned to the West. More exactly the West came to meet her, advancing through northern Italy where, in Milan, Verona, Vincenza, and other mainland cities, Gothic architecture was already acquiring its distinctive Italian character.

It is this Italian Gothic, a comparatively remote derivative from the architecture of the north, which now invades the lagoons where it was to undergo still further modification under the influence of lagoon conditions and of the slowly awakened Venetian genius. Least original and least attractive of the important buildings of the period are the great churches of the Frari and Santi Giovanni e Paolo (Fig. 8), buildings known to the traveler not for their own attractions but for their

Fig. 8, S. S. Giovanni e Paolo

incomparable contents and accessories. They differ little from churches previously erected in Verona and elsewhere save in their enormous size which gives us an idea of the power and wealth of their builders, the Franciscan and Dominican orders, in the fourteenth century.

Those who are familiar with our northern cathedrals will hesitate to call these churches Gothic, so completely do they lack the accustomed ornament and the secondary features by which we are too much accustomed to identify the Gothic style. Yet we notice that they have pointed windows, though small and widely spaced, and something of tracery. Their vaulting, too, is essentially Gothic, though of the simplest character. Even here, however, at the point where the Gothic principle is most clearly present, a change is introduced which is revolutionary. The northern builders had counteracted the thrust of their great vaults by building buttresses, huge masses of masonry set edgewise against the outer walls and even carried over by flying buttresses, or stone props, to the clerestory walls beyond, a device which is chiefly responsible for the picturesque appearance of a northern cathedral. But the Venetians prevented their walls from spreading, not by bracing them without but by tying them together within by iron rods running from column to column. These rods are unsightly within, though one soon learns to forget them. The elimination of the buttresses outside, however, completely changes the appearance of the building, leaving it smooth, featureless, and uninteresting, the more so as the Byzantine use of incrusted ornament was now abandoned. As a structural principle, however, this use of ties instead of buttresses is perfectly legitimate. It had been adopted earlier in the building of Saint Mark's, as the visitor to the galleries is made unpleasantly aware, and is by no means limited to Venice. It has the advantage of greatly lessening the mass of the building, an advantage of prime importance in Venice where rock foundations were impossible.

In keeping with this fundamental change if not necessitated by it there was an extreme simplification of the interior (Fig. 9). Round piers take the place of the expressive clustered piers and the interpretive, soaring shafts that so visibly support the groins in the northern cathedral while all the decorative arcades and panels that in our familiar northern churches repeat in infinite variety the structural forms, are lacking. Walls of brick, plain without and plastered and painted within, make us reluctant to recognize in these churches the embodiment of the true Gothic spirit. The glass, too, is colorless or worse, while the square Italian campanile,

Fig. 9, Church of the Frari, interior.

or bell tower, always badly out of perpendicular in Venice, is poor compensation for the missing towers and spires of the Gothic. Only slowly and half unwillingly do we recognize in these spacious interiors an element of dignity and harmonious proportion. With the exterior it is doubtful if we ever get so far.

It is easy to explain much of this as due to the nature of available materials, the soft foundation, and other physical conditions. Venice had no stone near at hand. She secured excellent stone from Istria across the Adriatic, but it was necessarily expensive. The common building material was brick. The result was that Venice developed a builder's technique based on brick.

In France where only stone was available, every building from a stable to a palace was built of stone. Common basements were vaulted over in a way that seems to us very beautiful but which was merely the easiest way of covering it with their materials. Practical devices of every sort gradually translated themselves into decorative forms as is always the case until we have the marvelous fabric of the Gothic church. In Venice all that was lacking because there had been no occasion for it. The friars of Saint Francis and Saint Dominic might conceivably have imported stone for their churches but they would have found no one who knew how to use it in the northern way. The builder's technique cannot be improvised, cannot even be very successfully imported. It was not possible to build a church of the northern type in Venice, and if built it would not have endured.

But while local conditions and local traditions explain this simplification of the Gothic style in these Venetian churches, they do not reconcile us to it. These churches are not masterpieces and they have the fatal defect of recalling the memory of churches that are. If Venice has any noteworthy contribution to make to ecclesiastical architecture it still lies in the future.

Fortunately the Gothic architecture found in the Venetian palace a more congenial opportunity and a happier adaptation. This was perhaps due to the limited nature of the opportunity, there being no possibility of Gothic structure in a building whose stories were separated in the ordinary manner by floors supported by wooden beams. The problem was merely that of the façade with the privilege of rearrangement and the substitution of Gothic for Byzantine details. This rearrangement and substitution was undertaken, timidly at first and under the lead of the mainland cities, then boldly and with magnificent originality. Nobody cares much for the Venetian Gothic churches. Everybody admires the Venetian Gothic palace, at least in its fully developed form. No doubt this is partly because we set more store by pretty details than by fundamentals — the churches having only the fundamentals and the palaces only the pretty details — but there is another and a better reason. The church architecture is all negative. It reminds us of the elements the builder could not use, the things he could not do. The palace architecture is positive. The builder has found something he could do, something not done before and much worth doing. His discovery is not epoch-making. He has made no addition to the list of basic principles, a list that is perhaps incapable of extension. It is a surface achievement, but by so much the more within our comprehension. The significant feature of the Byzantine palace we have seen to be the arcades running the whole length of the façade in both lower and middle stories but divided into a center and wings by some difference in scale or treatment. In the Gothic palace this difference is increased with the result that the wings cease to be parts of the main arcade but present the appearance of a wall pierced with windows. The arcade is thus limited to the central portion, both above and below. It thus assumes the character of an inset portico, or as the Italians call it when above the ground floor, a loggia, one of the most beautiful features of Italian architecture and one associated with almost every style. The unequal spacing of the arcade so characteristic of the Byzantine period now for the most part gives way to regularity, though the wider central opening is still sometimes retained even in the latest examples.

The most striking change, however, and the one chiefly associated in the popular mind with the Gothic style is the introduction of the pointed arch. It is a surprise, however, to learn that this change was made very gradually and in a most illogical way. Even in the Byzantine period the round arch, though semi-

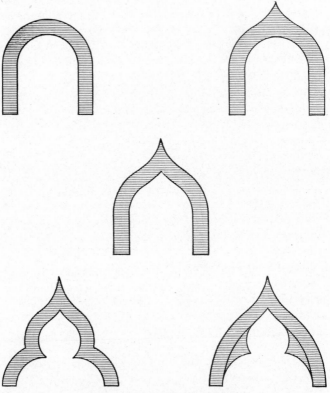

Fig. 10, Forms of Venetian Arches

circular in its inner contour, sometimes developed a point in the center of its outer margin. This was purely an ornamental feature and had no structural significance (Fig. 10). Eventually, however, the inner line of the arch followed suit and developed a point to

match that of the outer contour. This was a most unhappy compromise. The general shape of the round
arch was retained but with a capricious variation which
suggested only weakness and was inherently unbeautiful.
Gradually this outline changed. It is as though the
point were pulled upward, straightening out the awkward compound curve of the sides until a true pointed
arch was the result. The cusps were added dividing
the arch opening into three parts. These cusps were a
favorite feature of the Italian Gothic in arches of all
kinds. They are obviously related to the familiar
tracery of the north.

These arches in all their forms, incipient, intermediate,
and complete, are to be seen all over Venice, both in the
minor streets and on the Grand Canal, singly and in
groups. A favorite arrangement is to have a group in
the center and then one or two isolated windows in the
wing on either side. The latter were often of a different
variety from the former, variety being characteristic of
the style. This development was characteristic of the
thirteenth century. It involved no serious change in
the architecture of the Venetian palace. It merely
substituted pointed arches for round and used them more
sparingly in the wings, thus considerably modifying the
appearance of the palace but not its fundamental character. There was, however, one more change, which although superficial, had very considerable consequences.
This was the discontinuance of marble incrustation.
Whether the marble — largely taken from old buildings
— became scarce or was regarded as too expensive, or
whether there was merely a change of taste, we do not
know. There was much to be said for the frank exposure
of the brick, for good brick work needs no apology.
There was the alternative, however, very popular with
some, of covering the brick with plaster and painting it,

often with bright colors and ultimately with pictorial compositions. Both methods were uncongenial to the use of the inserted ornaments of which the Venetians had been so fond and which they evidently abandoned with reluctance. There seems to have been a little groping for a substitute, a quest, fruitless at first, but finally rewarded by a brilliant discovery which revolutionizes the Gothic façade of the fourteenth century and gives it the character ever afterward remembered as the Venetian Gothic. This was the work of a single man and the lesson was embodied in a single monumental building, one of the most remarkable buildings in the world.

We left the Doge's Palace a fortress or castle built at the beginning of the ninth century. This was burned down in 976 and rebuilt soon after, probably without much change. It was burned again and again and as many times rebuilt or restored, with how much of modification we do not know. There is reason to believe, however, that the last of these rebuildings, that of Doge Ziani in 1173–79 was a very complete reconstruction which both enlarged the building and gave it a genuinely palatial character, though one entirely unlike the present building.

The present building (Fig. 11) begun in 1301 marks an epoch not only in Venetian building but in Venetian history as well. This was the establishment of the Grand Council, the oligarchy of noble families which was henceforth to rule Venice under the name of a republic. The building was built in parts over a period of two centuries and a half. Begun in 1301, it was finished as it now stands in 1560. The first thing built was a senate chamber near the corner where the Bridge of Sighs now spans the canal. This, however, was ultimately demolished when the structure was finally completed. The end fronting the Grand Canal and containing the Hall of the Great Council remains as it was originally built, and this determined the character of the whole. For by a most remarkable exception to the practice of the early builders, when the rebuilding was resumed in 1422 it was decided to preserve the style of the preceding

Fig. 11, The Doge's Palace.

century in the interest of harmony. It is difficult to recall another instance before the nineteenth century where the style of the moment gave way to an earlier style in the interest of uniformity. Rarely, however, has the condescension been so well deserved.

The brilliantly original character of this building is seldom appreciated even by its admirers. It inheres in two things, the arcades and the heavy wall above them. Each is conditioned by the other.

The lower arcade at first seems attractive but not remarkable. It is massive as it should be, with broad capitals on short columns and perfectly plain pointed arches of admirable design. Only the capitals are ornamented and these are among the most beautiful in the world. (Fig. 12). Their octagonal shape perfectly fitting the moulded arches above is an immense improvement upon the four cornered classical varieties which have exerted such a tyrannous domination. Their sculptured leafage, too, is the best the writer knows. He has seen smaller leaves, leaves cut thinner, and all that, but nowhere a better understanding of the function of

Fig. 12, Doge's Palace; capitals from lower arcade.

ornament than here. Finally, there is the fullest play of the poetical and story telling tendencies of the early art. The sages, the heroes, the saints, the occupations, allegories, symbols, fruits, not excluding the broad humor which is characteristic of the age, are all present and executed in a faultless technique. It is amazing that the beauties of these capitals which, on their short columns are almost on a level with the eye, so seldom arrest the gaze of the traveler. Yet between the pigeons and trinkets of the Piazza and the gondolas of the Canal it is all but impossible to secure for these incomparable creations a moment's contemplation. They deserve hours of study.

It is the upper arcade, however, which made an epoch

in Venetian building. This arcade, much lighter than the other and with arches but half as wide, introduces the new feature of tracery. Apparently tracery had not been used in any Venetian building of the thirteenth century nor yet in the Gothic buildings of the mainland. It did not develop piecemeal like the pointed arch nor was it copied from the traceried windows or screens of the north with which it is structurally in sharpest contrast. It is the original conception of a brilliant mind motived, possibly, by the loss of the ornament which was previously inserted between the arches and which, as we have seen, had now been discontinued.

Fig. 13, Tracery of the Doge's Palace.

The pattern of this tracery (Fig. 13) is simple but rich, a circle set between two pointed arches and ornamented with four cusps which produce a quatrefoil pattern within. In appropriate conformity the arches are also ornamented with cusps which give them a trefoil appearance. It is doubtful if decorative design inwrought into structure has ever achieved a greater triumph.

But the remarkable thing about this tracery is that it is used to support the huge weight of a forty-foot wall, that is, to support the building itself. That is never true of our northern Gothic tracery which either bears no weight at all as in a rood screen or is enclosed in an arch that bears the weight of everything above it and relieves the tracery of all burden. Indeed it is just because the northern builders adopted the device of building a blind arch into their walls enclosing a group of windows which without this protection would have weakened the wall in which they were inserted, that tracery developed. Realizing that this arch bore all the weight they gradually perceived that they could cut away more and more of the wall which it enclosed until the group of windows became a composite window and the wall was transformed into the lace work that we know. But the tracery of this Venetian arcade is protected by no arch and is compelled to bear the burden of a solid wall of unusual height. It is, therefore, very substantial and so designed as to carry its burden safely and with no suggestion of inadequacy. The superficial resemblance of this tracery to that of the north (the resemblance is only superficial) must not mislead us. We are dealing with something new in architecture. This is burden-bearing or structural tracery while the northern tracery with which we are familiar is rather to be classed as ornament, its structural value being at the most that of window sash. As a result of this distinction Venetian tracery always remained simple and developed but few forms, while the northern tracery finally became utterly fantastic. Substantial duties are, in architecture as in life, the best safeguard against extravagance and caprice.

Incidentally we cannot disguise the fact that the architect with all his cleverness and creative power did a very doubtful thing in placing a forty-foot wall on top of an open arcade. Solid work belongs below, open work above. He understood this perfectly. He did what he did from necessity. The great assembly halls of the government, the meeting places of the Senate and the Grand Council, were necessarily on the upper floor and they required more space than the inner wall afforded. It is alleged that this enlargement of the upper story was an afterthought, the original intention having been to carry up the inner wall, that is, the wall behind the arcade, to the top in which case the arcades would have given us merely porticoes and would have borne nothing heavier than some simple cresting or ornament. In that case we might never have had the Venetian Gothic palaces as we now know them. But compelled in the course of construction to change his plans and enlarge the upper story he developed the heavy tracery required for the work and turned the whole course of Venetian architectural development in another direction.

But this was not the limit of his cleverness. To design tracery which would bear the weight of the wall was good engineering. Something more was needed to make it good architecture. It was necessary not only that the wall should not be too heavy for its supports; it must not *look* too heavy. This architect knew that there are ways of making a wall look heavier or lighter than it really is. A wall made of big stones is no heavier than one made of little stones but it looks heavier, much heavier. We are conscious that we could lift the little stones but not the big ones. Color, too, has its effect. Hence our architect has built his wall of small pieces of white and pink marble laid in pleasing pattern and the arcade bears it lightly. Had he built it of huge blocks of sombre hued stone the effect upon the arcade would have been crushing.

The rear part of the Palace, both the façade facing on the court with its famous staircase and that facing the Canal at the rear, finished in 1560 in the very different style of the Venetian Renaissance and perhaps its most elegant creation, will call for brief notice in the next chapter.

Fig. 14, Palace of the Embassy; early Gothic.

We have noted as extraordinary the fact that the style first adopted for this building was followed when, after the interval of a century, the interrupted work was resumed. It was a remarkable tribute to the impression which this unique work made upon the minds of both builders and people. It received a still greater attestation in 1574 when a fire completely destroyed the interior of the building leaving only the outer walls and the arcades standing. Had it been any other building in Venice with the possible exception of Saint Mark's the walls would have been torn down and a new building erected in the style of the time. This was indeed proposed and a celebrated architect urged it strongly, offering his own plan for the new building. For once, however, the profession waived its present advantage in behalf of a great historic monument. Influential architects including Sansovino, the architect of the beautiful Library opposite, put in their plea for the beautiful building and the Palace was restored without external change. The interior, of course, acquired the sumptuous and somewhat vulgar character of the Venetian Renaissance and Veronese and Tintoretto took the place of the Bellini and Titian in its decoration.

The influence of this great building upon the palace architecture of Venice was immediate and enormous (Fig. 14.) The traceried arcade fitted perfectly into the traditional Gothic façade occupying the middle space to which, as we have seen, the arcade was now restricted. On the ground level the simple arcade was retained as in the great palace (Fig. 11) or replaced by simple doorways (Fig. 14). In the middle story the traceried arcade was used, the tracery being usually that of the upper arcade or loggia already described. If an arcade was used in the third story a different pattern was chosen in the interest of variety as in the Ca d' Oro

(Fig. 15). The whole rectangle was often framed with a Gothic moulding as were also the independent Gothic windows used in the wings, while Gothic corner mouldings and other details diversified the façade, often in a very beautiful manner. The charm of the tracery lay in the fact that it supplied the place of the incrusted

Fig. 15, Ca d' Oro; late Gothic.

ornament which had disappeared with the general scheme of incrustation and the lack of which was plainly felt. As architectural ornament the tracery was immeasurably superior. The delicate reliefs set into the walls of the Byzantine palaces, though often very beautiful in themselves, were perfectly arbitrary in their location and at the distance of a few yards they were quite wasted. As contrasted with these extraneous ornaments this simple massive tracery forming a part of the wall and obviously doing a wall's work, carried its bold and rich design the whole range of the Canal. It was recognized as a success at once and is so still.   Not only the pretentious palaces of the Renaissance but even the earlier Gothic with their charming pointed arch arcades were forgotten in its presence.   Surely the brilliant thought of the great architect of the Doges' Palace carried far.   The traceried arcade is to the traveler the Venetian Gothic, that and that only.

The charm of this architecture endued it with unusual life.   It held its own into the period of the Renaissance and achieved its chief triumphs at the very end, somewhat, after the date which we have chosen as the convenient limit of our two century period.   The most celebrated and undoubtedly the most beautiful of the Gothic palaces of Venice, the Ca d' Oro or Golden House (Fig. 15) was built in 1421–36.   Here marble replaces brick and Gothic ornament, as restrained as it is elegant, exhausts its possibilities upon the exquisite façade.   A possible defect which is after all probably a matter of deliberate choice, is the lack of symmetry, the palace having but one wing.   The façade was once heavily gilded and picked out with color, a feature whose loss we can hardly regret considering the exquisite color which the pink Verona marble possesses in its own right. The house, now the property of the municipality, is destined, we may hope, long to remain as one of the most beautiful monuments of human art.

One more feature of the Gothic palace requires mention, the balcony.   The type of balcony used in connection with these palaces, except in a single case, seems not to be distinctively Gothic.   The single exception is the little Contarini-Fasan Palace (Fig. 16) known to every cicerone as the House of Desdemona.   The balconies here are filled with Gothic tracery of a rich and appropriate pattern which it is strange was not emulated. Usually, however, the balcony is surrounded by a tiny arcade of simple colonnettes surmounted by a rail which is pierced below by little trefoil arches like those in the railing of the upper gallery of the Doge's Palace (Fig. 13).

Fig. 16, Contarini-Fasan Palace, "House of Desdemona."

Small lions sit upon the corner posts. This balcony, though offering but a hint of the Gothic style, harmonizes perfectly with the arcade behind it which dominates the entire façade. Unfortunately these balconies have largely disappeared and have given place to a tasteless Renaissance style which for inscrutable reasons appealed to a later generation. This type has heavy, bulging balusters obviously imitated from wood forms and wholly out of harmony with Gothic architecture. Used on buildings of their own period they have the limited merit of being congruous. Installed on the graceful Gothic palaces of an earlier date they have none. How far the substitution was made as a necessary repair and how far as a needless concession to a later degraded taste we cannot say.

How stands it with other arts and with other matters of import in this year 1400 to which we have now come? Again we are impressed by the blanks that remain to be filled. The Venetians have been building empires and creating fortunes during these two hundred years and have added much to the embellishment and something to the comfort of their city. But some things have had to wait and like all peoples of the time they have judged that cleanliness and the ordering of the city with that end in view could best be postponed. Pavements are not yet universal and stone pavements are unknown. Horses are still used and stabled in the city — are to be used for centuries to come. None of the beautiful arcaded buildings that now surround Saint Mark's Square have yet been built. For them we must wait a hundred, two hundred, even four hundred years before the circuit is complete. The Square is still a market with its butcher and bake shops, its litter, its stone cutters, and its latrine. The broad quay that now separates the Doge's Palace from the waters of the Lagoon has not yet been won from the sea and the shallow water dashes its wavelets against the osier palings only a few yards from the palace foundations. The spacious Riva beyond is not yet the broad promenade and landing place for pleasure boats of a more leisurely age but a busy mart with unlading of ships and cluttered with bales of merchandise and rows of casks crowded in the limited space. For Venice is a busy place, oh, very busy, and what with administering an empire and conducting a world commerce and caring for family position and propitiating the unseen powers to avert the ever recurring pestilence, minor interests of comfort and careful housekeeping have sometimes to wait.

But in all this sameness we are not long in noting that in the prosperity which has transformed the Grand Canal, Saint Mark's has had its part. The Church of the Republic wears a glory now which was quite unknown two centuries before. There are pictures, too, upon church altars which have a new appeal and the painter's guild includes along with painters of houses and ships, certain members who paint saints and other symbols of devotion. The age of art has begun.

CHAPTER VI

ZENITH AND DECLINE

1400 – 1800

By the year 1400 Venice had reached her zenith. Up to this time all her struggles had ended in victory and all victories had brought increase of power. There were still struggles in store for her and these struggles were not infrequently to be crowned with victory, but victory was not to bring increase of power or wealth but rather poverty and exhaustion. This was due neither to corruption nor to mistaken policy but to forces wholly beyond her control. The stars in their courses turned and fought against her as against Sisera of old.

This change in her fortunes, however, did not take place immediately nor was it at once apparent when it began. For a time decay took on the aspect of health and specious acquisitions clothed loss with the habiliments of prosperity. Her commerce, if not maintained at its absolute maximum, was prosperous and as yet unmenaced and unburdened by the heavy outlays which were later required for its maintenance. Even when these conditions changed the change was at first very gradual and seemingly not incapable of repair. Eventually the change became more rapid and as the true cause was recognized it became apparent that the great days of the Republic were numbered. During the long period of decline, however, the Venetians by transferring their ambitions to another field succeeded in wresting from adverse fortune their most glorious triumphs. The event which conveniently marks the new era was the extension of Venetian authority to the mainland. This began with the annexation of Treviso in 1399 and continued by successive annexations for nearly a century until a large part of northern Italy was under Venetian control. Territorial acquisitions were no new thing for Venice, as we have seen, but hitherto her annexations had been in the East and of such a nature that they could be defended by her navy. Venice had always stood with her back to the mainland protected by the impassable barrier of the lagoon. But once she had crossed this barrier she was exposed to land attack along an arbitrary and almost indefensible frontier. This compelled her to develop an army and to measure herself with land powers which, in combination if not singly, were more than her equal.

This new policy has therefore been the subject of much criticism by later writers as indeed it was at the time by members of the conservative or anti-imperialist party, one of whom, the aged Doge Mocenigo, warned the Venetians against the election of the imperialist, Foscari, as his successor, a warning which went unheeded. But critics forget that nations are not always free to choose their policy but follow perforce the line dictated to them by circumstances. This was clearly the case with Venice. Venetian statesmen understood perfectly that in crossing to the mainland they were incurring grave risks and greatly weakening their position, but the alternative was far worse. The mainland was the source of the food supply for two hundred thousand people. Moreover it was through the mainland routes that Venetian commerce passed to the great markets of the North. So long as these vital interests were not interfered with the Venetians were glad to leave the mainland to itself. But at the time we are considering, political developments upon the mainland had taken a direction which was highly inimical to Venetian interests. The larger cities

had fallen under the control of powerful families like
the Medici of Florence, the Scaligers of Verona, and
the Visconti of Milan, men who were alike able, ambitious, and unscrupulous. By conquest, alliance,
intrigue, or purchase they were annexing neighboring
territories and consolidating the once disintegrated mainland. They were jealous of the power of Venice and
above all of her popular and liberal form of government,
which was a standing rebuke to their own. From these
despots Venice had nothing to fear in the way of direct
attack, but their control of her food supply and of her
trade routes gave them a strangle hold of which they
were not slow to avail themselves on occasion. Worse
still, these principalities of the mainland were in occasional alliance with greater enemies, the Emperor,
Hungary, and France.

It was not, therefore, in a spirit of reckless adventure
but after much provocation and in defense of vital
national interests that Venice embarked upon a policy
which, though perilous, involved the lesser risk. That
risk, so far as it was humanly foreseeable, was clearly
foreseen. Venice knew that it would involve war and a
military establishment and unprecedented expenditure.
She did not know that all this must be borne in a period
of decaying fortune. She did not foresee the new trade
route and the inevitable collapse of her commerce. But
for this unexpected factor which was as little anticipated
by conservatives as by imperialists her choice might have
been more obviously justified by the outcome. Even
as it was the new policy not only kept the trade routes
open for a couple of centuries but it offered in a considerable measure a way of escape from the ruin which no
foresight could have averted. Venice had been a nation
of sailors and merchants. She ended as a nation of
landed proprietors in her mainland territories, territories

which she had taken by force from despots who had
acquired and who held them by force but which she
reconciled to her rule by the excellence of her laws, the
uniformity of her justice, and the lightness of her taxation
so that, though repeatedly snatched away, they returned
voluntarily to her sway when free to do so.

For a time the venture prospered. The cost of acquisition was moderate and the advantages of possession in
the assured food supply and security to commerce amply
justified the outlay. Indeed the threatened disaster
from this quarter did not appear for more than a century
and not until Venice was weakened by losses from another
and far more dangerous source.

The situation in the East had long been changing to
the detriment of commerce. The gradual advance of
the Turks, an intensely militaristic but non-industrial
and non-commercial power, had reduced the Byzantine
empire to the limits of Constantinople itself and had
greatly reduced the industrial output of the whole Levant,
formerly the most advanced technically of all European
and Mediterranean lands. Venice was to experience
what modern nations are beginning to realize, that an
industrial and commercial people cannot grow rich in
an impoverished world. When the great struggle ended
with the fall of Constantinople in 1453 the population of
the city had dwindled to a fraction of its former number,
grass grew in the streets, and industry and trade were
stagnant. The conqueror made heroic efforts to restore
the prosperity of his new capital by offering the most
extraordinary inducements to Venetians and others to
re-establish themselves there and renew their activities,
inducements which were to have altogether unexpected
consequences in later centuries, but the mischief which
had been wrought proved incapable of remedy. Turkey
has had great rulers but they have proved unable to

correct the blight which everywhere results from the principles of Turkish rule.

The ruin of Constantinople was a serious loss to Venice but it left the more lucrative trade with Alexandria and other eastern ports comparatively undisturbed. With the improved situation in the West Venice might be said to be holding her own for the better part of the fifteenth century.

Toward the end of the century, however, fell another blow wholly unexpected and far more crushing. In 1486 Vasco da Gama rounded the Cape of Good Hope and discovered the sea route to India and the Far East. This route, though longer than the overland route which Venice had brought under her control, was vastly cheaper. All conditions were favorable to its immediate and effective exploitation. Portugal, the fortunate discoverer, was for the moment dominated by a spirit of enterprise in strange contrast to her subsequent lethargy and sloth. Other western nations were beginning to develop that maritime enterprise which was to give their peoples undreamed of expansion and power. On the other hand Venice was envied and feared as a great power and hated as a monopolist. It was known that she exacted a profit of one hundred per cent on every turnover. We know the result, the rapid expansion of the Portuguese Empire followed by the world overshadowing power of Spain. Then the rising power of Holland followed by that of France and England with their sanguinary struggles for control and their rapid development of a commerce with which Venice could not compete. Venice was a thousand miles farther away from India by the new route than Lisbon and even farther away economically from her customers in the North and West. Moreover her ships which were swift oared galleys, though outdistancing all rivals in the Mediterranean, were wholly unsuited to the long ocean route, a defect to be remedied, no doubt, but not at once and in the face of the most serious handicaps.

A suggestion was made in 1504 which if adopted would have reversed the situation and left the western powers again at a hopeless disadvantage. This was nothing less than the construction of a canal across the Isthmus of Suez. Whether the resources of the time would have sufficed for such an undertaking we can only speculate. Probably under favorable conditions the work might have been brought to a successful conclusion. But the conditions were not favorable. The canal could be built only with the co-operation of Egypt and while that country had suffered almost as much as Venice by the diversion of commerce from the Mediterranean, the splendid Caliphate of Cairo, weakened by corruption and internal dissension, was now tottering to its fall. The proposal to build a canal had unfortunately been coupled with a proposal to make war upon Portugal and the Sultan of Egypt quite naturally decided to begin with war. Though briefly victorious the war exhausted his resources and his kingdom soon succumbed to the rising power of Turkey under whose baneful sway all hope of a canal disappeared.

Meanwhile Venice had suffered another disaster which put an end to any heroic effort to retrieve her fortunes. Venice as we have previously noted had never been in favor with the Pope. Despite threats and blandishments the Republic had stoutly maintained its religious independence. In the age-long struggle, too, between the emperor and the Pope, Venice had skillfully contrived to hold the balance of power, preventing either from acquiring that ascendency which he sought. The powerful Pope, Julius II, determined to put an end to this state of affairs and in 1508 succeeded in forming the

League of Cambrai in which France, Spain, the Emperor, the Papal States, and certain of the minor Italian principalities, very nearly the whole of Europe in fact, were banded together against Venice. The latter suffered a severe defeat at Agnadello and was deprived of all her newly acquired possessions on the Italian mainland. Venice seemed ruined but her astute statesmanship saw the weakness in the new combination. The allies were traditional enemies and were but briefly united against a power that they all envied and feared. Venice played upon these antipathies and soon the Pope was chasing his allies out of Italy and courting Venice in the difficult task. Soon all her mainland possessions were back under her rule where they remained practically during the life of the Republic.

Despite these occasional favors of fortune the basis of Venetian prosperity had been hopelessly cut away. Desperately the Venetians clung to all that could be retained and sought substitutes for that which was lost. The annual fair, greatest of its kind, was maintained in undiminished splendor and its patronage continued long after its utility had ceased. Manufacture was fostered and not only Venice but the whole Venetian mainland became a hive of industry producing wares which could long be obtained nowhere else. Capital accumulations were enormous and profitably invested and even the magnificent spending to which the Venetians had become accustomed in the days of greater prosperity did not at once exhaust them. Venetian extravagance, indeed, gave to Venice a semblance of power long after the substance had vanished.

One supreme disaster awaited the doomed Republic. As the power of Venice waned that of Turkey increased. The extension of this purely military empire could not fail to be at the expense of Venice. Simultaneously

with the acquisition of territories upon the Italian mainland went the loss of territories in the East. These
gains and losses continued throughout the fifteenth century with the net result that Venice was crowded
toward the West. This coincided with the changed conditions already referred to. The East under Turkish
rule was no longer important either as a productive area
or as a way station on the way to the farther East beyond. There were Venetians who dreamed a new dream
for their country at this time, a dream which for a while
seemed not incapable of realization. Might not the
Republic, forced out of the East, acquire a dominating
position in Italy, perhaps the control of the whole peninsula, and thus enjoy a new lease of life as a great con-
tinental power? In the domain of law and civil administration, probably too in military science, Venice was
far in advance of contemporary nations. Might she not
legitimately aspire to the leadership of Italy and to a
foremost place among modern nations? Unfortunately
for Venice there were others that saw this possibility.
The plan accorded ill with the ambitions of France, of
Spain, of the Emperor, of the Pope, least of all with the
interests of the surviving Italian despots who had seen
so many of their number fall before advancing Venice
and who saw that their turn came next. Hence the
League of Cambrai and its half realized program.
Venice kept her acquisitions but after the annexation
of Cremona in 1499 she acquired no more. The dream
of a Venetian Italy was not to come true.

But while the accessions stopped, the losses continued.
Even the brilliant naval victory of Lepanto in 1571 with
its destruction of the Turkish fleet did not prevent the
loss of Cyprus in the same year with the exclusion of
Venice from the easternmost Mediterranean, though it
gave her a much needed respite of which, however, she

was able to make little use for the strengthening of her
position. Finally in 1644 the long awaited storm broke.
A powerful Turkish expedition launched ostensibly to
avenge an act of piracy which Venice was accused of
having instigated, attacked Crete, one of the two considerable possessions which remained to Venice in the
East. The expedition was in such overwhelming force
that no opposition was expected. The result, however,
was a war which lasted for twenty-five years, ruining one
contestant and permanently arresting the advance of
the other. Despite the extreme exhaustion resulting
from this struggle Venice did not hesitate twenty years
later to enter a new league against the Turk. An incident of the war which followed was the destruction of
the Parthenon in 1689. The Venetians recovered the
Morea (Peloponnesus) and held it for another generation when it was lost to the Turks. With it passed the
last vestige of imperial Venice. From that day the city
was reduced to the ignoble role of amuser of the nations.

Curiously enough it is to this period of declining fortunes that we owe the city's most memorable achievements in the arts and in the finer side of living. Up to
this time the Venetians had been too busy making money
to give much attention to the fine art of spending it, a
situation not without its parallel in times nearer our own.
If the life of the city had been arrested in 1400 not a
single Venetian picture would now hang in our art
galleries. In the more utilitarian art of architecture, to
be sure, the case was somewhat better. Saint Mark's
was there but there was no Square of Saint Mark's with
its surrounding arcades to give it glorious setting. The
Doge's Palace was there, at least the two outer façades
with their incomparable arcades, and not a few of the
Gothic palaces that we now admire on the Grand Canal.
But the best even of these were not yet begun to say

nothing of the stupendous piles, Lombard, Renaissance, and Baroque, which now overshadow their more graceful and modest predecessors. So with the churches which the traveller now visits in quest of works of art or historic associations. Barely two of the dozen or more now visited were then in existence. The earlier period had laid foundations and had accumulated colossal wealth for the superstructure which was to be reared in later and less affluent times.

Perhaps the most impressive change which took place at this time, doubtless very gradually and for the most part without recorded date, was the introduction of what we may call municipal housekeeping. It is incontestable that the Venetian, even in the great days, was careless in certain matters to which we have grown sensitive. Some of these were matters of appearance, others of vital importance, sanitary and otherwise. The two were closely related then as always.

To recall one of the minor features of fifteenth century Venice, it is difficult to imagine much of trimness and tidiness in the city so long as the streets were unpaved and the canals were bordered with stakes interwoven with osiers as was certainly the case up to the fifteenth century and later. The bordering of the canals with brick walls coped with stone and the paving of all streets, even the least frequented, with cut stone is perhaps the most noteworthy achievement of this period. Taken in the aggregate it involved enormous labor and expense, an outlay hardly paralleled in other cities.

More conspicuous and memorable if not more important was the transformation of Saint Mark's Square. This, as the reader has been often reminded, had hitherto been merely an open space surrounded by heterogeneous and indifferent buildings and devoted to utilitarian and even unseemly uses. It was apparently in the interest

of these baser uses and nowise in anticipation of its
later monumental character that the Square had been
enlarged in 1176. A large part of this area was given
over to stone cutters whose business requires much space.
The rest was an open market packed full on occasion
with booths, wares, vegetables and all the miscellany
which may be seen in the market squares of any Italian
town today. The ill concealed and unguarded latrine
added an offensive element to the uncomely scene. To
all of this must be added the fact that the Square was
unpaved, that it contained trees, apparently irregularly
distributed, to which horses were tied, and that it was
in all respects the counterpart of an ill kept square in a
country village.

The surroundings were hardly more attractive. The
site of Sansovino's great Library opposite the Doge's
Palace was occupied by the bakers and that of the Mint
adjoining by the butchers. Clustered thick around the
pillars of the Palace arcade, dentists, barbers, notaries,
and others conducted their interesting operations in
public. Behind, against the wall of the Palace, were
benches from which loungers watched these operations,
while boxes and other bulky articles encumbered the
arcade.

These conditions changed but slowly with the developing sense of decency and self respect. Nothing was done
until near the end of the fifteenth century when in 1495
the Square was paved with brick. This was an immense
improvement, for the unpaved square had been muddy
and nasty in the extreme in rainy weather. It was now
possible to enforce greater cleanliness which we may
assume was done.

But improvements once begun suggest other improvements and so on without limit. In 1496, the year after
the paving of the Square began an extensive reconstruc-

tion of the Square which distinctly foreshadows its monumental character. From the north side of the Square leads a street, narrow but yet the broadest in Venice, the Merceria, the most famous street in the city. It is the busiest shopping street in Venice today though the wares now displayed are very different from

Fig. 17, The Clock Tower seen from the Piazzetta between Saint Mark's on the right and the Campanile on the left. A portion of the Procuratie Vecchie appears behind the flagstaffs.

those of four centuries ago. The entrance to this street was now spanned by an arch above which rose the famous Clock Tower where the ancient clock with its twenty-four hour face still shows the hour in its peculiar fashion while knights in armor still beat the strokes upon the great bell with their huge hammers (Fig. 17). This clock tower, apparently pushed rapidly to completion, rendered inevitable the demolition of all the buildings on that side of the Square and their replacement by the beautiful arcaded structure which we know as the Procuratie Vecchie. This beautiful structure for which it would have been difficult to find a rival in its day was begun in the same year as the clock tower, 1496, whether as a part of one comprehensive plan or as an afterthought we do not know. It was not finished until 1517, perhaps because of difficulty in dealing with the owners of the land, more likely because the disastrous war with the League of Cambrai interrupted building operations.

This great embellishment of the Square seems to have reacted almost at once upon the sentiment of the people. To have stone cutters, latrines, and unkempt trees, vines and other farm-yard suggestions in the foreground of so elegant a building was an incongruity which the growing sense of taste and elegance could not endure. Hence in 1504 while the beautiful arcade was still building these unsightly elements were removed. The market of course remained, doubtless with better regulation and greater tidiness than in the earlier time. The barbers, too, still shaved and the dentists pulled teeth over by the columns of the Palace and the butcher, the baker, and the candlestick maker still carried on their trade in their premises across the way.

The butchers and the bakers were the next to move, not because their business was deemed offensive but because their premises were desired for public buildings. The proof is that when they were dispossessed in 1536 to make way for the new Library and the Mint (see Frontispiece) they were allowed to set up their shops near the foot of the great campanile where they were far more of a nuisance than before. Here they remained for nearly forty years and might have remained longer had it not been for a fortunate conflagration in 1574 which called for reconstruction and made removal possible. The Venetians with all their callousness to

unsavory sights and odors, had already in 1569 cleared
the Palace arcade of its disfiguring encumbrances. The
benches of the loungers were taken away, the boxes,
casks, and cases removed, and the dentists, barbers, and
notaries compelled to seek elsewhere a place to ply their
vocations. Quite naturally, therefore, the Venetians
took advantage of the conflagration of 1574 to remove
the bakers and butchers to an entirely different site.
The Square was now cleared of everything except the
market which was a temporary occupant limited to
certain hours and days and comparatively inoffensive.
This too was removed in 1580 and the great Square
became what it thenceforth remained, an imposing
monumental center of the city and the empire.

Architecturally, however, the Square was still incomplete. Only the northern side had attained its present
beautiful form. The southern side was occupied by
the hospital built, it will be remembered, by Orseolo the
Great, conqueror of the pirates, some six hundred years
before. This was a dignified building if we may trust
the representation of it in the great picture of Gentile
Bellini (Fig. 39, Page 190) painted about the time the
Clock Tower was built. It is a wonderful thing when
we stop to consider it, that a building on such a scale
should have been erected for such a purpose as early as
976. But in the course of six centuries it may well have
become obsolete. Whatever the cause, it was demolished
in 1584 to make way for the splendid *Procuratie Nuove*
(Fig. 1, Page 58) which were set somewhat back, thus
widening the Square considerably and exposing to full
view the campanile which had previously stood flush
with the hospital as Bellini's picture shows.

Framed thus in its two long arcades the Square stood
unchanged until the fall of the Republic. The end of
the Square was open save for the church of San Geremia,

which, situated originally in the middle of the present Square, had been moved back to this location on the occasion of the enlargement of the Square in 1176. It remained for Napoleon who had occupied the city in 1797 to give to the famous Square its finishing touch by erecting a palace at the west end with an arcade similar to that on the south side. Thus surrounded the noble precinct remained complete and inviolate save for the sacrilege of the traffic in baubles in these one-time halls of empire.

We have followed the development of the city thus far in connection with its famous square, but development was as active on the Grand Canal and in other parts of the city as here. The great majority of the palaces and churches in Venice date from these four hundred years. It is the period of the Renaissance and manifests the same phases as in other Italian cities, though with highly characteristic Venetian peculiarities. The architecture of this prolific period is almost totally ignored by the traveler who sees, not unjustly, in the Venetian Gothic the true creation of Venice. This later architecture, however, is significant and at times very beautiful. It falls into certain well defined groups or periods which the observant can easily learn to recognize.

First there is the early Romanesque, often called the Lombard Romanesque because of its apparent provenance. This is a simple, light, and graceful type of round arch architecture clearly of classical origin, avoiding equally the extremes of austerity and turgidity. It is essentially the architecture of the fifteenth century, though that century witnessed belated Gothic building and in turn left uncompleted work for the next century to finish. It first appears in minor examples like the gate of the Arsenal and the pedestal of the statue of Colleoni, a singularly pure example, too easily forgotten in the presence of the magnificent statue which it bears. In the Square it is represented by the Procuratie Vecchie, the early northern arcade built concurrently with the Clock Tower.   On the Grand Canal it is seen in the Pa-

lazzo Dario (Fig. 18) one of the first which the visitor passes on his usual tour, a narrow palace much sunken out of shape but with characteristic graceful arches and incrusted marbles, a feature borrowed from the Byzantine.   Its most magnificent example, however, is the Palazzo   Vendramin-Calergi (Fig. 19) the supreme monument of the period in the palaces of Venice.

Fig. 18, Palazzo Dario.

Most significant, however, are the churches and allied buildings of the period of which two are certain to be visited by every moderately careful traveler.   These are the church of San Zaccaria (Fig. 20) (famous for its wonderful Madonna by Bellini) and the Scuola (now Hospital) di San Marco.   The façades of these buildings, divided perpendicularly into three parts corresponding to nave and aisles and topped out with half and quarter rounds, are distinctly original and good.   Few if any of the later and more pretentious creations of the Venetian architects equal these early examples.

Most splendid of all the creations of this period is the rear portion of the Doge's Palace seen from the court and also from the canal in the rear.   Few things better illustrate the misleading power of sentiment than the

fact that every traveler goes round behind the Palace
to see the Bridge of Sighs, a wretched work of the most
degraded period which no one but the tourist ever sighed
over, and never looks at the magnificent building from
which the unsightly structure leads to the equally unsightly prison across the canal.   The visitor should

Fig. 19, Palazzo Vendramin-Calergi.

note with especial care the Palace front which faces upon
the court with its exquisite decorative details still kept
within the limits of legitimate decoration, its Renaissance
spirit, and withal its skilful adaption to the Gothic
front opposite.   It is a neglected masterpiece.

The change which took place during the sixteenth
century is best observed in Saint Mark's Square in the
contrast between the northern and southern sides.   The
difference of date is somewhat less than a century.   The
difference in character is pronounced, yet so closely are
the two akin that there is no sense of contradiction or

unpleasant contrast. The newer work is far heavier, the grouped supports more massive, the ornament more prominent and distinct. The architecture of the period is seen at its best in the Library (Fig. 21) built by Sansovino in 1536. Sansovino is the great architect of the period and this is his masterpiece. It must be accounted one of the masterpieces of the Renaissance, a fit challenge of this logical age to the fascinating heterodox Palace opposite, the preservation of which, it will be remembered, after the fire of 1574 we owe to the generous intervention of the aged Sansovino.

Fig. 20, San Zaccaria.

Yet admirable as is this architecture it shows tendencies which, to say the least, ought not to be carried much farther. The ornament is bold and stands out with an independence which is a little disquieting. Decorative elements are not quite willing to be forgotten, elements which emerge from the general whole rather than merge themselves in it. The movement is not yet one of open revolt. We might not question it if we did not know what it later came to. And Sansovino did not know. Whatever its limitation this architecture has a monumental quality which the earlier architecture lacks. It has exchanged grace for dignity, an exchange which if made prudently, architecture can always afford.

In the palace architecture of Venice this period was amply represented, among others by the Palazzo Corner

della Ca Grande (Fig. 22) a rather austere and frugally ornamented structure built by Sansovino just before he built
the Library. In church and allied architecture the façade
of the Scuola di San Rocco is a dignified and much praised
example quite in line with the examples above noted.

In church architecture, however, we have a distinctly

Fig. 21, The Library. To the right the Loggietta at the base of the
Campanile. Both are by Sansovino.

individual note due to the influence of a great and creative architect, Palladio, a man classical in his sympathies,
austere in his temperament, and original in his creative
power. The church of San Giorgio Maggiore (Fig. 23)
on a little island facing the Doge's Palace and perhaps
the most conspicuous landmark of Venice, perfectly
illustrates these ideals. The church is well worth visiting
for its details, its carved wood, and its paintings, but the
traveler need not leave the Piazzetta to see the essentials
of Palladio's art. Ornament plays little or no part in

this severely simple façade, the originality of which is only equalled by its intrinsic appropriateness. It was the constant desire of the Renaissance architects to adapt the classical architecture to con-

temporary needs. Unfortunately the front of a Christian church with its low side aisles and its high central nave was not at all the same shape as the front of a Greek temple. How adapt the architecture of the one to the shape of the other? In the opinion of the writer Palladio has most nearly succeeded.

Fig. 22, Plazzo Corner della Ca Grande.

But whatever recognition Palladio won from the Venetians, he did not win their sympathies. Venice was about the last place in the world to appreciate the austere, the severely simple,

Fig. 23, San Giorgio Maggiore.

the classic. Venice was not without appreciation and good taste as her achievements in painting and allied arts abundantly prove, but she was voluptuous, splendid, gorgeous, with the temptations that this temperamental choice implied. Palladio was not without influence on the subsequent architecture of Venice but it was the richer and more ornate style of Sansovino — still restrained and sober in his handling — that Venice adopted — and degraded — in the years that followed. To stand with the Venetians in the presence of these two great geniuses and note the way they beckoned, the choice which the Venetians made, and what it all came to is one of the great lessons of history.

The next century, the seventeenth (*i.e.* the sixteen hundreds), the perfectly logical sequel of this Venetian choice, ushers in that turgid, heavy, ornate style which

Fig. 24, Plazzo Rezzonice, the "Browning House."

in the following century became known as the Baroque. The word is of obscure origin and seems to have been first applied to jewelry where it connoted grotesque, extravagant, and meaningless forms. Its application to furniture and ultimately to architecture where it is now chiefly used, came in due course. The Baroque had almost universal vogue in the first half of the eighteenth century, a period later recognized as representing the very nadir of good taste.

In Venice the Baroque developed early. It is impossible, of course, to classify with any exactness the buildings that we characterize as Baroque. It is sufficient to cite a few examples.

The Rezzonico Palace, familiarly known as the "Browning House" (Fig. 24) because of its occupation by the poet, is a comparatively inoffensive example of this unattractive style. The baroque spirit is manifest in the columns with their heavy, protruding, rustico surfaces breaking the straight line of the shaft, the true beauty of the column. A general heaviness and gracelessness pervades everything. The Prison (connected with the Doge's Palace by the Bridge of Sighs) is another example of this cumbrous style, perhaps not so inappropriate for this purpose.

The depths to which this style could descend are best illustrated by the church of San Moisè (Fig. 25) which is on the route of every traveler as he walks from his hotel on the Grand Canal to Saint Mark's Square. It would be difficult to find a more extreme example of the vulgarity and effrontery of meaningless and obtrusive orna-
ment than the façade of this
utterly degenerate building.
It is not simply that the
ornament is big and bold and
bad, though it is all of these.
It is utterly meaningless.
There are two ways in which
ornament may have mean-
ing. First, in itself as symbol, narrative, or the like.

' Fig. 25, San Moisè.

Second, as decoration, through line, mass and arrangement completing, echoing, interpreting the building. The ornament of San Moisè has neither. Coarse and graceless forms intrude themselves upon the observer's attention with an irrelevancy that is sheer impertinence. And withal it is upon this ornament that the architect has wholly staked his case. You can strip off the ornament from the Parthenon, from Santa Sophia, from any good building and it will not be greatly missed. Good architecture never depends upon ornament even when it uses ornament. But San Moisè without its ornaments would be as uninteresting as with it. It is unfair to the architecture of these two centuries to judge it by this degraded example. There were buildings of real dignity and merit built in this period as we shall see in a moment. But it is legitimate to see in

Fig. 26, Santa Maria della Salute.

San Moisè the vicious ideal which was regnant at this time, not in Venice alone but, perhaps we must admit, in Venice more than elsewhere.

We have reserved for separate consideration one great church which holds a unique place not only in the architecture of these late centuries but in the general aspect of Venice, Santa Maria della Salute (Fig. 26). More than Saint Mark's or even its towering campanile, perhaps more than the Doge's Palace itself, the comely dome of this great church dominates the aspect of Venice. Begun in 1631, about a generation before San Moisè, this church is strangely free from the ornate buffooneries of the Baroque. It is first of all a building superb in its composition, a dome resting upon an octagonal structure. Interior and exterior alike are magnificent units instantly felt and comprehended as such. There are Baroque ornamental forms but they are easily overlooked. The building dominates its details as every good building must. Even the huge scrolls around the base of the dome, so unloved in their use in other Baroque buildings, the writer ventures here to admire as admirable supports for the dome and transitions to the broader mass below. The church is not above criticism but it is the best thing that this century produced and one of the most splendid landmarks of this or any other city.

Our attention has been given almost wholly to the exteriors of Venetian buildings, chiefly even to their façades. This is inevitable. Interiors for the most part are inaccessible and in the decadence of Venice they have rarely preserved their original character. A single interior, however, that of the Doge's Palace, is invariably visited and is highly characteristic of Venetian taste. The building, it will be remembered, was gutted by fire in 1574 and 1577. The time spent in reconstruction crowded the work of decoration into the period we have been considering. The work began, however, while Sansovino and Palladio were still alive and both are said to have contributed to it, though it is difficult to trace in any part of the work the distinctive taste of Palladio.

The striking feature of these great apartments is their

Fig. 27, The Sala del Senato, Doge's Palace.

ceilings, more particularly those of the Anticollegio and of the Sala del Senato (Fig. 27), the former perhaps to be adjudged the finest in Venice. These ceilings are divided into compartments, round, oval, square, oblong, and other shapes, containing paintings and separated from one another by massive gilded frames of carved wood. Nothing can well surpass the gorgeousness of these splendid surfaces ablaze with gold and color. Probably this general character makes its impression though in the writer's experience it seldom attracts conscious attention. Interest at once centers upon the paintings.

Guide book and ciceroni inform us that this is by Tintoretto, that by Veronese and so on with details of who
the Doge is and what he is represented as doing. In
short it is a picture gallery and we take it as such. If
our attention finds time to wander from the pictures to
the room and the ceiling as such we cannot fail to note
that the decoration gives no hint of structure, no suggestion of support. Its heavy mass hangs like a weight
from the ceiling whose ability to support it is not dis-
closed. In a word, these ceilings are art but they are
not decoration; they are gorgeous and splendid but they
are not interpretive of structure; they show no sympathy
with its purpose, suggest no contribution to the accomplishment of its task. All is characteristic of the
Renaissance, especially of the Renaissance in Venice.
It suggests the Baroque.

In accordance with the purpose of this book attention
has been confined to those visible things which are likely
to interest the traveler. It is with reluctance that the
invisible and intangible achievements of these declining
yet ever creative years are passed by. Along with the
rearing of palaces and churches there were never ceasing
activities in the building of hospitals, the sanitation of
the city, the artificializing of the lagoons, the deepening
of the harbor, the fight against malaria, activities much
in the spirit of our own time and augmenting as the
fortunes of the city declined. Not less noteworthy were
the constructive activities of Venice in the development
of law and judicial procedure, activities by which Venice
commanded the respect of Europe long after she had
ceased to inspire its fear. Not least memorable was
the long struggle with the church to establish the principle since recognized by every state in Christendom of
the supremacy of the civil courts in the enforcement
of civil law. This principle which Europe slowly

established by centuries of struggle had been established
in Venice from the first, and thanks to the powerful support of Paolo Sarpi, a Venetian Servite monk, it survived
the disaster of Cambrai. But these achievements will
not be evident to the traveler and can, therefore, find
no place in this book.

The four centuries under consideration here left Venice
essentially as we see it today. Another century and
more has since been added and vast changes have taken
place in the fortunes of the city. Great suburbs have
grown up on the adjacent mainland. New industries
have developed contrasting strangely with the old traditions. Above all the tourist has taken possession and
the impoverished population fawns before him. That
too is changing. Serious interests compete with tourist
toryism. Motor boats displace the picturesque but
dawdling gondolas and Venice lives again with a life that
is her own, the life of today. But all this has left little
visible mark upon the city. If the last Doge who laid
aside his cap in 1797 saying that he would not need it
again were to return to the city today he could name
every church, every palace on the Grand Canal. Hush
the motor boats and keep him away from the railway
station and he would feel at home after the lapse of a
hundred and thirty years. What other city has so
defied this era of change?

PART II

VENETIAN ART

CHAPTER VII

Venice, in common with the whole of Christendom, was heir to an art tradition from which she was slower than most to emancipate herself. Some knowledge of this tradition and of the remarkable art which it produced is necessary to an understanding of the individual and local developments which found in it their common origin.

The Byzantine tradition is not to be thought of as narrowly limited to Constantinople in its origin and as artificially propagated from that center by a process of conscious borrowing and imitation. General in both origin and practice it was essentially the Christian tradition, a tradition not unmodified by local and personal factors but manifesting a degree of uniformity which, viewed from a distance, quite overshadows these differences of detail. It is called Byzantine simply because of the unique eminence of Constantinople in wealth, art, and culture during this period when the western peoples were on too low a cultural plane to fashion a tradition of their own. Later these peoples awoke and, stimulated by renewed contact with the art of the ancients, gradually developed an art which expressed their character and varying individuality. This earlier tutelage and later emancipation was common to them all. Only the date was different and, in the case of Venice, very late.

There are few greater contrasts than that between the art of the Middle Ages and that of the modern period. We are familiar with the latter, not with the former.

Each has its conventions, that is, tacitly recognized deviations from nature in the interest of artistic effect. But we are so used to the conventions of the Renaissance art that they do not seem to us to be deviations from nature. We look through them, forget them, and get from them the impression of naturalness.

This is the normal way in which a people always regards an art which is truly its own. It seems incredible to us that the figures in a Japanese print should appear natural to the Japanese but they undoubtedly do. Similarly the figures of the Byzantine painter and mosaicist, whatever merit we may concede to them, seem to be totally unnatural. They did not seem so to people of that time. If we cannot say that people thought them altogether natural we may at least be sure that no one thought about their unnaturalness or was troubled by it. They were thinking about something else as the one who contemplates real art always does.

It is altogether useless for us to approach the study of mediaeval art from the standpoint of our own, comparing the unnaturalness of the one with the naturalness of the other. This is for the most part only a comparison of unfamiliar conventions with familiar conventions, of course to the disparagement of the former. Our object should be to discover that "something else" which the artist and his contemporaries saw in this art and which made them forget the conventions which in our ignorance become so obtrusive. For the soul of art is always to be found in that "something else." No artist worthy of the name was ever interested in mere naturalness of representation.

The characteristic of mediaeval art which most impresses a modern observer is its formalism and rigidity in which it rivals the art of Egypt itself. Of vivacity, spontaneity, personality there seems to be little or nothing. Everything seems to be prescribed; nothing left to the imagination. There is liberty of choice in matters that do not signify but seldom anything that could be called originality.

This characteristic was due, at least in part, to peculiar historic causes. When Constantine in the fourth century made Christianity the religion of the Empire he was moved thereto in part by the fact that it represented the largest body of united opinion in the realm. This unity he sought to make the support of his throne. But no sooner had he made Christianity supreme than this unity vanished. While the Christians were persecuted they were united, but with this unifying pressure removed they began forthwith to disagree and to develop those differences which have characterized them ever since. This alarmed Constantine who saw in the growing dissensions among Christians the weakening and possible destruction of his empire. To avert this disaster the Council of Nicaea was called with no less a program than the settlement of all the questions that were threatening Christian unity. Constantine opened the council in person, expressing no preference as between different views but insisting in the strongest terms upon the necessity of agreement. That theological and philosophical discussion was still immature and that the agreement reached by the vote of representatives many of whom had no opinion on the subject could be little more than verbal was hardly appreciated by an old soldier who was concerned more for peace than for orthodoxy. This continued to be the concern of his successors for centuries to come, especially in the East where theological differences continually led to armed conflict and threatened the very existence of the state. Two centuries after Constantine we find Justinian, a man very differently minded but not less a statesman, struggling with the same problem. Himself profoundly interested in theology and warned of the futility of attempted agreement through council decisions, he decided to settle the question himself. It is a pathetic picture, that of the great emperor sitting long hours at his desk in an attempt to indite and to promulgate by imperial authority the ultimate verities of Christianity.

We need not concern ourselves with the conclusion reached in the one case or the other. It is needless to say that the desired unity was not attained, though dissent was more or less silenced, probably with advantage to the state. The permanent result, however, was to establish the principle of intolerance, the right of the state and ultimately of the church to dictate the belief as well as the action of the individual. This principle which so sharply distinguishes historic Christianity from other religions is not inherent in its nature, is not due to Jesus or even to Paul. It is incident rather to the use of Christianity for the ends of state in a period of advancing dissolution.

But this right of dictation was asserted not only in connection with theology. It was extended by a later Nicene Council to art, the medium through which theology was chiefly inculcated. If it was necessary that men believe alike, it was obviously necessary that men paint alike, for the one in a large measure determined the other. Hence the Council which, whatever its differences, was a unit in its estimation of its own authority, delivered itself of a definite pronouncement on this subject. It did not pertain to the painter to decide what to paint or how it should be painted. That was the function of the holy church. The artist was but the instrument to execute its behests.

Art thus definitely taken under ecclesiastical control, became in a measure stereotyped and subject to formula.

It is this character which first strikes the beholder as he gazes upon a mediaeval mosaic in Constantinople, Venice, or Rome, or an early picture in Florence, Siena, or Umbria. Only slowly does he become aware of two important facts which are necessary to a judgment of mediaeval art.

The first is that this stereotyped and unnatural character is not arbitrary but is in large measure an adaptation to the purpose for which this art was created. As such it is an excellence rather than a defect, an expression of subtle thought and aesthetic feeling which our modern realistic art too often misses. No doubt there is helplessness in mediaeval art but not all its unnaturalness is due to helplessness. The artist had a reason for drawing and arranging his figures as he did, sometimes an excellent reason which we have all too much forgotten.

The second fact is that ideas, sentiments, and even personality are as truly susceptible of expression through conventional as through naturalistic forms, in certain connections even more so. Of course if art is merely the imitation of nature then naturalism is its goal, for anything else falls short of perfect imitation. But if art is a language for the expression of certain ideas, emotions, and concepts, then it by no means follows that exact imitation of nature is the best means to that end. Nature's forms are plastic in the artist's hands and may be modified to any degree that serves the purposes of expression. Mediaeval art was certainly not naturalistic but it may be doubted whether any other art has expressed so much or conveyed its meaning so successfully. There are plenty of imperfections in mediaeval art as in every other, cases in which the artist did not succeed in accomplishing his own purpose or in realizing his own ideals. But the thing to remember is that his achievements are to be measured by his ideals, not by ours.   We sometimes forget that like the people of every other age we are one-sided, and while sensitive to some things are blind to others which another age regarded as all important.   Our hobby is naturalness. It is hard for us to realize that this is not the whole of art'; that in some cases it is not art at all.

The church art of the Middle Ages was one of those cases.   For purposes of religion mere naturalness was of very little value, was even in some connections quite inadmissible.   The church demanded of the artist two things, things quite distinct and not always easily reconciled, but alike indispensable.

On the one hand he must make beautiful the church. This was *decoration*.

On the other hand he must tell the sacred stories, depict angels, saints, and apostles, inculcate virtues, explain dogmas, and guide the beholder in ritual worship. This we may call *instruction*.

Strange as it may seem there are very compelling reasons why the artist should depart from naturalness in the interest of both decoration and instruction.   Persons and things represented upon the church with a view to beautifying it must be harmonized with it and brought into sympathy with its character or they will only produce discords.   Hence the necessity for a whole series of decorative conventions.   Or again if our purpose is to instruct and guide the worshiper we shall be called upon to depart from nature in quite a different way. It might seem that naturalness would be an aid in all this.   Stories, saints, and dogmas would seem to gain by being represented as naturally as possible.   So thought Giotto and his successors.   They did not realize at first that when their stories became natural they would cease to be sacred and when the saints became lifelike they would cease to be saints.   But that is what hap-

pened and men like Fra Angelico saw it. For naturalness can be nothing else than conformity to our
experience, and our experience is not of things sacred
nor are our acquaintances saints.

The mediaeval artist with all his limitations was certainly conscious of these things as we are not. He
doubtless could not have been naturalistic if he had
tried but he certainly did not always try. On the
contrary he learned to deviate from nature in certain
regular and studied ways concerning which both artists
and their public gradually came into a large measure of
agreement and understanding. Hence the term, convention, *i.e.*, agreement, the original meaning of the word.
These conventions were developed in the interest, now
of one, now of the other of the purposes which he always
kept in view. Let us briefly consider each.

Decoration is not to be confounded with ornament.
To put beautiful things upon a wall will not necessarily
make it a beautiful wall. It may spoil it. Indeed it
is hardly an exaggeration to say that for the last five
hundred years it has usually done so, for the artist in
these later times in his search for naturalness has lost
the mediaeval instinct for decoration.

*Decorative art is art whose purpose is to make something
else than itself beautiful.*

Beautiful things will not necessarily do this. Unbeautiful things may conceivably do it. It is a question
not of their own beauty but of their effect upon the thing
decorated. The essential thing therefore is that we
should remember what we are decorating, that we
should understand and respect its character, that further,
we should express and interpret its character by means
of our decoration. No decoration is good, no matter
how beautiful in itself, if it absorbs all our thought in
itself and makes us forget the thing decorated. Above

all it is inadmissible that decoration should deceive us
about that which it purports to beautify or that it should
apologize for it or interfere with its nature or use. The
mere mention of these things reminds us how many
objects ranging from cathedrals to teapots have been
disfigured by mistaken attempts at decoration.

It is perhaps well to remind ourselves at this point
that decoration is not the only aim in art and that a
work may be very great art though a poor decoration.
The famous Sistine Ceiling of Michelangelo is a case in
point. As decoration it is open to the gravest criticism,
yet as a work of art it ranks among the three or four
greatest in the world. To assert that a work is not
decorative is not to condemn it; it is merely to classify
it. On the other hand we cannot but recognize it as a
merit when a work used for decorative purposes is decorative in character. This quality the mediaeval art possesses in a degree far higher than our own. The early
artists did not make pictures so beautiful or figures so
lifelike as those of a later time but they thought much
more about the church they were decorating. We must
judge their art, therefore, not by the stiffness of the
figures or the absence of perspective, but by the beauty
of the church which they achieved.

Instruction is less easy to define than decoration but
it is plain that like the latter it made demands upon the
artist which were quite at variance with realism. In
nothing does mediaeval art differ from modern art so
much as in the nature of its theme. The subject of
modern art, broadly speaking, is nature. Out of this
vast repertory it may sort and choose in infinite variety,
but its theme is always nature and naturalness is its
criterion. The subject of mediaeval art, on the contrary,
is the supernatural. No matter how homely or terrestrial
the scene of the story may be there is always something

about it that is above nature or other than nature. For such art, to be merely natural was flat failure.

But we have no experience of the supernatural and attempts to express the supernatural became of necessity merely a kind of unnaturalness. This in its turn was slowly formulated by tacit agreement into conventions which the people, like the artists, came to understand. The halo used in its different forms to designate saintly or celestial personages is a familiar example. The gold background used by the mosaicists and contemporary painters, adopted in the first instance for decorative reasons, later acquired an ideal and spiritual significance. To these must be added the multitude of symbols, colors, attitudes, and objects, which gradually constituted a language perfectly intelligible to the instructed and largely even to the ignorant of the time. This language of convention permeates the whole body of mediaeval art and is indispensable to the accomplishment of its purpose. The invasion of naturalism in the Renaissance destroyed not only these conventions but in large measure also the ideas and sentiments which they were devised to express, thus imposing a double task upon those who would grasp its meaning.

An effectual barrier to realism in mediaeval art was its exclusion of perspective. It is two-dimension art. The introduction of the third dimension is the achievement of the Renaissance and was a necessary condition of its program.

Why did the mediaeval art exclude perspective? Partly, no doubt, because it was beyond the painter's powers. Skilful as the mediaeval artists often were in their own way, the science of perspective presented difficulties which were to be mastered only after centuries of effort and by an age very differently minded from this. It is quite possible that some of the finest decorations of the Middle Ages would have been spoiled if the artist had been clever enough to do so.

But a further and more potent reason was the artist's love of gold and color and his feeling that the wall looked better that way.   This feeling hindered the introduction of perspective well down into the Renaissance.   When we recall that in Giotto's time it was still customary to stipulate in the contract for a wall decoration that a certain percentage of the surface should be covered with ultramarine blue we can understand that there were other than negative reasons for the use of flat backgrounds in gold and color.

But if these flat backgrounds excluded perspective and with it all the vast range of pictorial art, they had the immense advantage from the standpoint of decoration that they left the wall intact and undisturbed. Physically, of course, the wall is undisturbed in any case, but our impression or consciousness of it is greatly influenced by that which is put upon it.

Let us take an extreme illustration. The writer recalls a restaurant the entire rear wall of which was covered with a mirror.   This reflected the entire room and to a person entering, it doubled its apparent size and accommodations, so much so that customers frequently tried to find seats in this apparent rear.   Collisions with the mirror resulted until the proprietor was obliged to put up a sign on the mirror: "The rear of this restaurant is closed."   This is, of course, the absolute antithesis of decoration.   The mirror did not make the wall beautiful; it simply annihilated it.

Now a pictorial or perspective decoration has something the same effect as the mirror. It does not absolutely deceive us as to the existence or location of the wall — the pictorial decorator is usually pretty careful to avoid anything like illusion painting — but it carries us in imagination quite beyond the wall, which it can do only by inducing us to forget the wall, while we are thinking about the picture. There is thus an inherent conflict between perspective and decoration. Perspective which gives depth to a picture, knocks a hole in the wall in so doing. Physically the wall is intact but our consciousness of it is weakened and confused.

Let us remind ourselves once more that this is not necessarily a condemnation. Some pictures are worth infinitely more than the walls on which they are painted or the buildings in which they are placed. Leonardo knocks out the end of the room on which he has painted his "Last Supper," but we would willingly give any number of such rooms for such a picture. All the same it does not beautify the room or help us to be conscious of it. Even the chalky toned pictured walls of Puvis de Chavannes which differentiate so sharply between the picture world and the world in which we stand have for us as walls something less than one hundred per cent of reality.

Let us pass now from the mirror wall and the picture wall to the plain wall. We are fully conscious that it is and where it is, but ordinarily we do not think much about it or feel much impressed by it. For most purposes this is quite sufficient, but if we are to appreciate the room of which it forms a part and feel its beauty we must notice the wall and be impressed by it. Is it not plain that if the wall is covered with gold or with brilliant color it will make much more impression upon us than before? And this is precisely the purpose of decoration, to emphasize and make pleasingly impressive the thing decorated without destroying or disguising its character.

For similar reasons figures or other objects represented upon the wall must avoid extreme detachment and vivid relief. They must remember that they are upon the wall, that they are in fact a part of its surface. The mediaeval artist was perfectly conscious of this requirement. His figures are essentially flat. They seldom detach themselves from the wall nor are they lifted out in high relief by strong modeling. Draperies and other features are represented as far as possible by lines after the manner of a line drawing instead of by shading which is too vivid for decorative purposes. The artist wishes to avoid the suggestion of a hump or projection from the surface and so chooses the less vivid method of representation. Even the faces are left flat, eyes, nose, and mouth being represented chiefly by lines or spots.

But walls have more than surface. They have boundaries and lines of union, often of great significance and beauty, and are used in conjunction with other elements, pillars, mouldings, and the like, which vastly complicate the decorator's problem. As the wall introduces the problem of surface, so these involve the problem of line. It is not enough that the artist respect the surface of his wall by keeping his decoration flat. He must also respect the lines of that which he is decorating. This requirement seems to be much less appreciated. We not infrequently hear a composition praised as a good decoration simply because the artist has kept his figures flat, when he has sprawled over the surface random, lawless composition lines which show not the slightest regard for the compelling lines of the architecture about them. We are all of us conscious of the importance of harmony in sounds and usually in colors as well. But the realistic painters of the last five hundred years interested only in spontaneity and naturalness, have taught us to disregard the subtle harmonies of line which are quite as vital to artistic effect as the harmonies of sound are to music. Not only must composition lines be harmonious among themselves, a requirement that every painter recognizes, but they must be harmonious with the lines of their setting. This is the paramount problem of decoration.

Architectural decoration involves this problem of line in a very high degree. First of all the building has its own powerful and all important lines, the straight line of the pillars, the curve of the arches and the vaults, etc. These furnish the organ accompaniment, as it were, to all other lines that may be added, furniture, decorations, and the like. Such lines are necessarily subordinate. It is the organ that gives the tune.

Every true decorator is conscious of this problem. He may solve it well or ill but he knows that every figure and every object that he represents must be disposed with references to these compelling architectural lines. And since the dominant architectural lines are usually perpendicular, straight, sober, and dignified, the subtle process of architectural convention which is always at work tends to assimilate figures and all else to these architectural forms. Angels arrange themselves symmetrically and their wings unconsciously repeat the curve of the vault above. Saints and prophets stand erect and motionless, true pillars in the church. Their draperies hang in straight and simple folds like the columns below them. They have simply heard the organ playing and have learned to sing in tune.

No art in the world has ever so perfectly met these requirements of architectural decoration as the mediaeval art and in particular the mediaeval mosaics. Supreme examples are the Procession of the Maidens in Ravenna and the mosaic panels of Cefalù, works which have inspired some of the rare triumphs of the modern decorator, notably the superb series in the Pantheon by Puvis de Chavannes (the series usually ignored by the visitor, the *upper* series to the right on entering). Here, seen

between the compelling lines of the fluted columns stand
in dignified procession the most perfectly conventionalized figures of modern times.   There is no constraint,
no stiffness, no monotony.   The perfect harmony of
the whole is a matter of inner sympathy.   The triumph
of this great master of mediaeval harmony is the more
impressive by contrast with the nearby work of other
artists who are blind with their seeing eyes.   More
striking still is the contrast with the art of the late
Renaissance whose chief characteristic was ostentatious
repudiation of all dependence upon anything but itself.

But this problem of line harmony was one that permitted no absolute and complete solution.   Much as
we admire the Procession of Maidens and other like
compositions, we are compelled to recognize that life
does not altogether lend itself to processional arrangement.   There were stories which could not be archi-
tecturalized without becoming unintelligible.   In such
cases decoration had to content itself with gold background and flat figures leaving lines to go whither they
would.   To the writer these story mosaics, such as are
seen on the side walls of Monreale and in certain parts
of Saint Mark's, are an unhappy compromise, too
naturalistic to permit of decorative arrangement and
too flat to have the merit of picture.   This was where
decoration and instruction clashed with doubtful victory
to either.

Such conflicts, however, were exceptional.   For the
most part the gold background and the dignified, conventional figures which harmonized so well with the
architectural forms about them served equally the ends
of spiritual instruction.   Figures portrayed upon a gold
background and in an unrealistic manner were by that
very fact removed from our realistic, worldly environment.   It was thus easy to conceive of them as of another

kind and living in another world than ourselves. If
golden sheen did not perfectly connote celestial character
and environment it met the requirements of a childlike
imagination and the gold background became in itself
a symbol of abstraction and spiritual character. As
such it was restored by Fra Angelico in protest against
the destructive realism of the Renaissance. Even less
conservative artists continued far down into the Renaissance the practice of excluding perspective — already
quite familiar—from the representation of celestial beings
and scenes while terrestrial scenes were represented in
perspective in adjacent panels or even in other parts of
the same picture. Perspective was the medium of the
mundane, flat surface of the celestial, a distinction which
can still be traced.

As with the flat background so with the conventional
figure. Its stiffness and formality, whether determined
in the first instance by helplessness or by decorative
adaptation, acquired a sacred character serviceable for
the ends of edification. Only the exigencies of action and
incident found decorative conventions unsuitable and
forced such concessions as they might.

We have considered the mediaeval art thus far in the
form of mural decoration. In another and hardly less
important form, that of the altar piece, the same principles worked out interesting differences of result.

This branch of mediaeval art was in its nature far
more perishable than mural decorations and very few
mediaeval altar pieces now exist. For our knowledge of
them we are largely dependent upon later works of the
transitional or early Renaissance period in which the
mediaeval characteristics are still present.

The mediaeval altar piece was not merely a bit of
altar furniture but a part of the altar itself. As such it
had a quasi architectural rather than a purely pictorial

character. Not a picture hung to the wall by a cord or wire, it was the crowning part of a structure half architecture in character. The altar piece dominated the altar as the altar dominated the chapel. The altar was symmetrically placed in a chapel which was also symmetrical and as beautiful as the builder could make it. In this limited space with its impressive symmetries the altar was given the place of honor, a place necessarily exacting in its requirements. It was the altar piece which was to make the chapel beautiful, which was to catch the eye and direct attention down the long aisle or across the pillared nave to the place of devotion.

It is clear that the altar piece, as a structural part of the altar itself and placed in an impressive architectural setting, must, in the interest of decorative effect, assume a form, if not strictly architectural, at least harmonious with the architecture with which it was surrounded. It must have impressive symmetry and beauty of design, quite aside from its pictorial or intellectual character. This threw the emphasis heavily upon the structure or what we are wont to call — quite inadequately — the frame. The frame is all important in these early altar pieces, as witness the magnificent Gothic frames which are so conspicuous an ornament in our modern museums. It would hardly be an exaggeration in some cases to speak of the frame as the real altar piece and the painting as accessory. Certainly upon the one as upon the other the artist lavished his utmost care.

Hardly less important than this requirement of symmetry and architectural design was the demand for light and color. Gold and color not only had their decorative value but they were all potent to catch the eye and command the attention of the beholder. Nay, more. They were in no small degree the vehicle of emotional and spiritual suggestion. An ascetic or over intellectual age may disparage them as sensuous, but disparagement is itself an homage, often a mere affectation. The harmonious combination of color and gold is the visual counterpart of music and its age-long rival in appealing to human emotion. Sensuous, no doubt, but what art is not sensuous that appeals through the senses to the human spirit? The sensuous has ever been the direct road to the spiritual. The intellectual is a roundabout and much more uncertain way.

The mediaeval artist was not a scientist but a poet. He did not talk or argue or explain; he sang. His conventionalized figures, his rhythmical symmetries, and his color splendor are as far from the drab realities of nature as a song is from normal human speech. But who ever objected to a song on the ground that it was not a natural way of talking? How different the pages of the modern historian from the songs of Homer, but what historian would not be a Homer if he could?

Our modern art is so entirely different from all this, not only in its forms of expression but in its objective, that we who are its creatures need constantly to remind ourselves that it is but one of the many forms of human art and that it is no more legitimate than any other. The early art subordinated man and nature to its symmetries and its color music. The later art sacrificed music and symmetry to the representation of nature and man. The constraining symmetries of the architectonic frame have been abandoned in favor of the prosaic parallelogram of carpentered picture moulding in the hope that picture and frame may be forgotten and that with the shackle of symmetry removed from figure and action we may think of them alone. Gold is banished, even color is grudged, lest the witchery of its music distract attention from the all important theme of nature and man. For the hampering symmetrical composition is substituted balance, the feebler and less noticeable concession to the unescapable exactions of symmetrical space.

This too is all legitimate. Whether we are wiser in our day and generation than the artist of long ago we are not at present called upon to decide. Suffice it to note that our art is the natural expression of a scientific and sophisticated age and that the mediaeval art, whatever its merits, presupposes a childlike naiveté which we have hopelessly lost. Of this as of other heavens it may be said that "except ye become as little children ye shall in no wise enter in."

This is a long preliminary to the consideration of the art of Venice, but for some at least a necessary one. However familiar and recognized the principles of mediaeval art, the student who is heir of the Renaissance tradition will be constantly tempted to base his judgments upon its criterion of lifelikeness and spontaneity, a criterion which the mediaeval artist repudiated in the interest of what he judged to be higher ends.

CHAPTER VIII

MEDIAEVAL ART IN VENICE

As has already been noted the Venetians were not precocious in the development of the fine arts nor was their range as wide as that of some of their rivals. Their genius was ultimately concentrated largely upon a single art in which they not only won distinction but far surpassed all others of their own or earlier times.

Their achievements in architecture have been sufficiently considered in the preceding pages. These achievements were notable and highly distinctive but in last analysis superficial and of merely local validity. They discovered no great principles and built little or nothing that we should care to see built elsewhere than on the Grand Canal. But their development of burden-bearing tracery is highly original and it gave to their open arcades a fascination rarely equaled. If suited only to Venice they were at least superlatively suited here and this is much. But Venice was essentially a borrower in architecture and with the exception of this Gothic period she did not succeed in stamping her borrowings with a distinctive character of her own.

In sculpture the Venetians did not attain to eminence. There are notable works of sculpture in Venice, one of them a masterpiece for all time, but this one is hardly Venetian and those which can be so accounted are in general of but moderate interest. In the carving of architectural ornament the Venetian sculptors were unexcelled, but this bears little relation to true sculpture as the case of Venice and of other cities proves.

It was upon painting and the nearly allied arts,

especially mosaic, that the Venetians wisely concentrated their efforts. It is hardly too much to say that among the moderns they were the first real painters. The Florentines were greater artists than the Venetians and painting was their usual, not to say their chosen, form of expression. But the Florentines were not really painters even when they painted. The Venetians were.

But all this lay far in the future at the time with which we are now concerned. Throughout the whole mediaeval period and even for the first two centuries commonly accounted as of the Renaissance, centuries in which Giotto and Masaccio were winning immortal fame for Florence, Venice was a contented follower of the Byzantine tradition. The Venetians, essentially under the leadership of Constantinople in the eleventh and twelfth centuries, showed no tendency to develop an art tradition of their own. It is not even certain that the craft was seriously developed locally. For serious undertakings they had long been in the habit of calling skilled artisans from abroad, a thing made easy by the constant traffic with Constantinople and elsewhere. It is even probable that the simple icons of the Madonna and other saints, so necessary for chapels, public and private, were largely supplied by importation from the art metropolis. At least up to the capture of Constantinople in 1204 we have little evidence of any art activity on the part of the Venetians. A century, even two centuries, after that date when Constantinople had long since lost all prestige, art activity in Venice was feeble and showed little independence, though by that time the world had turned its back upon the Middle Ages and was headed resolutely toward the modern age. This somewhat lessens our regret that the Venetian painting of these centuries has so largely perished

The great monument of mediaeval art in Venice is

the mosaic decoration of Saint Mark's. Though executed at different times and covering altogether a period of nearly a thousand years, and though subjected to destructive restoration and even in part to ruthless replacement at the most unfortunate moment, these mosaics still retain to a remarkable degree their general mediaeval character and give us a better idea of what the mediaeval artist sought to accomplish than anything else in Venice.

We are impressed first of all by the gold ground which covers not only the figured areas but arches, pendentives, pilasters, in short the entire interior above the line of marble incrustation. The walls seem literally made of gold and yet far more beautiful than gold, for it is not garish or blinding but it glows with a softened lustre of incomparable splendor. The effect is in fact very much finer than that of a polished surface of actual gold. This is due to the peculiarities of mosaic technique. Mosaic is made, as is well known, of small squares of stone or glass set in cement. As developed by the Romans, the great mosaicists of the world, mosaic was used chiefly for floors and the material used was marble in the few familiar colors which were known to them. Later when used as wall decorations glass was substituted for marble as being more brilliant and permanent and capable of any desired range of color. The small pieces being laid with the fractured surface exposed gave gleams of almost diamond brilliancy. The decorative possibilities of such a medium are sufficiently obvious and also, we may add, its unsuitableness for pictorial representation, both to be so amply demonstrated in the later history of the art.

The event which glorified mosaic above all other arts was the discovery of a way to use gold imprisoned in glass. Gold leaf is laid between panes of red hot glass which are thus fused together and then cut up into the little squares required for mosaic. These are laid, not with the fractured surface exposed but with the smooth surface outward. These surfaces, however, not perfect planes in themselves, cannot be laid in a perfect plane but present, when finished, a somewhat undulating and irregular surface which reflects the light unequally and thus obviates the hard, metallic luster that comes from a polished metal surface. To all this is added the softening effects of time, for glass, as is well known, decomposes slowly on exposure and its surface takes on a slight film which still farther reduces the metallic gleam of the gold.

This use of gold was known at least as early as the fourth century when it was used, especially in vestments and other accessories, to suggest the celestial character of the wearer. As early as the fifth century, however, it is used as a ground against which figures and patterns were set off in color. This use is at first purely decorative, gold finding a rival in the glittering cobalt blue so loved in the sixth century in Rome and elsewhere. By the seventh century, however, the gold background holds the field and has come to stay. Saint Mark's knows no other.

Slowly this gold ground acquires a more than decorative character. Through long use in sacred and celestial representations it becomes the visible symbol of the celestial. Taken over later by the painters from the mosaicists it becomes the recognized setting for Madonna and saint, the symbol and suggestion of that glory in which the blessed move and have their being. The association may seem arbitrary to an age that has become shy of material symbols, but men seem to have found it natural and inevitable. How else could the writer of the Apocalypse express the glories of the blessed city? "The twelve gates were twelve pearls; every several gate was of one pearl: And the street of the city was pure gold, as it were transparent glass." If the naturalism to which we have been bred leaves little place for this color and sheen as a spiritual token we may well recall that Phidias did not disdain to represent his goddess in ivory and gold and that to the subtlest and most intellectual of the Greeks this splendor made her seem more divine.

This gold surface, so completely dominating the interior of Saint Mark's, is beyond doubt the most striking and, perhaps we may add, the most valuable feature of these mosaics. The effect is greatly enhanced by the fact that considerable areas were unsuited to pictorial or figure decoration, and that in many of those so decorated the figures are relatively few and occupy but a moderate portion of the space. A correspondingly large surface is left to the plain gold and to the borders, medallions, and the like which complete the decorative scheme.

At the risk of tiresome iteration the writer would enter his plea for this golden splendor. We moderns are afraid of appearing childish. We hesitate to applaud a beautiful melody. It is too simple. Anybody can like that and we don't care to belong to the "anybody" class. We applaud Stravinsky and try to make ourselves — and others — think that we like him. Perhaps we do or may come to do so. It is all right. Growth comes partly in that way. But it is a pity that in our program of strenuous endeavor we should so often feel called upon to spurn our childhood. The love of splendor is not dead within us. It is merely discredited, disparaged as barbaric, belonging to an age we have left behind. Why leave any good thing behind? "We are heirs of all the ages." Why limit ourselves to the last? The visitor to Saint Mark's will do well for one brief hour to be as "barbaric" as possible in his tastes and enjoyments. He will do no violence to Michelangelo or Titian by so doing.

Turning from the gold ground to the figures and incidents represented, the mosaics of Saint Mark's are less uniform and less satisfactory. The use of radial figures in the domes, though based on a sound decorative principle, is rather mechanical and uninspiring. The narrative

Fig. 28, Saint Mark's; a dome, detail of mosaic decoration.

portions encounter the difficulty that inheres in all narrative when used for decorative purposes and no particular skill has been shown in handling the difficult problem. It is when viewed in the large that the mosaics produce their best impression, which is not altogether a criticism.

Worthy of special attention and for the most part of

very high praise are the magnificent borders which decorate the face of the arches, the medallions in the center of the domes and vaults, and the scroll patterns used in the corners of the pendentives and like situations. Some of these are of extraordinary beauty and being in their nature far better suited to mosaic representation than figures and faces they are perhaps the most satisfactory of all mosaics. Their use to break the monotony of the extensive gold surfaces is in the highest degree felicitous.

We have thus far considered the mosaics of Saint Mark's solely in the aggregate, noting characteristics that are more or less common to all, or at least to those of mediaeval date and character. If we turn, however, from these general considerations to the study of individual mosaics we are at once struck by their diversity, amounting in some cases almost to incongruity among themselves. We notice first of all that they fall into two groups which can be distinguished by the veriest novice, the early or mediaeval mosaics and the modern. The latter, though of importance as completing the mosaic decoration of the church, are otherwise of little value. Though harmonized, as far as the artist was able to do so, with the older work, they were executed at a time when mosaic was not understood and the traditions of the great Venetian school of painting completely dominated the taste of the public and the minds of artists in every line. The single merit to be noted is their concession of the gold background in the interest of general unity together with something of the rich coloring of Venetian painting. But this advantage is limited by the pictorial habit of filling the space with crowds of figures and objects in several planes, thus leaving little room for the precious gold. In composition and arrangement these mosaics betray an utter lack of decorative feeling bordering at times upon the ridiculous, as when a genealogical tree is represented by a thoroughly realistic tree of large size growing out of an equally realistic man's body while his very realistic descendants sit life size upon the limbs overhead. Nothing could better illustrate the limitations of realism than this theme which the mediaeval artist, untrammeled by naturalism, was able to represent with significance and even with extraordinary beauty. The Venetian artist should have studied the Jesse Window of Chartres.

Our chief regret in connection with these modern mosaics is that in many cases, probably in all, they replace early mosaics of immensely superior quality. This we know in the case of the façade where the earlier mosaics are perfectly represented in the painting by Gentile Bellini (Fig. 39, page 190). We may safely infer it in the case of the interior. What caused the substitution we do not know. If the original mosaics were destroyed by earthquake or injured beyond possibility of repair we may accept the substitutes with resignation touched with gratitude. The suspicion arises, however, that in this as in so many other cases the arrogance of the late Renaissance wantonly destroyed what it thought to better but could not equal. Of the six mosaics represented by Gentile Bellini only one remains and that the poorest. Among the others now lost was at least one — that over the main entrance — which deserves to be counted among the noblest decorations ever executed.

The early mosaics of Saint Mark's are of various but unrecorded dates. A single chapel is said to contain mosaics of the tenth century, the century before the church was built. This hazardous conclusion can be accepted, therefore, only on the assumption that portions of the earlier and very different edifice were incorporated in the present structure. The mosaics of the domes are assigned by critics to the twelfth century, that is to the century preceding the capture of Constantinople by the Venetians. A single chapel, on the other hand, contains mosaics of the late fourteenth century, a period when painting was beginning and mosaic was being abandoned.

But the great mosaic period for Saint Mark's was the

Fig. 29, Saint Mark's; mosaic decoration representing the carrying of the body of Saint Mark into the Church. Note the presence of the horses added in 1204; also the absence of the Gothic details now so conspicuous.

thirteenth century. To this period belong the original mosaics of the façade, the mosaics of the vestibule, both side and front, and presumably the panel mosaics of the interior and most of the wall mosaics. The single remaining original mosaic of the façade (Fig. 29) gives us only one certain indication as to the date of these mosaics. It represents the carrying of the body of Saint Mark into the church and this includes a representation

Fig. 30, Saint Mark's; Vestibule with mosaic decoration.
Note the borders under the arches, and the medallion and scroll
decoration of the pendentives beyond. The numbering
of the bays in the text begins at the farther end.

of the church itself. In this representation appear the
horses of Saint Mark which were not brought to Venice
until 1204. The mosaic must, therefore, have been
executed after that date. The same was undoubtedly
true of the other mosaics of the façade and of the
apparently contemporary mosaics of the vestibule and
certain mosaics of the interior. The completion of the
mosaic decoration of Saint Mark's, already begun but
long interrupted, may therefore be regarded as a result,
almost as a memorial, of the victory of 1204.

This is not the place for a detailed study of individual
mosaics. The traveler, however, who cares to get an
idea of the possibilities of this magnificent art should
not content himself with general impressions. A careful
inspection of a few selected examples will add much to
the understanding and the enjoyment of the whole.
Fortunately this is unusually easy in St. Mark's. The
best mosaics in St. Mark's are in the narthex or vestibule
and in the unused part of it at that where the student is
seldom disturbed by either tourist or devotee. He will
do well to enter by the side door on the north side, *i.e.*,
opposite the Clock Tower. The vestibule is divided
into square bays or sections, each covered by a low
dome which is supported on pendentives rising from the
corners. The whole is decorated in mosaic and the
mosaicist is here at his best (Fig. 30) though not without unhappy modern intrusions.

The first bay is devoted to the story of Moses. The
dome with its wonderful center is the ideal of what such
things should be. Not less perfect are the pendentives
with their medallion heads and the exquisite scrolls
filling the corners. All is in perfect mosaic technique
and is an appropriate subject for the purpose. The side
walls which take the form of apses or lunettes are pictorially more ambitious and correspondingly more difficult

Fig. 31, Saint Mark's; a pendentive; detail of mosaic decoration.

and less satisfactory as decorations. The one opposite the entrance door is modern and atrocious.

The second bay, which is devoted to the story of Joseph, is probably by the same hand as the first and is not less admirable. Especially worthy of admiration as before are the dome and the lunettes with the magnificent border pattern on the arches on either side. As before the modern artist is represented — and at his worst — in the window niche. One of the puzzles that the student is continually called upon to solve is how that modern artist could have had the nerve to execute his new work alongside the old. Not that all new work is bad or all old work good. These assumptions are pitfalls — especially the second — that we should avoid with all care. But in this case the straightforward mind, taught or untaught, can come to but one conclusion. It is not always easy to appreciate mediaeval art even at its best. The feelings and the thoughts to which it was addressed have very largely passed away. But here is art that requires no learning, no sophistication, no acquired taste. It is as beautiful today as it was seven centuries ago. We do well to make the most of it.

The third bay is fine but not quite so fine and the fourth or corner bay is distinctly inferior as is the fifth. The artist was more interested in narration and less in decoration. The transition from purely decorative elements to those that quaintly depict bible stories is interesting but it hardly marks a decorative climax. The sixth bay which coincides with the great west entrance is altogether different, it is much higher and covered with a vault instead of a dome. All the mosaics here are modern and ill-suited to decorative purposes excepting, perhaps, the figures in the arcade among which the Madonna at least must be pronounced fine.

In directing detailed attention to the mosaics of the narthex it is not intended to disparage those of the church interior, many of which will equally repay individual study. Especially noteworthy are the beautiful panels with their single decorative figures which line the walls on either side of the nave. (Fig. 33.) Similarly

Fig. 32, Saint Mark's; Chapel of San Zeno; detail of mosaic decoration.

the Coronation of the Virgin over the entrance door, and finally the magnificent scroll border and medallion patterns which abound everywhere. The earnest traveler may well spend hours in the study of these mosaics which earnest artists spent centuries to create, divining as he may be able the reasons for their peculiarities and endeavoring to appraise their value as decorations and as expressions of mediaeval feeling and thought.

And now as to the place of these mosaics among others

of their kind. Despite the presence of exquisite portions it must be admitted that the mosaics of Saint Mark's do not as a whole rank high in their class. They repre-

sent a noble art but one already in decadence. They cannot compare with the mosaics of Ravenna or Cefalù or even of Rome. Constantinople, the source of Venetian art, was utterly decadent in the thirteenth century and in the absence of creative tasks the craft inevitably declined. Tradition and mannerism, not meaningless but with meanings half forgotten, are manifest in all the mosaics of the period and lessen our regret at the loss of an art which for decorative purposes has had no equal and which the intellectual and emotional con-ditions of our age make it impossible to restore.

Fig. 33, Saint Mark's; the Madonna. Mosaic panel from the nave.

When all is said, however, there are few buildings which mean so much to the decorator as Saint Mark's. Even the mistaken, modern, pictorial mosaics of the façade, when viewed from a distance, lose their incongru-ousness and blend in the opalescent hue which is the glory of Saint Mark's. Happy the visitor whose first view of the church is from the opposite end of the great Square and who, after all his studies of detail, takes his slow and lingering farewell from this same vantage point.

If the mosaics are the glory of the thirteenth century painting takes possession of the field in the fourteenth.

Painting had of course existed in Venice for centuries but apparently without attaining either to independence or to distinction. Very little of this primitive Venetian painting remains but we are in little doubt as to its existence or its character. It was the Byzantine painting which, as stated in the preceding chapter, prevailed throughout Christendom.

For some time previous to the period of which we write, certain parts of Italy, notable Tuscany and Umbria, had been stirring with a new and strange life. The greatest painter of the period and one of the most creative artists of all time, Giotto, had been called to Padua, the city of the mainland nearest to Venice, where in 1305 he had executed in the Arena Chapel that epoch making series of frescoes which constitute one of the chief monuments of Italian art. It is impossible for us, accustomed as we are to the more facile and resourceful art of a later time, to appreciate the amazing originality and freedom from tradition of these marvelous paintings, but of those who knew them in that day there were few who did not feel their startling newness and power.

And the Venetians knew them. Padua was near and a center of Venetian commerce. Communication was constant and the influence of Padua was marked as the history of Venetian architecture clearly proves. Yet Venice furnished no followers of Giotto. While all the painters of central Italy were following his potent lead and becoming as "giottesque" as their lesser powers permitted, it would be difficult to trace the influence of Giotto in any Venetian painting of the fourteenth century. Was Venice too unawakened as yet to respond to the quickening touch or were the Venetians too conservative in temperament to follow the great innovator? Certain it is that when Venice does at last cast aside the Byzantine tradition it is not to follow Giotto.

But though the new movement found no followers in Venice it none the less left its mark upon the city of the lagoons. The building of the Doge's Palace around which centered, as we have seen, the art activity of the four-teenth century, called for decoration on a large scale. It is significant that mosaic was not considered. The mosaics of Saint Mark's, now essentially completed, must have appealed strongly to fourteenth century taste. Had they acquired a sacred character from their use in churches which was a barrier to their employment in a civil edifice? It is impossible to say. But there were other and perhaps sufficient reasons. The mosaic art had been abandoned everywhere else for a century or more. Only in Venice did it linger and even there with intermittent and inadequate employment. Under such circumstances decadence was inevitable. And withal the rival art of painting had risen to new promi-nence and was carrying out vast undertakings not formerly regarded as within its scope. Finally there was another consideration to which the Venetians were never insensible. Painting was much less expensive than mosaic. Being withal a more facile art its substitution for the constrained and costly art of mosaics was inevitable as soon as the master painter appeared.

The decision to decorate the new Hall of the Great Council with painting was very possibly due in part to the work of Giotto in Padua. But though two gener-ations had elapsed since the completion of the Paduan frescoes, there seems to have been no painter in Venice who could undertake the task. Hence a painter was called *from Padua* to execute the work. Fragments of his work which was ruined by the fire of 1574 are still preserved. Nearly two generations later still, in 1420, we find the Venetians again sending for foreign painters to execute farther decorations in the Palace. The

Fig. 34, Altarpiece by Stefano da Sant' Agnese. Academy, Venice.

choice fell upon two admirable painters, Pisanello and Gentile da Fabriano, whose sojourn in Venice ought to have produced a greater impression than seems to have been the case. The Venetians who were later to make the art of mural decoration peculiarly their own were certainly slow to claim their birthright.

But the Venetians, if little influenced by the revolutionary art of Giotto, were not unresponsive to the stimulus of this awakening century. In the more conservative tradition which was their inheritance they display a new activity and produced in *Stefano da Sant' Agnese and Lorenzo Veneziano artists who rose distinctly above the ranks of craftsmanship to the level of art. The chief work of Lorenzo, an altarpiece in many compartments, hangs near the top of the stairway in the great hall of the Venetian Academy of Fine Arts. That of Stefano (Fig. 34) to which for convenience we shall chiefly direct our attention, hangs near by. It may be doubted whether anything in that famous gallery better deserves the visitor's attention or rewards with keener pleasure his careful and sympathetic study.

But the picture contains nothing of the modernism of Giotto. The painter has no new idea of what a picture should represent or how it should be represented. He is content to do the traditional thing, but aims to do it better than it has ever been done before. In this he is eminently successful, but his painting is essentially Byzantine and must be regarded from that point of view. If we look for naturalism in figure and action, for perspective, and for realistic environment as we do in the pictures of Giotto and in all that follow them, we shall find little to commend, and the picture, judged by such standards — standards which with us moderns have become instinctive — will be rated very low.

---

* Pronounced Stay-fah-no dah Sant Ahn-yay-zay.

We must again remind ourselves that the Byzantine artist, whether mosaicist or painter, aimed at something else than naturalness. A degree of naturalness was no doubt desirable and was aimed at so far as other considerations and the artist's limited powers permitted. But there were other considerations which to artist and public alike seemed more important. Nor was the public critical or exacting in matters of realism. If characters were identifiable and familiar stories intelligible, it was satisfied. But there were other matters to which the mediaeval public was acutely sensitive and these matters inevitably became the chief concern to the artist. They must in turn be the standard by which we judge his work.

We must recall in this connection the character of mediaeval art which was discussed in the preceding chapter. Whether mosaic or painting the purpose was primarily decorative, only secondarily narrative, and very remotely realistic. The individual painting is always a part of something else and is to be considered in its relation to that something else. It is to be considered further as an attempt to tell stories, to express dogma, and to inspire devotion.

The work under consideration is therefore first of all an altarpiece, that is, a structure essentially architectural in character. Our modern way of looking at the picture and ignoring the frame, our effort so to frame the picture that the frame will be unnoticed, all this must be reversed. The artist planned his frame in advance as a matter of paramount importance and lavished upon it his utmost skill and imagination. There was nothing in which he was more interested and nothing that better justified his interest. Its symmetrical design, its wealth of Gothic detail — far more appropriate in a work like this than in the façade of a Gothic cathedral — its judicious combination of dull and polished gold, above all its use of pale, turquoise blue, the best of all possible colors to pick out the design in contrast with gold, all this is art, possibly of a humble order but of exquisite perfection. The whole has rather the character of a colossal jewel in which design, ornament, gold, and color play their legitimately paramount part. To ignore all this and plunge at once into the narrative art of the several compartments, overlooking their studied adaptation to their setting and perhaps noting chiefly their childish naiveté and unnaturalness is an evidence not of perspicacity but of blindness and provincialism.

Turning briefly to these compartment pictures we note along with their obvious limitations a studied symmetry which is a familiar characteristic of Byzantine art. Panel is set off against panel with as complete a balance as possible in character, color, and light. In each individual panel, too, the composition is as symmetrical as possible with its apex and its balanced sides, when possible man for man and woman for woman, symmetrical too, when possible, in attitude and action. All this is unnatural but decorative. These artificially balanced groups fit charmingly into the ornate little niches of which the frame is composed. Indeed it is plain that the niches are responsible for the arrangement of the groups. We shall be quite willing to have it so if we appreciate the frame and the altar of which it is to be the glory.

The subject matter of the pictures requires little consideration. The representation is of the simplest and the themes are easily identified by those who are familiar with the bible story and the lives of the saints, a limited number in our day. Upon the large central panel, the Coronation, the artist has lavished his utmost skill, not in vain, we may add, though he is still the decorator rather than the diviner of the thoughts and intents of the heart. The setting of this panel, too, is peculiarly rich and beautiful.

And now, leaving our little pictures, let us end as we began by viewing the work as a whole and from something of a distance as was originally intended. Let us cross to the other side of the room, or better still, let us view the altarpiece of Stefano through the open door of the room opposite, the room which contains Titian's Presentation in the Temple. When we have made the rounds of the great gallery and admired as it deserves this masterpiece of the incomparable painter and open the door to go out, fortunate if at that moment our eye catches a glimpse through the opening of the masterpiece of Stefano da Sant' Agnese. A moment's contemplation of its soft radiance and — not all will give the prize to the work of the mighty Titian.

The art of this fourteenth century in Venice, an art of which these artists were the chief but not the only representatives, is in essence altogether Byzantine. It has the fundamental merits and limitations of the Byzantine art. It is not realistic, vivacious, dramatic, or subtle. But aside from its uniformly decorative character it has great dignity and occasional elements of rare beauty. The writer is perfectly aware of the manifold ways in which later representations of the ascending Christ surpass that of Stefano da Sant' Agnese, but frankly he would prefer this as a subject of daily contemplation. The angels in the foreground have had few rivals in Christian art (Fig. 35).

But Stefano was not a prophet. To realize how utterly alien his art is to the modern movement we have but to glance once more at Giotto's frescoes, already half a century old when Stefano painted, and note their vivid life, their studied and realistic action, their insistent if crude perspective, and their subordination of decorative to vital interests. Of all this our artist knows nothing. The old symmetries, the soft glow of gold and color, still charm him and seem to offer new possibil-

Fig. 35, Stefano da Sant' Agnese; the Ascension. (Detail of Fig. 34.)

ities of unattained perfection. The first great Venetian painter thus makes it his task to express perfectly the traditional ideals.

From these ideals the Venetians were exceedingly slow to depart. The great doings of the Florentine artists in the fifteenth century provoked no emulation.

For a century and a half after Stefano's time the Venetians still preserved the symmetrical as contrasted with the balanced composition whose greater freedom was so essential to the representation of action and life.   Constrained to admit perspective, they are prone to smuggle in their beloved gold in the mosaic covered niche in which they enthrone Madonna.   The great John Bellini, truest artist of them all, still stands astride the boundary between old and new, blending with marvelous skill the symmetry and glow of the older art with the deeper human insight of the new.   Venice had no Giotto.   Her art knew no revolution, no conscious break with the past. Foreign innovation and foreign triumphs are alike unheeded.   Raphael may imitate the Venetians but the compliment is not returned.   The artists of half Europe may waste their energies in futile emulation of the painter of the Sistine Ceiling, but the Venetians are not among them.   The movement gathers volume and quickens its pace but it is self contained, self directed, self inspired.   From Stefano to Tiepolo it is a consistent evolution, a logical development from that art which was her inheritance and which is perfectly expressed in the fourteenth century work of Stefano da Sant' Agnese.

CHAPTER IX

The opening of the fifteenth century, so epoch making in the political and commercial history of Venice, was equally noteworthy in the history of Venetian art. The preceding century, as we have seen, had shown a new interest in art and the development of skilled craftsmanship in this line but it discloses no new ideals, nothing distinctively Venetian. The fifteenth century was to witness the disappearance of the Byzantine tradition and the rise of a new art which was distinctively Venetian.

True Venetian painting begins, therefore, with the fifteenth century. To the foreign painters who were summoned to decorate the Doge's Palace it owes its incentive but not its character. Despite foreign stimulus and even foreign instruction that character is always distinctive, always Venetian. This is the more striking in view of the fact that other Italian cities were a hundred years ahead of Venice in art development and that their activities not only extended over the neighboring mainland but embraced the city itself in their extensive operations. Even this was not all, for the early Venetian painters, including some of the most influential, were obliged to seek employment much of the time in other countries where, owing to the form of government and the policy of the splendor loving despots, inducements were offered which were not yet forthcoming in the city of merchants and business interests. In spite of all, however, Venetian art shows surprisingly little foreign influence. Not even the Florentines with their early start and their pronounced individuality have developed an art more distinctively their own.

In 1411 the Venetian government, confronted in the decoration of the Doge's Palace with a task that exceeded local powers, called two foreigners, Pisanello of Verona, and *Gentile da Fabriano, an Umbrian, to do the work. Both were painters of ability as revealed in works which have been preserved. Their work in Venice, like so much else that followed it in that ill-fated building, has perished. The work was in progress, apparently, for some four years during which period it must have excited much interest in local members of the craft or those who aspired to become such. The work seems to have been in fresco, a medium familiar to Florentines and Umbrians but never popular with the Venetians who in this, as in all else, showed their characteristic independence

The two painters, whatever the relative value of their work in the great Palace, seem to have differed greatly in personality and in the influence which they exerted on Venetian art. Of Pisanello we hear nothing beyond the mere fact of his participation in the task. His work was probably satisfactory but it does not seem to have evoked applause. Gentile, on the other hand, not only won the approval of the Venetians but enjoyed an unusual degree of public and private favor. The government not only paid the price agreed but granted the painter a pension for life. A treatment so little in accord with the traditional thrift, not to say meanness, of these "grave and reverend signors" argues much for the work or for the painter's personality, more especially the latter.

It was probably due in no small degree to his attractive personality that Gentile developed a personal following among the younger members of the craft in Venice. A number of these were probably associated with him in the work in one capacity or another, for fresco painting

* Pronounced Jen-tee-lay dah Fah-bree-ah-no.

is a process which practically requires the co-operation
of several persons. The association seems, however, to
have been more than a professional one. These helpers
learned to like their master and in one case at least —
and that a most significant one — the liking became a
devoted and life-long attachment. The disciple left
Venice with his master and remained with him for years,
thus prolonging and deepening his influence. There
were other artists destined later to reveal the influence
of Gentile who as youths watched the painter at his
work and were perhaps admitted to his fellowship. In
a very real sense, therefore, Gentile, the Umbrian, may
be regarded as the father of Venetian art.

It is a matter for profound regret that the great work
through which this influence was chiefly exerted should
have disappeared without leaving a trace. Even contemporary description is lacking. Much of the artist's
other work has shared the same fate. Among the three
or four accredited works which remain two are easily
accessible to the travel public and are worthy representatives of his art. The first is a Madonna and Child
in the National Gallery, London, fortunately assigned
to a favorable position in the central hall. This extraordinarily beautiful picture perfectly represents the
conservative and transitional character of Gentile's
art. The picture is without perspective save such as
is involved in the careful modeling of the figures. The
painter even scatters gold rosettes or foliate ornaments
over the dark background quite without pictorial pretext
but with a pleasing jewel effect not unworthy of Stefano
da Sant' Agnese. The figures, however, are utterly
unlike those of Stefano and of mediaeval art in general.
While kept within the conservative limits of the early
art as regards motive and arrangement, there is a lifelikeness and a personal beauty unknown till now. It is

not too much to say that this is one of the most beautiful
Madonnas of the fifteenth century, a work which justifies
Michelangelo's remark that Gentile's art was like his
name, *gentile*, that is noble and refined.

More noteworthy is the famous altarpiece, the "Visit
of the Magi" (Fig. 36) one of the most popular of the art

Fig. 36, Gentile da Fabriano, Adoration of the Magi. Florence,
Uffizi.

treasures of Florence where it was painted in 1422, seven
years after the completion of the frescoes in Venice.
This work, executed in the fullness of the artist's powers,
is more elaborate than the foregoing and probably reflects
much more nearly the style of the frescoes. It is undoubtedly the masterpiece among his surviving works.
Perhaps no other painting combines so pleasingly the
mediaeval and the modern spirit.

Mediaeval are the chief actors in the scene who are

arranged with fine symmetry in the near foreground, their gorgeous costumes resplendent with rich and tasteful ornament such as no modern would dare to use. Mediaeval too is the shallowness of the stage on which the scene is enacted, a narrow shelf, as it were, barely sufficient for standing room. But the ease and relaxation of the figures, the naturalness of their attitudes, and the beauty and expressiveness of the faces are modern, not mediaeval. Modern, too, is the elaborate and over-emphasized perspective which opens long and rather needless vistas in the upper part of the picture while the foreground rises perpendicular and shows little sign of depth. The perspective is thus rather far fetched and irrelevant. For the composition proper he does not feel the need of it, but he is conscious that perspective is now in vogue and is expected, so he makes a sort of perspective annex to his picture which he enlivens by an otherwise unnecessary cavalcade. Evidently the artist does not yet see things in full perspective. The transition is not yet complete.

Most doubtful from the standpoint of sincere narration is the mass of irrelevant and distracting detail with which the picture is encumbered. The kings are accompanied by a vast retinue, as is the wont of kings, it may be argued, but not the less a distraction from the standpoint of the simple theme which the picture purports to present. There are pages to remove the royal spurs and equerries to take charge of horse and accoutrements. There are men and dogs and horses, leopards and monkeys and falcons bringing down their prey. This is explained by the fact that our artist is painting, not the scene as enacted in far away Judea, but the scene as presented in the pageant with which Florence was wont to edify — and incidentally to amuse — her citizens. That the scene as thus presented should lose its simplicity and be denaturalized by irrelevant and sensational additions was inevitable, and possibly we may say as much for the picture in turn. The Florentines knew what they were looking at and probably found pleasure in these menagerie details. But there is an element of superficiality in catering to such tastes and most artists chose the better part. Gentile had not learned the important truth that "painting is the art of leaving things out."

The art of Gentile was peculiarly fitted, by both its excellences and its defects, to bridge the gulf between old and new. In his love of splendor and his exquisite mastery of ornament he continued and glorified the old tradition while his striving for naturalness of figure and action and his ambitious if not wholly successful perspective reveals the new impulse.

The influence of Gentile was transmitted to Venetian art through two families, each represented by three members in the art of the fifteenth century. One of these, the Vivarini, lived, not in Venice proper, but in the close-lying industrial and residential suburb of Murano to whose semi-independent art development they were the chief contributors. Though clearly influenced by Gentile, their contact with him is unrecorded and was seemingly less direct. They will call for brief mention in a later connection.

It was the *Bellini, Jacopo and his two sons, Gentile and Giovanni (John), who were the direct agents of this transmission and the true founders of Venetian art. It was Jacopo who formed the attachment to Gentile which associated him for so long a time with that master. We do not know when Jacopo was born but there are clear indications that he was a youth in his early teens when he met Gentile, and probably served as his helper.

* Pronounced Bell-ee-nee.

With Gentile he went to Florence where we find him associated with the master in 1421. If, as is likely, the relationship had been continuous, the two had been associated already for ten years. It is probable that the association continued for some years after this. When in 1428 he married and the following year became the father of a son he named him Gentile in memory of the beloved master whom he is proud to mention as his teacher in the inscription placed beneath one of his most important works. These facts all point to a relation of affectionate regard which it is pleasant to note in a profession where jealousy and pettiness are only too familiar.

Jacopo found employment chiefly outside of Venice if we may judge from the very scanty record which has come down to us. He doubtless visited his native city from time to time and may have spent considerable time there but we hear of no extensive commissions in Venice until after he was sixty years old. On the other hand we hear of extensive works executed in Padua and find him high in favor at the court of the famous Este family in Ferrara whose great projects, however, seem not to have been carried out. Only in his old age was he called to Venice to execute an important series of paintings for the Scuola of St. John. He seems to have been specially interested in large and complex works of this kind, probably following in this the tradition of Gentile da Fabriano.

By a strange unkindness of fate not one of these larger works survives. His work in Venice was destroyed by fire. That in Padua was sacrificed to the baroque taste of a later age. His painting is known to us only through minor works, a crucifix in Verona, a youthful and quite inferior work, and several Madonnas, for the most part the small, half length figures which were painted for the private chapels then customary in the

Fig. 37, Jacopo Bellini, Madonna. Florence, Uffizi.

dwellings of the rich. These are of different periods and unequal value, but all seem at first glance to be "primitive," which is to say that conventions, now unfamiliar, tend to disguise for a time their real significance. There are two of these Madonnas in the Academy at Venice and another in the Uffizi, Florence (Fig. 37). The last is by far the most significant of his surviving works and deserves the closest attention. Underneath the formalism and somewhat rigid decorum which the age seems to have regarded (not wholly without reason) as essential to a religious picture, there is a striking beauty which will not fail to impress the discerning. In color especially the picture is singularly individual and pleasing, though not at all suggestive of the Venetian coloring of the classical period. It is a little thing upon which to base our judgment of an artist but it at least reveals him as a man of marked individuality and independence.

On the other hand it gives us no hint of his relation to the new art with its difficult problems of perspective, arrangement, and the like, the art that he had learned from Gentile and that he had certainly employed in his larger compositions. For this we turn to his sketch books which are remarkably voluminous and by a rare good fortune have been preserved to us through the pious devotion of his sons. These contain, in addition to possible studies for his paintings, a large number of drawings made apparently for his own delectation and therefore, we may assume, peculiarly representative of his temperament and art interests. From these sketches we can reconstruct in some measure his art as it was embodied in the larger works which we have lost.

Perhaps the most striking characteristic which these drawings reveal is his subordination of man to environment, the use of small scale figures in spacious architectural or nature setting, and his fondness for broad, open spaces. This tendency, which recurs in Giorgione half a century later, reminds us of the early landscape painters like Claude whose landscapes generally purport to be merely the setting of some historical or allegorical scene which is unobtrusively enacted in their midst. Not that Jacopo was a landscape painter. The world was not ready for landscape yet and a transition so violent as that from mediaeval decoration to landscape was unthinkable. None the less one wonders what Jacopo would have been if he had sat at the feet of Claude instead of Gentile.

It will be remembered that Jacopo named his first born son after the admired teacher, Gentile. This Gentile in turn became an artist and as he was born in happier times as regards his art, he is much better known to us than his father, though it is by no means clear that he was his superior in creative power. Chance has willed that of the great historic paintings upon which all the prominent artists of the period were so largely engaged, only certain of those of Gentile have been preserved. These represent to us, therefore, not only the work of an individual but the ideals and taste of an age. This gives to Gentile Bellini an importance which, as an individual, was possibly not his due.

Gentile seems to have been born in 1429, whether in Venice or in some of the mainland cities where his father was then chiefly occupied is not clear. We next hear of him as his father's helper in connection with a great painting in Padua in 1460. In what capacity he assisted him we are not told. His earliest individual work, a portrait and a very poor one, is dated 1465 when the artist was thirty-six years old. Gentile, like Titian and other Venetian painters, seems to have developed slowly. The precocity of Michelangelo and the Florentines generally was not a Venetian characteristic.

Other works executed about this time hardly enhance
his reputation but they are of interest as revealing the
powerful influence of Andrea Mantegna, one of the
outstanding personalities of this creative period and a
man with whom the fortunes of the Bellini family, both
professional and personal, were intimately bound up.
It is no disparagement of Mantegna to say that his
influence over the unformed art of Gentile was not happy.
Fortunately that influence was soon relaxed and Gentile
developed a style which was both Venetian and his own.
Indeed if we were to judge by existing works we should
be tempted to say that it was he who made it Venetian.
He certainly did his share to determine the character
of Venetian art.

Gentile, like his more celebrated brother, John, was a
profoundly religious man, a fact attested by much
evidence quite outside his art. Unlike his brother,
however, he lacked the power of expressing religious
sentiment in its subtler forms through his art. Perhaps
he realized this and for that reason rarely attempted
the all important theme of the Madonna. We have but
two from his hand, the one very early and almost incredibly helpless and inept, the other dating from his prime
and extraordinarily beautiful though less pronounced in
its religious import (Fig. 38). It suggests little kinship
with the unrivaled series of Madonnas which we have
from the hand of John.

Possibly this choice was due to circumstances rather
than to predilection, for it so happened that Gentile's
first great patron was a Scuola, *i.e.*, a guild or club to
which his father had belonged for many years and in
whose service both his father and his brother were also
employed. His success in this work led to his employment on what was virtually a life appointment by the
Venetian state, a service interrupted by a strange foreign

Fig. 38, Gentile Bellini; Madonna. London, National Gallery.

episode and by a later and more extensive commission from the Scuola di San Marco, the only one of all these huge undertakings which survives. All of these commissions required of the artist large and complicated historic scenes and necessarily turned his activity in this direction. Had he found time to paint devotional pictures for private chapels as did his brother and to some extent his father before him it is possible that his achievements in this line might have been more noteworthy. As it is we must judge him chiefly by the great canvases which are distinctive both of the art of the time and of his own.

Gentile was engaged in 1466 by the Scuola di San Marco to continue the work begun by his father, a work on which his brother was employed about the same time. This was only a year after the painting of the unsatisfactory pictures already mentioned as exhibiting the unfortunate influence of Mantegna. In all probability this manner still dominated his work. If so it would help to reconcile us to the destruction of these works by fire soon after their completion, though the loss of the work of both father and brother, work for which they have left us no counterpart, is a matter of profound regret. It was probably in this long continued task that Gentile worked out his problem and developed the style that we know and recognize as Venetian.

Meanwhile a peculiar occasion had arisen for his services. The great frescoes of Gentile da Fabriano and Pisanello, finished half a century before, were in a serious condition. Disintegration had begun almost as soon as the work was completed, and repeated efforts to arrest it had been but temporarily effective. This was a plain warning to the Venetians not to work in fresco, a medium apparently unsuited to the climate of Venice. This warning, as we have seen, the painters took to heart.

Gentile seems to have taken a personal interest in the preservation of these epoch making frescoes to which his father, but recently deceased, doubtless attributed his start in life. Gentile, whose filial and fraternal sentiment was very marked, offered in 1474 to undertake the task of restoring these frescoes "for the present and for the future" without payment except for expense incurred and the rent of a broker's stall, a sinecure which Venice not infrequently assigned to artists in her employ. It is interesting to note that this position of official painter was later held on the same terms by John Bellini and then by Titian and Tintoretto in turn.

Gentile spent, all told, fifteen years or more in this task, not without side employments and interruptions one of which was of no small importance. His efforts, however, like those that preceded, were unavailing and it was ultimately decided, doubtless with much reluctance, that the honored frescoes must be entirely replaced. This Gentile undertook, with the aid of his brother and others, oil painting upon canvas (a recent innovation) being substituted for the perishable fresco. The series of paintings thus executed undoubtedly constituted the monumental work of the century. They all perished in the great fire of 1574 together with works by Titian and other later masters, a loss beyond estimate. A couple of drawings alone remain to give us a hint of their character.

Deprived thus of the early and middle periods of Gentile's art we turn to the third and last. In his old age after completing the work in the Doge's Palace he undertook a vast commission for the Scuola di San Giovanni Evangelista consisting of three huge canvases which he was able to complete and which are fortunately preserved. Following this he undertook a similar task for the Scuola di San Marco with which his family had long been connected and for which, it will be recalled, the Bellini, father and sons, had executed a series of decorations which had perished by fire soon after their completion. The whole establishment was rebuilt on a splendid scale and in 1493 Gentile offered to execute the necessary decorations on his usual extremely generous terms. For unknown reasons this offer was not accepted for more than a decade. In 1504 the commission was at last awarded but on the seemingly ungracious condition that the work be begun at once and pushed as rapidly as possible to completion. The fact that the artist was over seventy years of age and no longer in good health probably motived this ungenerous stipulation. The condition was loyally accepted and the work pushed as rapidly as failing strength permitted. Dying before its completion he left the strictest of injunctions to his brother, John, to complete the work which the latter did with that affectionate loyalty which characterized the relation of these brothers through life. This work which is also preserved is therefore a composite, the work of Gentile as regards conception, composition, and drawing, but in color and finish the work of the more gifted John. Fundamentally, therefore, it is the work of Gentile and for our purposes we may so regard it.

To these *scuole* we are therefore indebted for four monumental pictures which embody not only the work of an outstanding painter of the period but in an important sense the art achievement of Venice during this epoch making century.

What were these **scuole?* The word, *scuola*, means school and is as often used in Italian in that sense as the corresponding term in English. But these *scuole* were not schools. They never gave instruction or fostered

---

* Pronounced Squo-lay; the plural of *scuola*.

learning. They were private organizations like our modern clubs with the addition of certain features of our secret orders and mutual benefit associations, though local in character. Like all such organizations they existed primarily to advance the interests of their own membership principally through the life of the *scuola* itself but also in all manner of relations outside. The basis of membership was sometimes occupational, sometimes racial, sometimes cultural, convivial, or arbitrary, but one and all were devoutly religious. They had their own chapels and burial grounds and their patron saints. They had their headquarters or hall, usually adjacent to the church of their chosen saint and in some cases an establishment of great magnificence. Examples familiar to every traveler are the Scuola della Carità, now the art gallery of Venice, the Scuola di San Marco, now the hospital, and the Scuola di San Rocco preserved as a national monument to the genius of Tintoretto. All the *scuole* were dissolved long since, their halls turned to other uses or in many cases destroyed and their art treasures scattered or transferred to the great collection now installed in the largest of their appropriated premises.

These confraternities, extremely numerous in this and succeeding centuries and representing every degree of size and wealth, became zealous patrons of art and had much to do with determining the character of its development in Venice. The little *scuole* that possessed but a single room doing duty for chapel and hall alike, covered its meager walls with the story of their order or the life of their patron saint, while the *scuole grandi* whose vast halls rivaled the Doge's Palace and whose large membership represented immense wealth and influence, sought for the decoration of their palatial apartments the great canvases which we have noted.

Even so early a painter as Carpaccio writes of a picture which he had painted twenty-five feet high, an ambitious dimension for almost any age but completely eclipsed by the later canvases of Veronese and Tintoretto. Thus all departments of Venetian life, the church, the state, the *scuola*, and we may add, even the family as represented by the wealthy palace owners, conspired to develop the huge, panoramic picture designed for spacious setting and long range view. This in turn influenced the artist in his technique, his composition, his choice of subject, and his art ideals. It favored the bold, the dramatic, the objective, characteristics which increasingly dominate Venetian art. It militated against refinement, intimacy, and subtlety, qualities not lacking at the outset but which disappear as art adapts itself to the conditions thus imposed. The direction thus given to art was congenial to Titian, Veronese, Tintoretto and Tiepolo. It was less suited to the Bellini, to Carpaccio, and to Giorgione, though they found themselves constrained to work chiefly in this line.

Of the four large pictures which we have noted as examples of Gentile's art the most important represents (Fig. 39), an incident in the history of the Scuola di San Giovanni Evangelista. This confraternity, one of the largest and wealthiest of the *scuole grandi*, had the proud distinction of possessing a priceless relic, a fragment of the true cross which was kept in a costly reliquary made in the shape of a cross. The miracle working powers of such a relic were taken for granted in an age when men believed with alacrity and resented investigation, and several miracles were deemed definitely accredited to it. These miracles were naturally the subject of Bellini's pictures.

In the case under consideration a citizen of Brescia, while absent in Venice, learned that his son had been seriously injured. The great pageant of the Scuola was then in progress, the sacred relic in its jeweled reliquary and under a golden canopy being borne in solemn procession through the Square of Saint Mark. The anxious father throws himself before the sacred object and implores its aid. In the same hour he later learns, his son is restored. How does Gentile tell this story?

Fig. 39, Gentile Bellini, the Miracle in Saint Mark's Square.

We have first of all the Square with the church at the end and the buildings on either side as they then were. All this is represented not with the light touch and suggestive style with which we are now familiar, but with meticulous exactness. We see the buildings on the right which have since been replaced by the Procuratie Nuove, the mosaics of the façade of Saint Mark's later so tragically displaced by feeble modern substitutes, and much else which is of the liveliest historic interest. As a document the picture is invaluable. The procession, too, is treated with impartial exactitude from beginning to end. There is none of that subordination of part to whole, of background to foreground, of bystander to actor, which makes Rembrandt's Night Watch a work of superlative art — and which, incidentally, caused its rejection by those for whom it was painted. Every figure is a separate study, every face apparently an individual portrait. This impartiality must have been highly gratifying to the confraternity.

But where is the miracle? Look close. In a tiny space just behind the gilded canopy is a kneeling figure, the only one in the picture, unobtrusive almost to the point of invisibility, as he may very well have been in fact. The picture tells us much about Saint Mark's Square but nothing about the miracle. We overlook the kneeling suppliant and when at last we discover him he means nothing to us. It is not that the artist, like so many of later date, is without interest in his nominal theme and makes it a pretext to paint something else. He is doing his best to paint the miracle. He is an able painter but he has a most naïve theory of art. Called upon to portray something that happened in Saint Mark's Square he assumes that he must first paint the whole Square with everybody and everything in it. And having done this honestly, even skilfully, the incident finds its place in literal and proper scale, merely one detail among a thousand others, all treated with the same pitiless impartiality. Imagine what Titian would have done with such a theme. A limited space, a hint of Saint Mark's in the background and an arch or two of the neighboring arcade, enough to tell us where we are but subdued enough to be forgotten; then half a dozen figures variously cognizant of the kneeling father whose agony of supplication would dominate the scene; finally a few bystanders and a hint of the moving procession, revealing little but suggesting much. Oh, Titian would have painted the miracle, and no surroundings however interesting and no personages however important would have been allowed to divert our attention.

There is much reason to believe that Gentile's picture is representative of the Venetian panoramic art up to this time. It reminds us of the Visit of the Magi, painted nearly a century before by that other Gentile, his namesake and the father of Venetian art. We may safely assume as much of the famous frescoes in the Doge's Palace and in general of the great canvases that replaced them. There was too much accessory, too many figures, too little subordination of the thousand and one irrelevant things with which nature always crowds her stage. Thus the poor story teller puts in all the things that happened and mentions all the people who were present, unmindful of the fact that nine-tenths of them were merely intruders and cumberers of the ground. Only slowly do we learn to omit the irrelevant and subordinate the accessory. Venice has still to wait for that simplification and concentration which is to be eventually the supreme characteristic of her art.

Another of these famous pictures represents also a miracle (Fig. 40). Again there is a procession and the reliquary is carried in state. But in crossing a crowded bridge the bearer is jostled and the sacred relic falls into the canal. Numerous bystanders at once plunge into the canal but the relic eludes their grasp, even that of a priest who hastens to the spot. Not until the official keeper of the relic appears does it both allow itself to be seized and even makes its way toward him unaided. The miracle, it will be seen, consisted in the fact that the relic recognized its own.

In many respects this picture is like the other. The bridge, the canal, the water, the buildings, all with their windows, doors, and chimneys accurately represented, are faithfully and impartially included. The people, too, on the bridge, along the banks, and in the water are correctly depicted. But there is something more which cannot be explained as realistic incident. On an arbitrary platform in the lower foreground are a number of kneeling figures in an attitude of formal devotion. To the left along the quay stand a row of rather portly female figures in court dress and excessively formal attitude in which critics believe we are to recognize Catharine

Fig. 40, Gentile Bellini, Miracle of the Cross. Venice, Academy.

Cornaro, the ex-queen of Cyprus, and her suite. These figures are not chance bystanders. They were not present nor can we imagine them to have been present, least of all in the attitude of fossilized decorum which characterizes them. They are dragged in to represent the homage, religious and courtly, which is the relic's due. This is a departure from realism, from matter of fact, but one which competes with the central theme instead of contributing to it. To us to whom relic and homage are alike alien, it is difficult to characterize these

features as otherwise than stupid.   But this is our bias.
The man of that time did not think so.

The last of the great paintings, the one undertaken
for his own *scuola* and finished by his brother, represents
Saint Mark preaching in Alexandria (Fig. 41).   In this
the artist was put to a new test for he could not represent
a real square or a real canal but must imagine the scene

Fig. 41, Gentile Bellini, St. Mark preaching in Alexandria. Milan,
Brera.

entire.   The result indicates poverty of imagination.
The scene is laid in an open square which is Saint Mark's
Square somewhat studiously and rather absurdly disguised.   A church closely resembling Saint Mark's save
for two preposterous buttresses forms the background.
A minaret, a camel, and a giraffe help us to get our bear-
ings.   A huge, isolated column in the rear suggests that
the artist had heard of Pompey's Pillar.   Saint Mark,
the least imposing figure in the picture, speaks from a
low platform to one side.   The center of attraction is a
group of sitting women who with strange headgear and
veiled faces listen to the address.

Despite the redeeming touch of John Bellini's brush
this last work is inferior to its predecessors.   It reveals

our painter as lacking in creative imagination and unable to depart from literalism without becoming grotesque. While in this case the theme is discoverable and something more of concentration and focus are apparent, it may be doubted whether this was not the result of accident rather than of growing skill.

One episode which has been omitted deserves mention before we take our leave. While he was engaged on the great pictures in the Doge's Palace, Venice received a request from the Sultan Mohammed II of Turkey to send him a skilful painter and Gentile was chosen for the delicate mission which he seems to have discharged with eminent success, not only satisfying the demands of his dangerous patron but winning his personal friendship. He remained at least a year in his service painting various subjects of which one at least has come down to us, the portrait of the monarch himself. It is an admirable work presenting the powerful but somewhat dreaded monarch truthfully but with that careful choice of the better self which is always the artist's privilege. The superb technique manifest in both the portrait and in the unusual but exquisite accessories make us regret that Gentile was not allowed to devote himself more to those simpler works for which he here shows himself fitted.

Another work of miniature proportions but of the most exquisite beauty now in the Gardner Collection in Boston probably dates from this period. It shows a marked Persian influence quite unlike anything else which bears his name. It heightens our regret that the work of this period has so completely disappeared and suggests possibilities of Persian influence on western art which we can not help wishing might have been realized.

It was in the year 1507 at the advanced age of seventy-eight that the brush at last dropped from his hand. He left a record of honest workmanship, of unceasing industry, and solid technical achievement. If he produced no great art, he shares with his father and brother the honor of having created Venetian art. In its most distinctive form, the great, panoramic picture, we owe it to the three, but we owe our knowledge of it solely to Gentile.

If he had shortcomings as an artist they were amply compensated by his high character as a man. His family loyalty, his public spirit, his generosity and unselfishness have rarely found their counterpart in the lives of artists. These qualities must be equally accorded to his brother and, so far as our limited knowledge goes, to his father as well. It is a satisfaction to note that through the art of another member of the family if not through his own, these qualities of gentle distinction and nobility found adequate expression.

CHAPTER X

THE MASTER WITHOUT A MASTERPIECE

The temptation at this point is to proceed at once to the consideration of the art of John Bellini in whom the art of this remarkable family undoubtedly culminates. For this study, however, one more preliminary is necessary, a preliminary which may seem at first territorially and artistically something of a digression. In a word we must go back to Padua where, as we have seen, the Bellini, father and sons, first found employment and acquired reputation. It is significant that at the moment when Venice was politically and commercially at her zenith she gave no employment to artists. The cities of the mainland were far in the lead in their patronage of art. Padua, as we have seen, had employed Giotto a century before Gentile and Pisanello were called to Venice and this tradition of art patronage continued in full force. Other mainland cities were hardly less interested. These cities had passed under the rule of despots who were normally given to ostentation and to the patronage of art while Venice, ruled by hardheaded, money making merchants, was proverbially thrifty.

The early Venetian painters, therefore, sought employment upon the mainland. Here they were subject to influences altogether unlike those which prevailed, or were destined to prevail, in Venice. They saw work executed by Florentines and others of pronounced individuality and highly developed technique. Above all they met the artists themselves and in some cases came into close personal and professional relation with them. Certain of the relationships thus established exerted a marked influence upon their own development.

One of these relations was of such importance that it cannot be ignored in any study of Venetian art.

The Bellini, it will be remembered, were long employed upon the mainland. Jacopo was court painter at Ferrara for a number of years. He was also employed, and ultimately his sons with him, upon important commissions in Padua where he sojourned more than once and apparently for considerable periods of time. Here he seems to have become well known, to have established a studio, attracted pupils, and enjoyed a reputation that aroused the jealousy of his rivals.

Among these rivals was *Squarcione, a strange and, at this distance, rather an amusing figure in the history of art. His service to art was unique and considerable but not primarily as an artist. He early became interested in the ancient art of which he was an enthusiastic if not always a discriminating collector. Not only were the antiques then gathered for the most part mediocre and very much overrated — there is no criterion of beauty so misleading as that of mere antiquity — but Squarcione was a painter and he shared the quite erroneous notion then prevalent that the proper training for a painter was the study of ancient sculpture. This of course ignores the fact that both painting and sculpture have their conventions, that is, they diverge from nature as their material and processes require, but necessarily in quite different ways. When the painter copies sculpture he not only adopts conventions which are alien to painting and therefore quite palpable defects, but he loses all that is most vital to his art because the sculptor has necessarily and quite properly left it out. The tendency is therefore to develop a hard manner insistent upon form and sharpness of outline but lacking the mellowness and warmth which come from

---

* Pronounced Squahr-chee-o-nay.

color. Further, the artist who has developed especial sensitiveness to line is tempted to give undue prominence and unnecessary precision to detail, not only in his figures but in the non-essentials of their environment. He will treat with quite unnecessary exactness, for instance, the architectural setting of his picture, its ornament and other details, which should be merely suggested and reduced to proper subordination by obscuring shadow. On the other hand line has a witchery of its own and a master who realizes its possibilities may reconcile us to its limitations. The sculpturesque manner with its emphasis upon line and form rather than upon color has very great achievements to its credit and counts among its devotees such names as Botticelli and Michelangelo.

Squarcione was neither a Michelangelo nor a Botticelli but an honest craftsman of very moderate ability but with considerable reputation as a teacher according to accepted standards. Among his pupils was one, Andrea *Mantegna, who was a genius of a very high order. He was born in Vicenza, a flourishing city less than twenty miles away, but he had come to Padua as a child where we find him inscribed in the guild of painters at the ripe age of ten years as an apprentice of Squarcione, whose sculpturesque manner seems to have been congenial to his temperament. His progress must have been rapid if we may judge from the fact that we find him at twenty a finished painter and charged with commissions of the highest order, which he executed in a manner that still excites the greatest admiration.

Mantegna was still a youth in the studio of Squarcione when Jacopo Bellini opened his studio in Padua. Jacopo represented a school of painting which we must regard as naïve, but it was not based on antique sculpture and

---

* Pronounced Mahn-tain-yah.

was unhampered by its perverting tradition. The art of Jacopo grew naturally into the great Venetian painting of a later day. That of Squarcione could never have done so. Withal Jacopo was a far more talented man than Squarcione.

Whether Mantegna realized all this we do not know. Judging by his later work we should hardly think so, for with all his ultimate mastery his art remained sculpturesque to the end. But there were other attractions which drew the young painter irresistibly to the new studio. Jacopo had a daughter, Nicolosia, who caught Mantegna's eye and whose charms quickly outweighed all technical considerations. The outcome was that Mantegna married Nicolosia and was received both into the studio of her father and into the bosom of the family. The relation seems to have been wholly harmonious and sympathetic, a fact the more noteworthy in view of their divergent temperaments and the natural irascibility of the new comer. Evidently the spiritual serenity which characterizes the noblest works of John Bellini had its foundation in the family character. The entire Bellini family was remarkable for the affection which seems to have subsisted between all of its members, the irritable brother-in-law included, an affection which was extinguished by neither separation nor death. When Gentile Bellini on his death bed adjured his brother to finish his great picture for the Scuola di San Marco, he offered as the greatest possible inducement the precious album of their father's drawings which, with filial piety he had long affectionately cherished. The inducement was quite unnecessary for the brothers were united by lifelong affection. That Nicolosia shared this affection cannot be doubted, and through her Mantegna became its beneficiary. It is pleasant to note that in his different way he reciprocated and between himself and the gifted

John there was a friendship of the strongest and most enduring character.

Mantegna never worked in Venice nor did his art ever become in any true sense Venetian. It is interesting to speculate as to what he might have become had he known Titian or Tintoretto. But in the hands of the Bellini, Venetian art had not yet developed its powerful tradition. The Bellini did not copy statues but they were still meticulous students of form and hardly realized the opposition of temperament between themselves and their brilliant associate. Affection and sympathy led to a sincere effort on each side to master the secret of the other but it not did make Mantegna a Venetian or check the development in its true character of that Venetian tradition which begins with the Bellini. Among the artists of this wonderful century Mantegna, judged by any just standard, must be assigned a high place. If the limitations of the sculpturesque manner, its hardness, its lack of warmth, and its over interest in detail, are more in evidence in his case than in that of the great Florentines, so also, we may add, is his music of line as manifest in draperies and other details too often graceless and prosaic. Note, for instance, the draperies on the little attendant in the picture of the Circumcision (Fig. 44). That figure alone would make the picture a masterpiece. And yet it is the draperies that, all unconsciously to ourselves, give the figure its charm.

To the influence of Squarcione was added the far more potent influence of Donatello, the mighty Florentine who spent a decade in Padua beginning when Mantegna was thirteen years old. We have no record of any relation between the two, but none is needed. That the enthusiasm felt by the Paduans for the wonderful work which Donatello was executing for the great church of the Paduan saint did not leave our susceptible youth untouched is abundantly proved by his later works. To a degree, of course, the influence of Donatello reinforced that of Squarcione and his antiques. Donatello was a sculptor and while his statues were not at all like those in Squarcione's collection they were still statues and expressed their meaning through form and line. But to Donatello he owed another characteristic which was a matter of temperament rather than of sculpture as such. Donatello was dramatic. He loved to represent incidents and situations that were tense with passion. There are few things in the whole range of plastic arts that in dramatic intensity surpass the "Feast of Herod," a little bronze relief in Siena. His "Deposition" in Padua is one of a long series of these powerfully dramatic but not always pleasing representations, for Donatello, like most of those who become interested in action and passion, cared very little for facial beauty.

There was much in this that appealed powerfully to Mantegna. Like Donatello he cared little for that meaningless type of beauty which we call prettiness and was better able to express his meaning through a plainer and more austere type. He was less dramatic than Donatello and his portrayal of themes of the Christian tragedy are quieter and far less impassioned. But he became profoundly interested in these harsher themes which appealed to the austere heroism of his nature.

Still a third influence was to contribute to the shaping of this extraordinary man, that of the Florentine, Paolo Ucello, who was in Padua during Mantegna's youth and through whom he became deeply interested in the problems of foreshortening and perspective which were the passion of the Florentine. These, of course, were no novelty, but Ucello had carried his studies much farther in these subjects than any of his contemporaries. He never painted anything that was worthy to be called a picture but he filled canvases with men, horses, and accoutrements seen sidewise, endwise, quarterwise, all in the interest of foreshortening and perspective. Perspective, in his work, does not exist for the sake of the picture; the picture exists for the sake of perspective.

It becomes somewhat so in the work of Mantegna. Not that Mantegna's pictures are ever lacking in serious content but they not infrequently contain foreshortenings and elaborate vistas which are not necessary to the content and which challenge more of our attention than they deserve. Mantegna, like every man who becomes absorbed in the problems of a developing technique, tended to become a technician, to make technique an end rather than a means. That tendency is manifest in all the art of the fifteenth century. It was an age of problems and of absorbing, technical interests and only the very greatest were able to hold these means in proper subserviency to the higher ends of art. There are few who do this in any age. Technique is the great winnower. It is not that so few master technique but that so few have any art left in them when they have done so. Said a lady to the writer: "I do so love to hear Paderewski because he has so completely mastered his technique that he can forget all about it and think about music." How many are like Paderewski?

Despite all that has been said Mantegna must be reckoned of the number. His powerful imagination, his unfailing dignity and loftiness of conception, his nobility of spirit survived all the influences that shaped — and in a degree misshaped — his art. If he cared little for prettiness and sometimes rejected it where it would have been in place, there is in the gentle earnestness, the profound but tender seriousness, of Madonna, child and saints (Fig. 42), especially those whom the years have subdued into gentleness, a beauty that the

Fig. 42, Mantegna, Madonna and child with saints. Dresden.

observant cannot fail to perceive and perceiving cannot fail to admire. This gentle seriousness easily lends itself to the suggestion of mysticism and so to the expression of religious sentiment, undoubtedly a sincere purpose of the artist as it was of the art of this sincerely religious century.

Mantegna's enthusiasm for the antique which grew with the years and led him into serious archaeological studies was not limited to sculpture but embraced every phase of ancient — that is, Roman — life. He knew Roman architecture, arms, accoutrements, costumes, furniture, in short, everything Roman. This became the absorbing theme of his art, rivaling even the Christian themes which were the themes of his time and to which he was also sincerely devoted. Things Roman are first the accessories and ultimately the avowed subjects of his art. The trial of Saint James (Fig. 43) takes place in front of a Roman triumphal arch, a masterpiece of design and detailed representation. A child in the foreground plays with a helmet and shield while another helmet lies on the pavement near by. In the "Triumph of Caesar" at Hampton Court his antiquarian imagination runs riot. There are statues and vases and nameless objects of beauty and price. There are arms and armor and battle standards of the foe. There are soldiers and captives and cattle and horses and elephants, all the jumbled miscellany, in fact, that Mantegna conceived as having graced one of these miserably vulgar shows. But Mantegna's show is not vulgar. The Romans who pass before us have the dignity of Rome. Even the miscellany ceases to be junk in his hands. Persons and things alike are endowed with that character which he perceives in Roman civilization. With all the coarseness, the harshness, the callousness and sordidness of Roman life there is an imperial quality

Fig. 43, Trial of Saint James.   Padua, Eremitani.

about it which — totally missed by an author like Gibbon — the world has sensed and Mantegna has immortalized.

These great qualities help us to judge more leniently certain incongruous features in his art which are chargeable to the usage of his time and locality as well as to the eccentricity of patrons. Such is the use which he makes of still life. The value of still life as a subject in art is not here in question. If an artist wishes to paint fruits and flowers there is no objection to his doing so. Those may look and enjoy them who can. But when he hangs them in heavy festoons over a Roman tribunal or over Saint George and his slain dragon or when he enthrones a madonna in a niche constructed for a horticultural fair, no conceivable skill of representation can save them from being ridiculous. It is to be noted, though hardly as a sufficient justification, that Mantegna was simply following the absurd practice of the north Italian artists, a practice not unknown in Venice itself where a highly realistic cucumber was regarded by some as an appropriate gift to lay at the Madonna's feet. His most pronounced extravagances, moreover, were due, at least in part, to the influence of Isabella d'Este, the great bluestocking of the age, who had the genial custom, in ordering a picture, of telling the artist how to paint it. The "Triumph of Wisdom over the Vices" in the Louvre painted under her direction represents alike the limit of Mantegna's skill and of Isabella's preposterous suggestion. The age had its foibles and its absurdities from which even genius was not exempt.

Mantegna's coloring, somewhat influenced by Bellini, is only occasionally successful. Here and there in details he makes the happiest of choices as in the slain dragon in the famous little picture of Saint George. There are, as it were, clear notes and beautiful single chords but

Fig. 44, Mantegna, Circumcision (detail).   Florence, Uffizi.

never a symphony in color such as becomes a common-place in the work of the Venetians. The use in his draperies of changeable colors, that is of fabrics which reflect one color in high light and another in shadow, always a sign of a weak color sense, mars the beauty of some of his noblest creations like the Madonna with Saints in the National Gallery, London.

Over against this fitful uncertainty of color may be set his unfailing mastery of line, a mastery not merely scientific but artistic as well. His draperies, avoiding the extravagance of Botticelli and the stiffness of the earlier Bellini, endue his figures with both dignity and grace. So in the figures of the Triumph of Caesar; so in the attendant of the Circumcision. (Fig. 44.)

We may well close our study of this imposing figure of the fifteenth century by a closer view of the last mentioned work by which, rather than by almost any other, our artist might well consent to be judged. The whole art of Mantegna is here, his dignity, his insight, his realism, his sympathy, his mastery of line and form, something too of his foibles and limitations. We note the old priest, austere but not unkindly, the plain but not unbeautiful mother so oblivious of all in her sympathy, and the child turning instinctively toward her in his distress. The little attendant with his roll of surgeon's lint and other necessaries adds a touch of realism which some will find excessive, but we can forgive anything in a creature like that. Notice the sculpturesque precision of form and outline (how differently Titian would have painted that beard); also the detail that utilizes all vacant space in every part of the picture, resigning no nook or corner to the tempering shadows which play so important a part in the later art. But whatever its limitations there is in the solicitude of the mother, the appeal of the child, and the kindly interest of the priest a manifestation of insight and sympathy which make of this difficult theme a subject of the highest art.

We may say of Mantegna as has been said of Carlyle; he was a master without a masterpiece. His faults and limitations are conspicuous but they never drop him to the plane of the commonplace. The problems of art were too great, too absorbing, the synthesis proposed too vast, to permit of all round achievement in a single lifetime. Mastery was beyond the reach even of the master.

Such was the man who now entered the studio of Jacopo Bellini. The antithesis even at that date must have been somewhat felt. Jacopo was no ultra colorist like Tiepolo three centuries later. There was still a long way to go before the painter could see in the complete dissociation of color from form a legitimate ideal of painting. Jacopo's art, based on that of Umbria, was still the compromise art of the period. But color and form were certainly held in better balance than in the art of Squarcione. Whether Mantegna perceived this we do not know. Anyhow he came and came to stay. Squarcione was angry and ungenerous. There are clear indications that he and Jacopo were rivals and he could not brook the loss to his rival of his most brilliant pupil. He turned from praise to criticism and with that amusing inconsistency which is humanity's inalienable privilege, he declared that Mantegna's figures looked like statues. Mantegna, always irascible, was deeply offended but he had the good sense to see that there was truth in the charge and to set himself with the aid of his favorite brother-in-law to correct the defect. As we have seen he did not altogether succeed.

We do not know how long the Bellini and Mantegna were thus personally associated but to judge from the result it must have been a considerable time. The influence thus exerted, though unequal, was mutual and profound, especially upon John whose relation to Mantegna seems to have been particularly sympathetic and close. Ultimately the two seemed to become completely merged in their art personality, two minds with but a single thought, and that thought chiefly Mantegna's. So complete is this merger that modern experts are frankly perplexed to determine the authorship of their unsigned works of this period. There seems to have been no actual collaboration between them. Indeed such a collaboration is almost as unthinkable in the case of Mantegna as in the case of Michelangelo. It was rather a personal attachment and spiritual partnership in which Mantegna was clearly the dominant partner. At its height his influence seemed to have perverted and almost to have supplanted the artistic individuality of the gentler Bellini. But an individuality that is worth preserving seldom succumbs to such influence no matter how powerful. The influence of Mantegna, to be sure, is traceable long after the personal association terminated, but it is a lessening force which yields increasingly to Bellini's recovered individuality. It was perhaps well for both that the relationship ceased while they were still young.

Mantegna's great frescoes in the Church of the Eremitani, begun at the age of twenty-two and finished at an unknown date but before he was twenty-eight, had made an epoch in art and had called forth an admiration which has never since been withheld. They are second only to the frescoes of Giotto among the art attractions of Padua. Long before they were completed Mantegna was the most famous painter in northern Italy. His fame attracted the attention of Ludovico Gonzaga, Marquis of Mantua, who invited him to come to Mantua as court painter. He seems to have been extremely reluctant to accept. He was devotedly attached to Padua, so much so that after he had left with little prospect of return he was still accustomed to sign himself, Andrea Mantegna, citizen of Padua. We shall not go far wrong in attributing this attachment to the presence of the Bellini family, though other reasons were not lacking. He had fame and lucrative employment in this city which had now passed under the mild Venetian rule and not unnaturally hesitated to exchange these advantages for the uncertain favor of princes. The invitation was repeated, however, and the inducements increased, and so at last Andrea and Nicolosia took their reluctant departure from city and family and went to Mantua never to return. Mantegna, now twenty-eight years old, began a service to the Mantuan family which lasted for nearly half a century and in the course of which he served three generations of the ducal family. He died in Mantua in 1506 at the age of seventy-five.

The influence of Mantegna upon Venetian art, more particularly upon the art of John Bellini, is at first striking and unpleasant. It is a period of conscious influence, a period in which the artist remembers Mantegna as he works and is consciously striving to do things in his way. Such an effort is seldom successful. In the present case it was more than usually unfortunate. The two men, perhaps equally talented, had very little in common. Their achievements were not only different; they were to a large extent incompatible and mutually exclusive. When Bellini tried to paint a harrowing scene of the passion in the austere, dramatic manner of Mantegna, he not only fell short of his model, but he necessarily excluded from his picture that spiritual serenity and mellowness of tone which was his birthright. He became a lesser Mantegna at the price of ceasing to be the great Bellini. Gradually he perceived this and the period of conscious influence comes to an end. Bellini became himself and painted in his own inimitable way. The sharp outline disappears. Contours are mellowed by the rich environing shadow. Color comes into its own. Bellini displaces Mantegna and the glory of Venice is here.

But the thoughtful admirer of Bellini will note that along with his exaltation of color and his mellowing shadows Bellini retains a wonderful integrity of form and expressiveness of attitude. The forms are subdued but the forms are correct. The outlines are softened but the outlines are right. In this as in much else we see the ideal of Mantegna. May we not see in it also in a measure his influence, the unconscious influence which is alone wholesome and lasting?

CHAPTER XI

The evolution of human art taken as a whole utterly transcends our comprehension. We cannot trace its beginnings nor can we anticipate its end. But fortunately for our purpose, the movement is subdivided into lesser movements which have limits and a character of their own. These movements often have beginnings that we can trace and ends already attained. They have their problems which they have solved and their ideals which they have measurably, perhaps perfectly, expressed. In the great, ever continuing movement these lesser movements are but steps — perhaps missteps — on the pathway toward the unseen goal. But for purposes of study they have a peculiarly satisfying finality. We see what they are trying to accomplish and can measure their approach to the goal.

The art of Venice in the fourteenth century is one of these definite and self contained cycles. It knew what it wanted to do, struggled manfully and patiently with the difficulties it encountered, and in the end achieved a measure of success which approaches perfection. The best works of John Bellini — a limited but not insignificant number — have a quality which it is difficult to designate by any other word. The epoch-making achievement of Giorgione and Titian is not to be interpreted as an improvement on Bellini. Their works belong to a different cycle and are to be measured by standards of their own. Before the Madonna of San Zaccaria these supreme geniuses could only throw up their hands. There is no going farther along this line. "What can the man do that cometh after the king? Even

214

that which the king hath already done." To repeat with no hope to surpass was not a program to tempt men like these. They go away and try something different, start a new cycle with new ideals, new problems, and in the end, new triumphs. They were immensely indebted to Bellini. They had learned their art in his studio and continued to keep in touch with his ever perfecting art as he with theirs. But their art is not a continuation of his. He closes one cycle; they begin another.

John Bellini was the brother, almost certainly the younger brother, of Gentile Bellini. We do not know the date of his birth but it probably followed soon after that of his brother who was born in 1429. This would make him near the age of Mantegna who was born in 1431. It must be confessed, however, that our grounds of inference are slight and that considerable divergence of views is noted in this connection. The question is of secondary importance but not wholly without interest. We are also in the dark as to the date when the family moved to Venice. They were in Padua in 1460 when all three are recorded as occupied with a great fresco in one of the churches. They were in Venice in 1465; how much earlier we do not know. Probably they left as soon as the fresco was completed. To a family like the Bellini the departure of the Mantegnas in 1459 must have greatly lessened the attractions of Padua.

All three found employment as we have seen on the great pictures for the Scuola di San Marco, the Scuola of the family. Their work here was destroyed by fire soon after its completion. Then Gentile becomes official painter to the Republic and endeavors first to restore and later to replace the great frescoes of his earlier namesake in the Doge's Palace. John meanwhile drops out of sight. He was not idle — he was never idle — but the numerous commissions which he executed for private patrons at this time and upon which his later fame was in no small degree to rest, seem to have called for no record.

When in 1479 Gentile was sent to Constantinople, John succeeded to his work as also to his official title and emoluments. These he seems to have retained after the brother's return and resumption of the work. Had the Venetians already discovered that the younger brother was the greater master? Here was an excellent chance for jealousy and estrangement, but such things seem to have been unknown in the family of the Bellini.

The work on these huge canvases absorbed years of our artist's valuable time only to perish like that which had gone before, in the fire of 1574. Of the pictures which he painted at this time nothing remains, not a sketch, not even a contemporary description. The subjects were undoubtedly historical and their aim was the glorification of Venice. From what we know of such pictures, those of Gentile and of other painters before and after, we may be sure that the canvases were crowded with figures and that most or all were contemporary portraits. It would interest us much to know how our artist mastered the difficulties which all this involved. Were his pictures diffuse or did he succeed in giving them focus and concentration? Did he know how to subdue the obtrusive prominence of his portrait figures and did their egotism permit him to do so? Were his pictures better centered and more intelligible than Gentile's procession in Saint Mark's Square? Perhaps so. They were the work of a greater man. But we shall never know. Much as we may regret the loss of these great canvases, however, we may be thankful that it was these rather than other works that perished. It is by no means certain that John was at home in this kind of painting. The probabilities are that he was not.

Were they still in our possession it is almost certainly not upon them but upon works of a very different character that we should base his claim to fame.

Rarely has an artist shown such capacity for continued improvement as John Bellini. Genius is apt to reach its zenith and pass into decadence in the lifetime of the individual. Sometimes the rise is rapid and brief and the decadence long and melancholy. Not so with John Bellini. His long life of more than eighty years was a continuous progress from very crude beginnings to almost unsurpassable perfection. He was at his best at seventy-five and to the last his eye had not dimmed nor his hand lost its cunning. It is interesting to follow his work in chronological sequence so far as that can be established. But other considerations have their importance and counsel the consideration of his works by groups in each of which the sequence may be observed.

Least satisfactory and least characteristic of Bellini's works are the dramatic or passion pictures which he painted under the influence of Mantegna. It will be remembered that Mantegna had a predilection for such themes, the inspiration for which he apparently drew from Donatello. To Donatello these themes were wholly congenial; to Mantegna they were less so; to Bellini they were altogether alien. Donatello's characteristic is passion; Mantegna's, austere dignity; Bellini's, pure beauty and deep, spiritual calm. These characteristics are very unequally suited to the demands of dramatic or passion art. With Donatello the adaptation is complete. Mantegna, who cared as little as Donatello for facial beauty, sacrificed little in accepting these harsh and exacting themes. Bellini sacrificed everything. It is interesting to note his sense of this loss and his wistful reaching for the missing beauty which he could not plausibly include nor yet willingly spare.

This group consists of a considerable number of pictures scattered through his long career. The subjects include the Agony in the Garden, the Crucifixion, and the Entombment. Other but allied subjects are the Transfiguration, the Resurrection, etc. It is in these works that the influence of Mantegna is most clearly apparent

Fig. 45, John Bellini, Pietà. Milan, Brera.

and by the same token it is here that we can most easily trace Bellini's emancipation from it.

The Pietà in Milan (Fig. 45) may be taken as a type of this group. It is an early work painted at a time when Mantegna's influence was at its height and is therefore the most mantegnesque of all Bellini's works. It has all of Mantegna's limitations. At first glance it seems to have much of his power. The figures, whether nude or draped, are entirely sculpturesque. The landscape, too, so far as revealed, has the same hard and formal character unmitigated by atmospheric haze or color. Facial beauty is completely and unnecessarily sacrificed as was the case in the analogous works of Mantegna.

But on closer examination we see that the resemblance to Mantegna is superficial. Forms and draperies are sculpturesque but they are very bad sculpture. The curled hair of St. John is preposterous. The folds in his draperies are arbitrary and unnatural. Note the quite impossible folds at the throat in the border of the garment as though made of a strip of metal. Even the sentiment or passion expressed is far from convincing. Our judgment of this picture must not be influenced by the consciousness that it is the work of an artist of great gifts and of indubitable later achievement. This picture does not reveal those gifts, is not in itself a notable achievement. It interests us as part of the record of the artist's evolution.

The Pietà in Berlin is later and marks a significant change. Donatello would have called it less successful, doubtless quite rightly, but it has the merit of being less ugly. Later and more striking still is the Pietà of the National Gallery in London (Fig. 46). We will not dwell for the moment on the changed conception of painting here manifest, the disappearance of the hard-featured landscape and architectural detail and the partial submersion of the figures in the shadow which fills the space and permits only the essentials to appear in varying degree as suits their importance. This revolutionary change which was the condition of his later triumphs will come up for consideration in its place. For the present let us note the subordination of tragedy and passion and the transformation of the whole in the interest of beauty. Anatomy is no less perfect than before but it is far less obtrusive. The Christ suggests less of pathos

Fig. 46, John Bellini, Pietà. London, National Gallery.

but far more of beauty, while on the angel to the right the artist has lavished his unrivaled powers. This exquisite creature may fall somewhat short of that self-effacing devotion to the Christ which the integrity of the theme requires but the face is one of the most beautiful in Venetian art. The other angel is less successful for the simple reason that the artist in this case has tried to express the passion of grief, a theme which as we have seen is ill suited to his temperament. Insensibly the tragedy in his hands ceases to be tragic, emotion becomes quieter, the group dissolves into its component individuals, and each is treated as a theme apart. The advance indicated in these works is not a progress in the portrayal of passion but a furtive quest of beauty which, however irrelevant, is its own sufficient justification.

If we turn from figure to environment the movement away from Mantegna is still more marked. The settings used by the artists of this period for their figure pieces fall roughly into three groups, architecture, landscape, and shadow. They may be used singly or in any degree of combination.

Architecture forms a plausible setting but it is prosaic, tempts to over elaboration of detail, and rarely attains high pictorial value unless relieved by landscape or subdued by shadow. It is Mantegna's favorite setting. Landscape is likewise plausible but unlike architecture it is potentially emotional and capable of very high artistic treatment, though liable to challenge undue attention. It is sparingly and unskilfully used by Mantegna and becomes the favorite of Bellini until a late period in his career.

Shadow, when dissociated from objects and used by itself, is completely arbitrary and artificial but for that very reason it is completely docile and the most poetical of all possible environments. It enables the artist to show just what he pleases and as he pleases, revealing, concealing, and suggesting as artistic purpose requires. While thus completely subservient it is unobtrusive and claims no attention in its own right. It is to this environment of shadow that Venetian art owes its magic. Shadow environment is unknown in the work of Man-

Fig. 47, Mantegna, Agony in the Garden. London, National Gallery.

tegna. As an independent and sufficient environment in itself it is apparently to be credited to John Bellini.

But this was later. In the period which we are considering, the choice lay between the two more realistic settings with a distinct preference on Bellini's part for landscape. Not unnaturally we find in him a far higher appreciation of its poetical or art value. Compare Mantegna's "Agony in the Garden" (Fig. 47) with Bellini's "Pietà" (Fig. 48) in the Doge's Palace. The alleged land-

scape in the former is hard and unsympathetic, a mere
assemblage of rocks and trees and houses seen in vacuo.
In the other the figures in moderate scale are surrounded
not by a miscellany of natural objects but by nature.
Rocks and trees and houses are merged and blended into a
unity under the influence of atmosphere and sunlight

Fig. 48, John Bellini, Pietà. Venice, Doge's Palace.

and shadow. When we remember that the figures and
the theme were required by the terms of his commission
but that the setting was almost certainly left to his
choice it is not difficult to see where our artist's interest
lay. Not that he painted the sacred themes and characters perfunctorily or without interest. Very much the
contrary as we shall see. But it is significant that at a
time when no one had conceived of landscape as in itself
a theme for art he should have gone so far to develop

its possibilities. His achievement was not an accident nor the result of a sudden inspiration. He struggled from painfully low beginnings as his "Pietà" in Milan (Fig. 45) and his "Transfiguration" in Venice, both painted with Mantegna's rockeries as a millstone about his neck, abundantly prove. Nor was his advance even and consistent. The later are not always better than the earlier if the accepted chronology is correct. But at his best we have in him a mastery of landscape which was foreshadowed in the work of his father and reflected in the work of his great pupil, and then — forgotten. Humanity was too egocentric as yet to find pleasure or meaning in the contemplation of impersonal nature.

But the fame of Bellini rests not upon passion or portrait or historical composition or landscape but upon the Madonna. He is the Madonna painter of the world. Others may have painted more beautiful pictures under that name but in his grasp of the true spiritual significance of the theme John Bellini has no rival. It is here that he differs most markedly from his brother. Gentile, as we have seen, seldom painted the Madonna. At least, very few examples from his hand survive. Nor can it be said that the few we have enhance his reputation. Save for the brief sojourn in Constantinople his life seems to have been devoted to the huge, panoramic pictures which the ostentatious civic life of his time required. There can be little doubt that these great commissions were regarded with especial favor and that the artist who was kept constantly employed upon them was esteemed fortunate. If so, then Gentile was the preferred of the two brothers, a contemporary judgment which posterity has not ratified.

John, as we have seen, was also employed upon these huge compositions, with what success we shall never know. But at first he was obliged to content himself with private commissions. The character of these commissions was predetermined. There was little of the miscellany which characterizes the modern household. The Venetians were religious and the tradition of art as a handmaid of religion was still dominant. Every household from the least unto the greatest had its sanctuary. It might be no more than a tiny icon in the common living room such as the Russian peasant keeps in his hut or the sailor in his cabin as the talismanic object of his superstitious reverence. Or it might be a stately chapel elegant in its appointments where the object of devotion engaged the resources of the highest art. Somewhere in this long scale stretching from humblest poverty to princely affluence artists of high and low degree found their opportunity.

The usual cult picture of a Venetian private chapel was a half length figure of the Madonna with the full length figure of the child held by the mother in various attitudes, more often standing, but also sitting, reclining, even at the breast. Occasionally the timid interest of the Christian art in the nude found in the child its innocent opportunity, an opportunity sufficient rather to demonstrate its ineptitude than to develop its skill. The draped figure of the Madonna involved the usual problems and offered the ordinary mild attractions. But the half figure representation inevitably focused attention upon the face. Represented in comparatively large scale and in connection with a theme where facial expression was of supreme importance, this naturally dominant feature challenged the artist's skill. It is a commonplace of art criticism that Christian art is an art of facial expression as contrasted with the art of the Greeks who "made the body eloquent."

To this humbler but far more sensitive art John Bellini devoted his early attention. No subject could have been more congenial to him and no artist was ever more fitted to the task. Probably many of his Madonnas have been lost or destroyed but the number that remain is remarkable. Still more noteworthy is their extraordinary variety along with their schematic uniformity. Barring the monumental Madonna groups which we shall consider later, the Madonna is uniformly represented in half figure, the child in full. Almost invariably, too, the Madonna is represented standing behind a sort of parapet or balustrade of which only the flat coping appears in the lower part of the picture. On this the child stands, sits, or is partly supported while reclining in the mother's arms. In rare cases this is enriched with carved ornament but the artist never distracts attention by the obtrusive rendering of classical details after the manner of his Florentine contemporaries and notably of Mantegna, his much esteemed exemplar.

But along with this uniformity of outward form there is a diversity of personality and spiritual suggestion which no other painter can equal. Always seemingly using a different model yet always charming her into that spiritual mood which to him was of the essence of his theme, his art manifests an unusual and happy variety while converging steadily upon that spiritual type which was his supreme achievement. It is most fortunate, however, that the development of this type was long deferred and awaited the maturing of his technique and perhaps, too, of his spiritual character.

His earlier Madonnas are essentially sensitive and spiritually conceived interpretations of lovely, madonna-like women. We feel instinctively that whatever charm and spiritual suggestion they manifest belongs to them rather than to the artist. He has chosen wisely not only the particular woman but also that particular one out of her many moods which he has known how to value and to evoke. In a word, with all his choosing and his conjuring we feel that the work is essentially realistic. We wonder who that woman was who is there represented. Whoever felt like asking that question about the Sistine (despite the fact that in that case we do know who she was) or about the Madonna of the Rocks, or for that matter, about Bellini's own Madonnas of the later period, the Madonna of the Trees or of San Zaccaria? Slowly the conjuring power increases, the spiritual mood becomes regnant and the individual is lost in the idea. In no other artist's work can we trace so perfectly the gradual ascendancy of the idea over the individual chosen as the vehicle of its expression. The madonna-like woman at last becomes Madonna.

It is impossible within the limits here proposed to trace the evolution through the long series of extant Madonnas. It must suffice to note a single contrast between early and late examples. The Madonna from Milan (Fig. 49) is a wonderfully sympathetic study of an altogether lovely woman, a woman whose beauty is of the spirit far more than of the flesh. But it is she, herself, a real woman, seen as men saw her, or at least as Bellini saw her, and in a character not alien to her nature. Her attitude is simple but natural, free from all suggestion of the conventional. Signs of her sacred character are conventional and negligible. In so far as she is Madonna it is because of what she is, not of where she is or what she wears. The child is less successful, less significant, but still only a child. By no sign or emblem does he announce his divinity. The background is simple yet amazingly subtle. Those feathery clouds that suggest immeasurable space belong to the most recondite phase of art.

There is much in this early Madonna that Bellini never surpassed, some things indeed that he rarely

Fig. 49, John Bellini, Madonna and Child. Milan.

equaled in his later work.   But if we turn to the Madonna of the Trees (Fig. 50), a work of much later date, we are at once conscious of a profound transformation. Certain defects remain, may even seem increased.   The child is still stiff and formal, anything but a real child, but after all what can we expect of a baby who has to suggest omniscience?   There are defects of drawing, too, if we care to look for them.   The right hand of the Madonna is surely misshapen while the absence of modeling, often very perfect in like case, will strike the observant.   Finally the color is comparatively crude and harsh in peculiar contrast with the usual rich mellowness of Bellini's coloring.   Much of this is due to a barbaric ordeal of restoration which this great picture in common with a number of others in Italy was compelled to undergo at a time when art appreciation was at lowest ebb. The surface, presumably cracked and defaced, was softened by the use of chemicals and scraped down until all defect was removed after which it was repainted.   This treatment which seems not to have been applied to the landscape vistas at the sides and probably not to the faces accounts for crude color and for missing modeling, but not for all the defects we have noted.   We must frankly recognize that the picture lacks the glorious spontaneity and freedom of the later art.   For Bellini is not Titian.

No, nor need he be, for in his way, a very high and significant way, he is something more.   This is Madonna as is no other.   What is the meaning of Madonna in Christian art?   Not the Jewish mother of Christ.   This original of the sacred theme hardly for a moment engages the attention of the Christian artist.   Not mere feminine beauty, not in the fifteenth century at least.   Madonna is less than this, more than this, something altogether different in kind.   The significance of the Madonna

Fig. 50, John Bellini, Madonna of the Trees.   Venice, Academy.

theme is to be found in Christianity, not in femininity or even in humanity as such.

The Madonna stands for the spirit of Christianity expressed in the face of a woman.

Viewed from within and in contact with its minor phases that spirit is difficult to define. Augustine and Francis of Assisi, Peter the Hermit, and Wesley are hard to harmonize. But viewed with the detachment which we habitually adopt toward Buddha or Confucius the meaning of Christianity is not doubtful. It is the striving of mankind to grow a soul. The experience has been not joyous but rather grievous. It has involved self chastisement, self discipline, self denial and suffering. Even its ecstasies and its triumphs stand relieved against a somber background of penitential sorrow. The end sought and in a degree attained is character chastened by suffering, spiritual poise amid the turmoil of passion, and sympathy born of remembered pain. How far these peaceable fruits of righteousness have been actually gathered as the result of this millennial effort is not here the question. What concerns us is the effort itself, the maintenance through unimaginable complications and against all possible counter influences of this conscious ideal. It is this ideal that the art of Christianity has striven to express through the only possible medium, the face of a woman.

As thus conceived the Madonna of the Trees is *the* Madonna of all Christian art. In mere physical beauty she is surpassed by scores of inferior creations. In naturalness and ease she is not to be compared with the Madonnas of Titian or even with the earlier works of Bellini himself. There is no dramatic motive, no centering of interest on a supremely significant moment. We may concede all this and more. But in realization of the Christian ideal she stands supreme. The Madonnas of

Titian and Raphael, masterpieces in their way, do not even deserve mention beside her. Only the unfathomable souls conceived by the great Buonarroti may challenge her supremacy. Self contained but not exclusive, reserved but not haughty, submissive but not weak, sympathetic but not sentimental, the list may be prolonged at will by any who can read the most unambiguous of meanings in the human countenance. Let those who will dwell upon the purely formal defects of this wonderful picture or indulge in irrelevant criticism of the ideal which the artist has striven to express. It is a great message greatly uttered, the one adequate expression of that vision which had hovered before the devout mind for a thousand years.

These simple Madonnas, as we have seen, met the demand of private homes as the great panoramic pictures met the requirements of the vast state apartments of the Republic. There was still a third claimant and one very different from either, the church. For church purposes the panoramic picture with its numerous figures, its elaborate setting, and its dramatic action had not yet acquired vogue. On the other hand the half length figure of the Madonna with the child was hardly adequate. The need was for an altarpiece that should be monumental, imposing. There had been developments more or less in this direction in Venice and elsewhere. Even the household Madonna was occasionally accompanied by attendant saints as in the case of Bellini's wonderful pictures which hang on either side of the Madonna of the Trees in the Bellini sanctuary of the Academy in Venice. These works which far surpass their great companion in technical perfection and approach it in spiritual value will call for consideration in another connection. The point to be noted here is that each contains four figures instead of the traditional two. Though obviously suited still for a private chapel rather than for the church the addition of the attendant figures led naturally to the monumental Madonna group which soon appears and which in its Venetian, fifteenth century form we must recognize as the fullest expression of Bellini's temperament and the ripest product of his genius.

John Bellini may be described as a conservative progressive. It is doubtful if the works of any other artist shows so long a record of consistent progress. Though living to a very advanced age he knew no decadence. It is a record of constant study, ceaseless experiment, and steady advance, the final result being the evolution of forms and types distinctly new. But in all this record of change there is no revolt, no bravado, no spirit of innovation. The canons of the older art are not uncongenial to him. He finds within their traditional limits the opportunity for unlimited improvement. He is less intent upon creating new art forms than upon realizing the possibilities of the old. His goal is not innovation but perfection. Yet perfection is perhaps the greatest of all innovations.

This progress along conservative lines is admirably illustrated in the monumental Madonna group, Bellini's principal achievement. The group from the Academy (Fig. 51) is representative of the new type. The Madonna no longer stands behind a parapet but sits enthroned. The throne is high and stately, a monumental thing in itself. It is symmetrically placed in an apsidal niche, the architecture of which is imposing and represented with extreme care. The vaulting is coffered, the pilasters richly decorated, and the half dome embellished with the mosaics which remind us like so many other works, of the enduring influence of Saint Mark's.

The compelling symmetry of this architectural setting is necessarily followed in the arrangement of the figures

Fig. 51, John Bellini, Madonna and Saints. Venice, Academy.

grouped about the throne. There are three saints on either side, one of them nude and two darkly clad. The three musicians who sit upon the steps of the throne are arranged in a symmetrical group. The niche and throne are seen in exact front view. The artist would seem to have accepted without qualification the mediaeval law of symmetry. Yet in fact while faithfully adhering to this principle of symmetry in general arrangement the whole picture is pervaded with an opposite principle which greatly relaxes its rigor. Thus of the two outer musicians sitting at the foot of the throne one is in high light and the other in shadow and the same contrast is noted in the half dome above. Physically we have symmetry but pictorially we have not. Similarly of the two nude saints which are obvious counterparts, one stands near the throne with the draped figures behind him while the other is farther away with a draped figure in front of him. There are farther contrasts in matters of detail where exact similarity would have been easy, such as position of the legs, the pose of the heads, and the like. This attitude of the artist toward the conflicting principles of symmetry and liberty is significant. Like others of his time he aims at naturalness and spontaneity, but he thinks these requirements can be met without sacrificing the fundamental symmetry so long recognized as necessary to monumental composition. Titian would have put it the other way — that the essentials of monumental composition could be secured without the symmetry so hampering to naturalness and freedom. And both artists in their work quite justified their contention. Despite its perfect symmetry there is no more natural or unforced group in all art than Bellini's Madonna of San Zaccaria, while Titian's Madonna of the Pesaro Family, though completely rejecting the ancient symmetries, is unrivaled as a monumental composition. Art has its laws as much as physics but there is as much freedom under the one as under the other.

But the new monumental Madonna of Bellini's creation did not at once attain perfection. Indeed at the outset she seems inferior to her humbler private counterpart. The enthroned Madonna of the Academy which we have thus far considered, though interesting as a new and significant departure in art, cannot for a moment be compared with its humbler predecessors as a study in the spiritual theme of the Madonna. The artist would seem to have been too much engrossed in the problem of composition to lay his accustomed emphasis upon spiritual values. Only with slow mastery of these difficult technical problems is the old balance restored.

The Madonna of the Frari (Fig. 52), perhaps the best known of all the artist's works, marks a distinct advance, both technical and spiritual. It is peculiar that in this, one of his later works, he returns to the obsolete form of the triptych or threefold picture, the only attempt of this kind in his entire career. It seems as if he were bent upon demonstrating that even the most conventional and stereotyped forms of art could be made to serve the ends of modern naturalism. The triptych, as is well known, was orginally a picture furnished with doors for its protection when not specially exhibited. It was an obvious necessity that these doors when open should not be unsightly. Hence the practice of painting a secondary picture on each door, sometimes quite unrelated but more often connected in one way or another, often the portrait of the donor and his wife kneeling in adoration on either side. When the doors were discontinued in favor of curtains, art did not at once readjust itself. The threefold picture had become traditional and for a long time no subject was deemed capable of artistic representation that did not show this threefold division.

The three part picture therefore continued though the sides no longer took the form of doors but assumed such form and character as the artist chose. The threefold

Fig. 52, John Bellini, Madonna and Saints. Venice, Frari.

frame thus became an elaborate and often very beautiful thing in itself and one which both artist and public were loath to give up. When finally it yielded to the painter's desire for unity and the whole was included in a single frame the picture still long continued to show the influence of the ancient threefold division. In this period falls the work of Bellini. His monumental pictures invariably show this threefold character and would require but slight modification to fit into the traditional triple form. But this division is wholly superficial. The sense of unity is complete.

In the Madonna of the Frari Bellini deliberately returns to the three part picture and the triple frame. This form, though still retained by humbler or more conservative painters, was for the higher purposes of art essentially obsolete. It made too much of the frame and too little of the picture and rendered difficult that unity in the interest of which the simpler form had been adopted. Bellini seems to have wished to show that unity is a thing of the spirit rather than of material conditions and adopts the divided picture for the purpose. His triumph is easy and complete.

The frame is designed in Renaissance architecture. Beautiful pilasters divide the central space with its domed niche from the side compartments each occupied by two apostles or saints who turn reverently toward the Madonna. But a second glance reveals that the pilasters do not really separate these groups at all. Back of the pilasters at some little distance and on either side of the enthroned Madonna the painter has represented other pilasters of exactly the same pattern as those of the frame. It is apparent that between these pilasters, front and rear, all is open and the saints on either side are all in the same room as the Madonna and Child, of whose presence they are devoutly conscious. We thus have the elaborate and elegant frame which the altar was so loath to spare, but a single group symmetrical in arrangement and perfectly unified in spirit. And withal, though the startling and dramatic are carefully avoided, no more natural portrayal of the human figure is anywhere to be met with than here. The lesson is that of all Bellini's art. The old forms are not a bondage. Naturalness, individuality, unity, freedom, all are possible within the time honored limits. Only the decorum which religious art requires and which is seldom lacking in great art of any kind sets a limit to the artist's freedom.

If we turn from the question of form to that of spirit we note a great advance over the Madonna of the Academy. The Madonna has much of that deep, spiritual beauty touched with unconscious pathos which is peculiarly the characteristic of Bellini. The little musicians on the steps of the throne, more particularly the one on the right, have been among the worthiest of popular favorites. But after all we have not yet reached the level of the Madonna of the Trees. The work seems too complex, makes too many demands upon the artist's attention to permit of that complete focusing of interest upon the spiritual theme which characterizes the simpler work.

It is in the Madonna of San Zaccaria (Fig. 53) that Bellini attains that rare goal of mortal endeavor, perfection. Not that this is the greatest of all pictures or even the greatest of Madonna pictures. Personally the writer bows in deeper reverence before the Madonna of the Trees. But with all her soulfulness the Madonna of the Trees lays no claim to perfection. Even making allowance for the mutilation and defacement which the picture has suffered the picture has shortcomings which are quite its own and which are apparent — and all too apparent — to the casual observer. In the Madonna of San Zaccaria all these disappear. The old symmetry is retained but all trace of mechanization disappears. Each figure stands in an unconstrained posture of its choice, the whole suffused with a gentle harmony which is of the inner spirit. There is an infinite suavity about these wonderful figures which baffles analysis. Compare

Fig. 53, John Bellini, Madonna and Saints. Venice, Church of San Zaccaria.

for instance the figure of Saint Peter with the closely similar figure in Titian's Madonna of the Pesaro Family. (Fig. 84, page 326). Closely similar, recognizing the same type, perhaps painted from the same model, yet a world apart. Titian's Saint Peter is mundane, splendidly, worthily so, but mundane none the less. The atmosphere is kingly, the dominant note one of magnificent manliness. Bellini's Saint Peter and Saint Jerome are no whit less splendid and virile but they are subdued into infinite gentleness by an influence which radiates unseen from the wonderful creature who sits enthroned between them. No person susceptible to spiritual suggestion through art can gaze upon this picture by the soft light of a Venetian afternoon without being in a measure won over to its temper of serenity and peace. In this most vital sense it is a religious picture without a rival.

While the spiritual problem of his art was ever in the foreground of Bellini's attention he was an industrious student of technique and within the conservative limits which he seems voluntarily to have chosen he was an acknowledged master. As a colorist no Venetian ever surpassed him. It is to him that we owe that blending of color with shadow which is so characteristic of Venetian painting. In Titian it is bolder, in Tintoretto sensational, in Veronese neglected. In Bellini and above all in the great picture which we must count his crowning triumph it is infinitely subtle and refined. It is indeed largely to this delicate play of shadow that the picture owes its power of spiritual suggestion as also its pictorial unity. Note the impartial subordination of face and figure by the shadows which are implied by the niche and its location. How easily Peter in his character as chief of the apostles might claim a prominence and a distinctness of representation incompatible with the shadowed position in which he stands. Yet a failure to subject him to the dominance of normal shadow would have ruined the unity of the picture which inheres very largely in this environment of light and shadow, the most spiritually suggestive of all sensuous elements.

Fig. 54, John Bellini, detail of Fig. 53.

Like the true idealist that he was Bellini's idealism is built upon a foundation of exacting realism. The Madonna of San Zaccaria illustrates this in matters both trivial and important. Thus the niche in which the Madonna sits enthroned is stiffened with the iron rod which we have seen was used in Venetian arched construction. The pilasters on either side of the throne are exact copies of the pilasters in the frame. The pavement is a faithful copy of that in the church and thus makes the niche as near as may be an extension of the church itself. The lamp hanging above is painted so realistically that in a photograph we cannot tell whether it is a real lamp that got in the way of the camera or a part of the painting. Some of these details are trivial, some even doubtful, notably the attempt to make the niche an extension of the church interior, an approach to illusion painting which a Florentine or an Umbrian would have carefully avoided. But as applied to the larger aspects of architecture and above all to the superb figures Bellini's realism is above all praise.

The daring modernism of Giorgione and Titian speedily developed in the Venetians a taste unfavorable to the appreciation of Bellini and until a comparatively recent date his greatness was unrecognized. Against the judgment of an age which was dominated by the outward and the sensational we may set the opinion of Albrecht Dürer, the foremost artist of transalpine Europe in his day and a critic without rival. Visiting Venice in 1506 he writes of Bellini: "He is very old but is still far the best in painting." Dürer had seen the Madonna of San Zaccaria which had been unveiled in the preceding year.

But Dürer writes something else that it behooves us likewise to remember. He found the painters of Venice jealous and hostile not only toward the newcomer but toward one another. The petty jealousies that have so often marred the personal history of art were sadly in evidence. He was even warned to be circumspect about accepting food or drink from unknown persons lest malice find there its opportunity. A single exception he records with gratitude. "But John Bellini praised me much to many of the nobility and the people all tell me what an upright man he is so that I too feel greatly attached to him." It is pleasant to record this tribute, confirmed as it is by all that is recorded of him during his life of more than eighty years. Artists have not always exemplified in their lives the spirit which they have sought to represent in their art. Was it because of this harmony between life and artistic endeavor that John Bellini attained perfection?

CHAPTER XII

We have now to consider a cross current or back eddy in the development of Venetian art, almost the only one which the history of that art records. In general the progress of Venetian art is a singularly consistent one. Great changes took place from generation to generation but they impress us always as natural changes, changes that follow logically from that which had gone before. There is the utmost diversity among the personalities of Venetian art but that diversity seems always subordinate to the broad unity which we call Venetian. However jealous and hostile the painters may have been as individuals, as artists they were first of all Venetians and actuated by an essentially common purpose. It would be difficult to find in Venetian art any such antithesis as that between Ghiberti and Donatello or between Masaccio and Fra Angelico.

But Carlo Crivelli is an exception. In a period of active art development and defined progress he stood apart viewing the movement with little sympathy and opposing to it, for the most part, at least a passive resistance. He has been called a reactionary, certainly with some justification, but like all reactionaries he was inconsistent, clinging to old methods yet striving for new effects, devoted to old ideals but introducing modern elements which were plainly, sometimes ludicrously, inconsistent with them. Like reactionaries in general his influence seems to have been slight. He did not guide the development of Venetian art; he did not appreciably delay it. The world has a way of passing the reactionary by and ignoring his protests. We might do

the same with little detriment to the logical completeness of our subject. But Crivelli's pictures are conspicuous in some of our greatest collections and by their
weirdness and oddity if nothing else challenge attention.
Since reaction is always an incident of progress, this
solitary Venetian reactionary deserves our brief attention.

We know almost nothing about Crivelli save what
his pictures tell us. We do not know when he was born
or where. We do not know where he studied or with
whom, or when or where he died. We know nothing of
his family life or his personal character. He is not
mentioned by Vasari or by any other chronicler so far
as the writer is aware. But we have his pictures, quite
a number of them, pictures whose authorship it is impossible to mistake, for Crivelli never imitated anyone and
no one seems to have imitated him. Moreover his
pictures are signed and dated, nearly all of them, a
practice which the historian could wish that other
painters had followed. His pictures, therefore, constitute
a sort of record, rather more of a record indeed than the
pictures of other painters for the reason mentioned.

From these pictures we learn that Crivelli was a Venetian for he was careful always to sign himself *Venetus*
though he lived most of his life and did most of his work
outside of Venetian territory. We infer, therefore, that
he was born in Venice, or at least in its immediate
neighborhood and that he was proud of the fact, though
from his pictures we might not guess either the birthright
or the pride. We learn further that he was painting at
least as early as 1468 for one of his pictures bears that
date, and that he painted at least as late as 1493, the date
of another picture. It is all but certain, however, that he
painted considerably earlier than the date first mentioned
for we have an undated picture, unmistakably his, which
is far more crude than the picture of 1468. How much

difference in date this crudity implies we can only guess, probably a number of years. From these very inadequate data some have inferred that he was born as early as 1430; others think as late as 1440. In any case — and this is the important thing — he was a full contemporary of Gentile and John Bellini and Mantegna, all of whom were born about the year 1430. He was probably slightly their junior. Giorgione and Titian were grown men when he died, though whether he lived to know them as artists is less certain. Venetian painting was thus approaching its zenith when Crivelli produced the remarkable pictures which we have now to consider.

How far Crivelli was acquainted with the art of the wonderful century in which he lived we can only conjecture. He certainly sojourned little in Venice and the district in which he spent most of his life, the Marches, was relatively isolated and probably little influenced by Venice. Still it would be difficult to believe that he was ignorant of the art of the Bellini, scattered as it was over the mainland, or with that of Mantegna whose activity was wholly on the mainland and not so very far from the scene of his own. Indeed we shall find in his pictures pretty conclusive evidence that he knew something of both the Bellini and Mantegna and that he was influenced by them, or possibly we should say, he was influenced by that which influenced them. But he was certainly not a disciple of Mantegna, least of all of John Bellini. The mood of reaction is not favorable to discipleship nor were his personal characteristics compatible with the great master's spirit. He apparently knew a good deal that he did not care to use or used only exceptionally just to show that he knew it. One is reminded of Fra Angelico who certainly knew more about the realistic art of his time than his usual practice would indicate. But the resemblance is limited to this general fact. The two men were so different in their spiritual and aesthetic qualities that we hesitate to admit even this resemblance.

Crivelli's art is fundamentally Byzantine. This is true both of his art conceptions and of his technical methods and that in spite of the fact that he occasionally tried his hand at a picture constructed on modern lines and even in the most mediaeval of his pictures introduced elements that no mediaeval painter would have dreamed of. With all that, his pictures never became really modern. The modern elements do not connote the modern spirit and make the impression of incongruity. In this respect he is far less happy than Fra Angelico whose modern mediaevalism is always harmonious, always beautiful, while that of Crivelli is weird, incongruous, sometimes laughable.

Crivelli continued to paint in tempera, the Byzantine medium, which the Venetian painters were abandoning for oil, the far more flexible medium which Antonello da Messina, the southern painter, had brought from the Netherlands. Tempera is a method of painting in which solid pigments are mixed in glue, white of egg, or gum of some sort dissolved in water. It has its advantages. It gives clear colors and a smooth glossy surface resembling enamel. It perfectly suited the purpose of the Byzantine flat, decorative painting. But tempera is an inflexible medium quite unsuited to the new, three-dimension painting with its soft gradations of color and shadow. For such purposes oil is vastly superior as the Venetians were quick to recognize.

Not so Crivelli. Whether he was ignorant of oil painting or too isolated to acquire facility in its use, he stuck to tempera and in so doing largely determined his choice of subjects and his career as an artist. Whether he painted in tempera because it was best suited to the kind of picture he chose to paint, or whether he painted this kind of a picture because it was best suited to the only medium he knew we cannot tell. The two went together.

But Crivelli does more or less force his medium and try to make it meet modern requirements. There is an unmistakable attempt at toning and soft transitions in his pictures which is more or less foreign to tempera but which was too popular to be ignored. In this Fra Angelico was wiser. He used tempera as tempera and never sought to make it render a service which was foreign to its nature. Who does not admire in his altarpieces the clear enamel-like surfaces of blue or pink or olive set off against the gold of the background?

Quite consistently Crivelli painted by preference and with most success the ancona, a picture largely frame but subdivided into many compartments, all more or less like niches, each suited to receive a single figure. The ancona was primarily a decoration and not, strictly speaking, a picture at all. The separate compartments were much like the niches sometimes seen in a great, monumental building, each containing a statue. No general theme, no unifying action was possible in such a work. And since unity of theme and action profoundly interested the Renaissance the ancona was rejected as unsuited to its purpose. That in the face of this rejection Crivelli should have revived it and painted it whenever he got a commission tells us much of his attitude.

But Crivelli's mediaevalism did not stop with the use of tempera and the revival of the ancona. He was fond of combining relief with painting, a well known Byzantine practice but one wholly inconsistent with pictorial painting. Thus, the mitre of Saint Peter is executed in gilded relief and set with imitation rubies, emeralds, and the like. Croziers, jeweled crosses, brooches, and many other articles of adornment were similarly treated, even the sarcophagus of the Savior being unplausibly thus adorned, a pretty sure indication that our artist was fond of this sort of thing. He even went beyond relief

Fig. 55, Crivelli, Madonna with Saints. Milan, Brera.

and attached wholly disconnected objects to his picture by one means or another. Thus when he represents St. Peter holding the keys (Fig. 55) he makes the keys of wood, gilds and ornaments them, and attaches them to Peter's painted finger by a real string. All this of course had its Byzantine precedent. The purpose would seem to have been to give an added vividness and sense of reality by the use of these actual objects. Of course the effect is just the opposite. Real keys tied to Peter's painted finger only emphasize by contrast the unreality of the finger and of the whole painted representation. But Crivelli probably had no philosophy in the matter. Byzantine painters had used relief and incrustation with imitation jewels in all sorts of connections, plausible and unplausible, and Crivelli followed the tradition because it was the tradition, as Sargent did in the Boston Library with greater skill but with less ingenuousness and spontaneity.

But with all his reaction and mediaevalism Crivelli is a man of the fifteenth century and is far more influenced than he knows by the currents of modern life. Even the most mediaeval of his creations, the great ancona of the National Gallery, London, contains elements that are wholly modern and out of place in a mediaeval picture as for instance the fruits and vegetables that hang on either side of the Madonna. In this phase of still life Crivelli was very greatly interested. He cares little for flowers but fruits, including the humbler varieties commonly classed as vegetables, seem to fascinate him. He is fond of the apple, the pear, the peach, but above all of the cucumber which he paints with superlative skill and never omits from his offerings.

And now that we reflect upon it, we have met something of this sort before. It will be recalled that the great Mantegna hung festoons of fruit over Saint George and his dragon and even constructed the most incredible niches and canopies of foliage and fruit as a setting for his Madonna. This fondness for painting still life seems to have been the one thing which Mantegna was unable to hold in its proper place. Admirable as is his workmanship it cannot but be accounted a weakness in his art.

In this, however, we see the characteristic, not of Mantegna whose whole temperament was of another sort, but of the Paduan school. This sort of painting was a fad in Padua, not in Venice. Paduan painters all learned it and indulged in it; Venetian painters rarely if ever.

Where, then, did Crivelli, the fruit painter par excellence, learn his trade? The records, we have seen, are silent but the testimony of his pictures is far more convincing. A tradition of this kind is not one to be developed by a single individual, least of all in an environment which had no sympathy with it. Crivelli undoubtedly studied painting in Padua and in all probability at a time when the rival studios of Squarcione and Jacopo Bellini were still in operation there. It would be hazardous to assume that he was a pupil in either but he must have had some knowledge of the ideals and methods of both. Can we trace that knowledge, that influence, in his art? Possibly we may.

As Crivelli continued the exercise of his craft the pressure of modernism inevitably increased. He abandoned the ancona, probably because commissions for so complicated and expensive an undertaking were difficult to secure, and devoted himself to simpler compositions, Madonnas, usually with attendant saints, something after the fashion of the large groups painted by John Bellini but of a far more primitive character. There was little of perspective and nothing of the mellowing shadow with which that great painter has made us familiar. In a single case, however, Crivelli seems to shake off his conservatism and tries to be genuinely modern. The Annunciation (Fig. 56) is Crivelli's challenge to the modernists. In sharpest contrast with his other works it is spacious and naturalistic in its setting, a far reaching vista carried back by imposing architectural perspective into the loveliest of gardens where the slender tips of

Fig. 56, Crivelli, Annunciation. London, National Gallery.

the cypress curve in delightful sympathy with the arch through which they are seen. In a charming Venetian apartment the Virgin kneels while the angel does obeisance in the passageway before the open window. To be particularly noted is the small size of the figures in comparison with the imposing height and spaciousness of the architectural setting.

Where did our painter of anconas and triptychs get the idea of a picture like that? Did it come from himself unprovoked and unaided in defiance of all his habits and traditions? We cannot be sure but we cannot but be struck by the fact that the nearest counterpart we can now find for this picture in the art of the day is one of the sketches in the album of Jacopo Bellini. To him in particular we owe the idea of spacious setting and figures drawn in small scale; to him also the use of architecture to frame his spaces. It is not his monopoly. It may not owe its origin exclusively to him. But it was his idea of a picture. And Jacopo was painting a great picture, undoubtedly of this sort, in Padua in 1466, perhaps when Crivelli was there, a picture which then or later he must have seen.

But as we have already said, Crivelli was no disciple of Jacopo or his sons. With all its innovations the picture is still his and his alone. It is beautiful in its conception and its setting, beautiful, too, in its voluminous detail, the rug, the peacock, the bird cage, yes, and the cucumber which as usual proudly holds the front of the stage. It is beautiful too in its general harmony of color, a harmonious golden brown which pervades everything and unites with the color of everything in perfect sympathy. But with all its beauties upon which the writer feels strongly disposed to insist the picture has eccentricities which make it ridiculous. The angel is clad in a costume which involves the utmost extravagances of fashion and gestures with quite impossible affectation to the boyish ecclesiastic, who, disregarding the sanctity of the occasion, chooses this most inappropriate moment to present a model of his church. The seclusion of the Virgin in her own inviolate apartment — apparently in suggestion of her virginity — while the angel and the ecclesiastic kneel in the street outside is an original feature which involves new difficulties. A necessary part of the traditional theme is the descent of the Holy Spirit in the form of a dove following a ray of light. But the Virgin is in doors and there is a heavy wall in the way. We might assume that this would be no obstacle to divine power but Crivelli is more naïve. The builder, apparently anticipating the emergency, has constructed a comely apperture for the purpose at the right spot.

It would be hard to find in the art of this whole transitional period a more astonishing combination of good and bad than in this amazing picture. It is packed full of bits of exquisite painting. The peacock, the rug, the apple, the cucumber are perfect save for the simple fact that they are superfluous and out of place. So with the youthful ecclesiastic and his model, the angel's coiffure and preposterous costume in which superfluity becomes positive impertinence. But the artist's skill is shown in greater and nobler things, in the architecture which a builder might envy, in the garden with its charming vista, in the cloud-flecked sky, in the upper terrace with its guests, in the half shadowed objects seen in the Virgin's room behind the beautiful curtain. The list of things to admire, great and small, is a long one. But the theme is sacrificed, not wantonly and in the listless, blasé temper of the decadence but by the sheer exuberance of undisciplined craftmanship that has not yet learned the difficult art of leaving things out.

While the Annunciation stands among Crivelli's works in a class quite by itself it is in essence quite akin with the ancona and the other works executed in the more conservative Byzantine manner. For manner, be it mediaeval or modern or what not, is after all only a language through which the artist expresses, often quite unconsciously, his spirit and that of his time. Crivelli was no exception. He might paint in the old medium and conceive his pictures in the old way or make brief excursions into the new, but he was a man of the fifteenth century as were those with whom he lived and for whom he painted. Crivelli was no producer of spurious antiques but a seeker after beauty which he tried to express in the medium most familiar to him. What did he find? What is the ideal content of Crivelli's art?

As judged by this standard we can not assign to Crivelli a very high place. He was a magnificent craftsman whose mastery over a refractory medium was altogether extraordinary like that of his great Florentine counter-part. But here the analogy ends. Fra Angelico eschews all irrelevancies, accepts cheerfully the limitations of his medium, and with masterly simplicity expresses a type of beauty which will charm to the end of time. Crivelli enriches — or swamps — his theme with superb and wholly irrelevant detail but gives us childish stories enacted by indifferent or impossible saints. To lay side by side and compare carefully copies of the Annun-ciation by Fra Angelico and by Crivelli would be a most useful exercise in the study of art. If the comparison be extended later to the Annunciations of Titian, Tinto-retto, and Veronese it will furnish a perfect epitome of Venetian art as represented in the work of these different masters.

On rare occasions, as in the Madonna of the Brera,

Crivelli gives us a comparatively beautiful face, but the beauty is outward, formal, and cold, never spiritual or seriously significant. More often his ideal creations are weirdly impossible. The Saint Catherine of the great ancona and the Magdalen of Berlin are not to be explained by the peculiarities of the model. Their impossible fingers and noses are a personal fancy which it is difficult to imagine as meant to be beautiful. Worst of all are the male saints, especially those whose age usually presupposes something of dignity and nobility. Their sharp, ill favored features are unsympathetic and uninspiring. Peculiarly unsatisfactory is his conception of Peter, a countenance always pinched and snippy and at times even sinister as in the triptych in Milan (Fig. 55). He is simply travestied by an honest but inept attempt at representation. Finally we have to note the painter's rare but wholly unsuccessful attempt to express passion as in the Pietà in the Lateran Museum, Rome. Anguish degenerates into mere grimace and the artist's clear intent miscarries. From these impossible bewailings and these unplausible saints we return with something of reconciliation to the faultless cucumber lying at their feet.

The modern critic sometimes objects impatiently to such observations: "What if the stories are unplausible and the saints unsaintly and the cucumbers out of place? Who cares about such things?" To which the reply is that the people who ordered the picture cared and the painter cared or pretended to do so. We are but measuring what he did by what he was trying to do, surely not an irrelevant standard. It is true the time came when the artist did not care for the saints he pretended to be painting but made them a pretext for something that interested him more. But art did not profit by the change.

Crivelli certainly was not of that time. Art is still sincere, even to the point of naïveté. But the great lesson of subordination, concentration, and simplification had not yet been learned. It was the learning of that lesson that was the crowning achievement of the next century.

Crivelli was a still life painter who was called upon to depict passion and portray saints. He worked sincerely and cleverly but rather ineffectually because he never attained to true unity of purpose or real knowledge of himself. He would have been at home in the Netherlands in the seventeenth century. Fate placed him in Venice in the fifteenth at a moment when art had other and vaster prospects.

CHAPTER XIII

Gentile and John Bellini and Mantegna were all born about 1430 and Crivelli not far from the same date. Mantegna and Crivelli, as we have seen, lived and worked on the mainland leaving Venice itself to the Bellini who soon acquired there a leadership in their profession which was unchallenged to the end of their very long lives, for John Bellini died in 1516 at the age of eighty-five or six. The leadership then passed unchallenged to Titian, a pupil of John Bellini but nearly half a century his junior. It was a little like a dynastic succession in which an abnormally long reign outlasts the lifetime of the heir and the succession passes to a grandson. One generation seemed to be crowded out of the leadership, not solely because of the prestige of the great Bellini but because, it must be admitted, it lacked the ability to challenge his supremacy.

That generation, the generation half way between Bellini and Titian, is represented by artists of whom a single one demands our attention, Vittore *Carpaccio. Again we are dealing with a painter whose life is veiled in obscurity. He was probably born in Venice, though even that is not certain. He must in any case have lived in Venice from a very early age. The date of his birth is not recorded and is variously assigned between 1455 and 1465, about the date when the Bellini, father and sons, returned from the continent and made Venice their permanent home. He grew up, therefore, while they were establishing their position and was a witness of their achievements.

---

* Pronounced Car-patch-o.

But Carpaccio was not a pupil of the Bellini. Painting had developed rapidly in Venice during the half century since the Senate had called strangers to decorate their great hall. There were now a number of studios in Venice, all thronged with pupils and exercising an influence upon Venetian painting not only through the work of their masters but through the instruction to which some of them gave much attention. There was, for instance, the studio of the Vivarini in the adjacent island of Murano, a community with much local pride and interest in art. This studio had been founded by two brothers who, like Jacopo, had worked as helpers of Gentile da Fabriano on the great frescoes of the Palace, but unlike Jacopo had not followed him home. The studio, now under a younger representative of the family, was popular and influential, long rivaling that of the Bellini but ultimately overshadowed by it. There were other studios, how many and how great we do not know. From one of these, that of Lazaro Bastiani, emerged Carpaccio.

More important, however, than any question of apprenticeship or instruction was that of the general environment in which the young artist found himself. In common with other students and artists he had viewed with wonder and admiration the great panoramic, historical pictures executed by Gentile and John as one by one they were unveiled to the public. He had seen the Madonnas as they in turn issued from the studio, among the rest the Madonna of the Trees, unspoiled as yet and peerless among all devotional pictures. When in 1490 he undertook his first great commission, the Saint Ursula series for the *Scuola* of that name, the two brothers had completed their great series in the Doge's Palace, the most imposing achievement in painting that the world had ever known. Concurrently the Bellini began a new

series on an almost equal scale of magnificence for the
Scuola di San Marco. Certainly the painter's environment was stimulating, how stimulating we can not now
appreciate. We honor the Bellini but for us they are
Hamlet with Hamlet left out. We may be thankful for
what we have, thankful even that fate left us the Madonnas rather than the panoramic pictures, but the destruction of the latter has nevertheless taken the heart out of
their work. How much of an idea would we have of
Michelangelo's painting if we had lost the Sistine Ceiling?
The cases are somewhat analogous.

These serial panoramic pictures are the specialty of
this age. They owe their origin in Venice to the frescoes
of Gentile da Fabriano and Pisanello, later replaced by
the great canvases of Gentile and John Bellini. Then
come the great confraternities, the *scuole grandi*, beginning with the Scuola di San Marco of which the Bellini
were members. Last come the little confraternities
in emulation of the great.

It was with these that Carpaccio found his chief
employment. This begins with the Saint Ursula Series
painted for the Scuola di Sant' Ursula, an institution
devoted, it is interesting to note, to the care and education of orphan girls. This series occupied him for five
years, from 1490 to 1495. A second series was painted
for the Scuola di San Giorgio degli Schiavoni (Saint
George of the Slavonians or Russians). The chief
subject was of course the life of Saint George, the patron
saint of the Slavs. This series was begun in 1502 and
finished, doubtless after many interruptions, in 1511.
Still a third series was executed for the Scuola di San
Stefano at a later but uncertain date. Carpaccio of
course painted altarpieces and other minor works during
the intervals between these major commissions and
while they were in progress. But he also had other

great commissions including decorations for the Doge's Palace for which he executed at least one large picture and we read of his working upon another in collaboration with no less a person than John Bellini. These perished like all others in the Palace in the great fire of 1574. There is the clearest evidence that he was influenced by the Bellini, particularly by Gentile, whose panoramic style appealed to him and was in fact the basis of his own.

Though the Saint Ursula series is Carpaccio's earliest dated work and shows signs of immaturity, it is the one upon which his fame chiefly rests. Since we are interested in the general character of his art rather than in cataloging his works we may take this as a type of his panoramic style, limiting our consideration of the other series to the briefest mention.

The legend of Saint Ursula, already familiar both to popular legend and to art, may be briefly summarized as follows. Ursula was the daughter of Maurus, King of Brittany. Her hand was sought in marriage by the King of England for his son and heir. Her father welcomed the proposal but Ursula had a mind of her own. She had decided upon the religious life and against wedlock but finally compromised and offered to yield upon certain extraordinary conditions. The English King and his people were to embrace Christianity and were to furnish her an escort of eleven thousand virgins for a pilgrimage to Rome which she had already vowed. The conditions were accepted and the pilgrimage was made. Her fiancé, quite appropriately excluded from the company, naturally followed by another route and reached Rome ahead of them. The Pope's blessing having been received, Ursula announced that she had received a revelation in a dream to the effect that they were all to suffer martyrdom in Cologne on their return. This her converted lover, the Pope, and a number of ecclesiastics decided to share and all met their death at the hands of the pagan Huns as predicted.

This story was depicted by Carpaccio in a series of nine pictures which covered the entire interior of the small room which served both as chapel and assembly hall of the little *Scuola*, a room long since destroyed but now exactly reproduced in the Academy as regards pictures, furniture, and everything. The subjects of the individual pictures, comparatively easily identified, are (1) The English ambassador makes his petition to King Maurus and (in the same frame) Ursula's answer; (2) Dictating the conditions of marriage; (3) Reading the conditions to the prince; (4) Ursula meets the prince and leaves for Rome; (5) The arrival in Rome; (6) Ursula's dream; (7) The arrival at Cologne; (8) The massacre of the pilgrims; (9) The glorification of Saint Ursula.

The earlier scenes in this series which are undeniably the best are noteworthy first of all for their spacious and elaborate setting. The figures are drawn in very small scale and move in the amplest spaces. So Jacopo had planned his pictures if we may judge by his drawings and so Gentile had followed in the procession in Saint Mark's Square and presumably in all his panoramic pictures. The same was probably true of the pictures of John Bellini and indeed of all the panoramic painting of the period. The effect of this was to remove the action farther from us, to lessen its vividness and dramatic intensity, and to throw the emphasis on the setting. All this was quite to Carpaccio's liking. He loved to paint detail both indoors and out. From his numerous interiors the antiquarian can derive an almost complete picture of Venetian domestic life while his outdoor scenes are hardly less complete. The antiquarian is naturally enthusiastic over Carpaccio. Titian, on the other hand, gives him nothing at all.

Carpaccio thus becomes in reality a genre painter. Of course genre in itself was not a subject for art in the fifteenth century. It had to find its place as an accessory to saints and sacred legend. The latter Carpaccio painted with perfect sincerity, quite unconscious of the fact that he was subtly disparaging them in the interest of the accessories that he loved.

It goes without saying that this setting upon which Carpaccio bestowed such affectionate care is entirely Venetian. He knows nothing about Brittany or England, and if he had known and represented them ever so truly he would have mystified rather than edified his public. As it was, the Venetians felt at home in the setting which he created and its studied unnaturalness made the story seem natural.

But while buildings, walls, towers, bridges, ships, rocks, and all the objects in the landscape are painstakingly and ably represented, the picture is not a landscape. A landscape does not consist of objects. Its essence is an intangible — perhaps we may say a spiritual — something which embraces all objects and merges them into a unity. We speak of this intangible something inadequately as atmosphere, overcolor, reflected light, etc. Those who know Turner are familiar with this spiritual essence of nature sometimes almost divorced from its material counterpart. Later painters have represented the two in more normal balance. But the day for the appreciation of this aspect of nature was yet afar off. For the Italians that day hardly came at all.

Yet scattered here and there through this series there are bits that seem to anticipate that later day. There are vistas framed by houses and trees through which we behold the sky, its blue passing softly into amber at the horizon as is its Venetian wont. There are dreamy bits of water where the light shimmers and the surrounding

buildings and ships and sails are mirrored softly in
its surface. These are foretastes of a later age, bits of
dreamland furtively introduced on a stage reserved for
martyrs and saints. The thoughtful observer will note
these things as both delightful and significant, things
done for love while other things seem done from necessity
or for pay.

Turning from outdoors to indoors the balance inclines
still more in our artist's favor. Carpaccio does not give
us landscape but he does very nearly give us its counterpart, the interior. The term, interior, as used in art
does not mean the walls that bound a room and the
objects which they enclose. It means rather the lights
and shadows, the colors, and all the intangible elements
that make the soul of indoors. To these the walls and
the objects must be subordinated, subdued, into a spiritual unity. This, as is well known, is the theme of the
Dutchmen, a theme rendered with infinite subtlety by
the little Dutchmen and exalted by the great Dutchman
to a stage set for the magician.

Carpaccio is not a Vermeer, much less a Rembrandt,
but in the Vision of Saint Ursula (Fig. 57) he has given
us perhaps the nearest approach to a true interior in all
Italian art. The whole room, of course, is represented,
floor, ceiling, and walls, as nearly as it is possible to do
from the outside standpoint assumed by the painter.
Similarly, every article of furniture is painted with
scrupulous care. The genre program is carried out completely. There is also a dainty touch of decorative design
in the plants that adorn the window, one of the loveliest
things in color in all Carpaccio's art. On the other hand
the persons are almost ruled out of the picture. Of
Saint Ursula only the pale face is seen at the extreme edge
of the picture. The angel is almost equally incon-
spicuous on the other side. The room, extraordinarily

lofty and spacious for the purpose, is the real subject of the picture.

But the room is more than walls and floor and ceiling, more than the furniture and objects that it contains.

Fig. 57, Carpaccio, Vision of Saint Ursula. Venice, Academy.

Nothing is more admirable than the way in which the shadows play over these objects, subduing them, blending their colors, and expressing the mood of the place. That Carpaccio has appreciated this is clear from the fact that he has cleared the room of all competing interests. The angel does not challenge attention, scarcely even attracts our notice. The furniture, despite its scrupulous completeness, is equally modest and unobtrusive. Not the things, not even the persons, but the interior, the spirit of the place as expressed in lights, shadows, and color, appeals to our feeling and wins our sympathy.

This quality of the interior is present in the series as a whole. In open pavilions and half interiors the shadows are studied with scrupulous care. They are not played up and exaggerated as with the Dutchmen. The artist's aim is to be realistic rather than poetical, but realism in things poetical gives us poetry just the same.

One thing more we must place to the artist's credit. He was the best colorist of his age except John Bellini. His coloring approaches closely to the type that we call Venetian, a type that owes much to him. But to the mellowness and transparent shadows of Bellini's later work, especially the Madonna of San Zaccaria, Carpaccio could lay no claim.

We have now to return briefly to what we too easily assume to be the real subject of the picture, the story itself. No doubt the artist would have subscribed to this as the essential thing in the picture. To us to whom the story means nothing and who are interested in tracing his loves and his fancy in the things not required by the theme, the story may well be of secondary importance.

To the writer's mind the story, the human element, the portrayal of the characters and of their action, is the least satisfactory thing in Carpaccio's work. It has certain qualities, to be sure, which appeal to the popular fancy. The story is objective, easy to follow and naïve. The characters are cheerful and kindly. But these are very far from meeting the requirements of great narrative art. It is not necessary to provoke comparison with the subtleties of the high Renaissance although Carpaccio was a full contemporary of Leonardo. It is sufficient to cite Giotto, who painted nearly two centuries before. Never a superfluous figure in his art,

Fig. 58, Carpaccio, the Ambassador before the King. Venice, Academy.

never an inexpressive face or attitude, never an unintelligible action. Note the attitude and expression of the Sultan's priests in the Trial by Fire or that of the centurion and the soldiers in the Crucifixion as examples of whole narrations expressed in a single gesture or expression of countenance.

Of all this Carpaccio shows not a trace. In the more passive parts of the story where the king sits upon his throne and the ambassador kneels before him and presents his petition (Fig. 58) Carpaccio is equal to the situation though the action is tame and the characters devoid of expressive personality. The open spaces, too, are

Fig. 59, Carpaccio, Death of Saint Ursula. Venice, Academy.

sprinkled with irrelevant figures and defects of drawing and action are apparent even to the novice.

When, however, we come to the more stirring and tragic parts of the narrative the painter's lack of dramatic faculty is almost ludicrously apparent. The scene of the massacre (Fig. 59) is incredibly lacking in all that should characterize such a scene. The commander of the Huns is a sentimental and lackadaisical creature whose followers display the savagery of a girls' archery club. The martyrs pose for the shooting as we now pose for the kodak. No doubt the good taste of the artist has always tended to moderate the brutality of these harsher themes. We do not want the blood curdling realism of a Rubens. On the other hand to burlesque the tragic and divest it of all reality is a proof of ineptitude or an abuse of the artist's privilege.

While we are gazing upon these pictures the query inevitably suggests itself, what were the Bellini pictures like, those great pictures in the Doge's Palace which had been Carpaccio's inspiration and those others in the Scuola di San Marco contemporary with his own which must have been the object of his constant emulation? Were they dramatic and intense? Were they vivified by personality and motived by passion? Almost certainly not. For Gentile at least the scanty existing remains are conclusive and the spirit of serenity and noble repose so universally manifest in the works of John is hardly less so. Let us hope that the subjects which they chose were suited to their great qualities. Had they painted the Saint Ursula series they would have improved it in many respects but it is doubtful if the massacre would have been more of a massacre than as it stands. The most that can be said is that it probably would not have been ridiculous.

No, the age of dramatic painting has not come yet, though it is at hand and its master, the dramatic painter of all time, stands by waiting with youthful restiveness for the time to show his powers. The painters have mastered the art of pageant, of calm and dignity and orderly arrangement. They have become subtle in their perception of character in its nobler moods of serenity and repose. They are skilful navigators on calm seas, but the tempest of passion and inscrutable destiny is reserved for more adventurous spirits.

One picture remains in the Ursula Series, one that is seldom discussed and yet one which from its position must have been intended as the climax of the series, the Glorification of Saint Ursula (Fig. 60). The writer can

Fig. 60, Carpaccio, Glorification of Saint Ursula. Venice, Academy.

sympathize with the conspiracy of silence which has shielded this picture from frank discussion. Carpaccio, whatever his limitations, has the faculty of winning our sympathy. Even when he is ridiculous we do not like to have him know that we are laughing at him. His characters are not real characters but children playing the grownup's game. We laugh at them behind their backs but we are demure in their presence.

But the Glorification calls for consideration not only because of its prominence as the crowning piece of the series but because it alone puts to the supreme test the artist's creative imagination. All the other scenes are terrestrial and can be expressed in terms of the artist's experience. He had seen ambassadors come to Venice and present petitions. He had witnessed state betrothals and had seen girls' bedrooms in houses of the wealthy. He had probably been spared the view of massacres which may account in part for his faulty portrayal at this point. But broadly speaking Carpaccio was able to tell his story in terms of what he had seen. His Breton ambassador disembarks from a Venetian galley in front of a Venetian palace which is approached by a Venetian footbridge which spans a Venetian canal; all rather unplausible, perhaps, but we will not quibble. Similarly the panorama unrolls itself throughout in intelligible Venetian terms.

But Carpaccio had never seen a saint glorified in heaven. For this the ordinary furniture in his extensive store would not serve. Something new must be created, imagined. It is the common test of all Christian art. All themes logically end in a glorification, in a beatific existence "where beyond these voices, there is peace."

Not by the remotest stretch of charity can Carpaccio be said to have met the requirement. In a space void of all those homely surroundings which Carpaccio painted so well and which so charm his antiquarian admirers, the eleven thousand virgins — they are nearly all there — kneel in a densely packed mass, a mass so dense that their heads actually come together on all sides. Being of uniform size and type the serried ranks of heads only the tops of which can be seen save in the front row, resemble nothing so much as a cobblestone pavement. The palms to which as martyrs they are severally entitled are all gathered together into a tightly bound sheaf on the top of which, somewhat precariously, Saint Ursula stands. Her expression, like that of the few of her associates whose faces are visible, is wholly inane.

This picture is simply stupid. It is a stultification of our common sense to affect to admire it. It is hardly fair, even, charitably to pass it by. Carpaccio was the best genre painter that Venice ever produced. He made creditable progress in the difficult problem of the interior and catches glimpses of the possibilities of landscape. He translates the Christian legends into a child vernacular which has the charm of all that recalls childhood. All this and more may be freely and gladly granted. But a man who knew next to nothing of the springs of human action, whose characters play their part as demurely and as mechanically as dolls in a puppet show, a man above all whose creative imagination was capable of a performance so helpless and so ludicrous as this is no wise entitled to that place of eminence in art which enthusiasts like Ruskin and Molmenti on essentially irrelevant grounds have assigned him.

Among the other confraternity series already mentioned that of San Giorgio degli Schiavoni is by far the most important. The writer feels little disposed to discuss Saint George's adventure with the dragon (Fig. 61), the representation of which holds the place of honor and has been the subject of what seems to him extravagant praise. The saint who tilts at the dragon on his hobby horse is as unreal as the chief of the Huns, and the dragon, that theme of unlimited possibilities for the creative imagination, is the tamest of monstrosities. What would Carpaccio have thought if he could have gazed for a moment upon the creation of some Chinese artist who was decorating the Dragon Throne? Nor do these pictures seem by their setting and accessories to claim a

Fig. 61, Carpaccio, Saint George in Combat with the Dragon. Venice, San Giorgio degli Schiavoni.

place alongside the better numbers of the Saint Ursula series. Here again the artist was required to go beyond the known and to imagine what was beyond his powers.

It is with relief that we turn from these to Saint Jerome in his Study (Fig. 62), a picture which shows us Carpaccio at his best. The scene is of course frankly Venetian. The room is a delightful interior which no doubt had its counterpart in many a Venetian palace. The niche at the end holds a statue of the Christ with a candle stick on either side and a crozier leaning near. An alcove nearby shows an open book mounted upon a lectern after the familiar Italian fashion. The saint sits pen in hand at his table which is piled with books. Other books stand open against the low platform on which the table

is placed while others are laid side by side on a shelf
opposite beneath which, ranged in a long row, are tiny
statuettes, vases, and other bric-a-brac not ordinarily
included in the inventory of a saint's belongings but
suitable enough for the home of a Venetian merchant.
Suited to both is the chair and desk which serves the

Fig. 62, Carpaccio, Saint Jerome in his Study. Venice, San Giorgio
degli Schiavoni.

purposes of devotion, for the fifteenth century Venetian
did not neglect his devotions. Nor has the painter forgotten the little dog that awaits with lively expectancy
some sign of the relaxation of his master's intellectual
labors. As genre painting this picture is worthy of all
praise and is perhaps to be accounted the artist's masterpiece.

But if we pass beyond genre to the ostensible and more
vital theme, if we turn from the setting to the saint,
our verdict must be less favorable. This vivacious
figure who interrupts his work to gaze with unaccountable

excitement out of the window has his attractions but he is not a Saint Jerome. One moment's comparison with Bellini's wonderful Jerome in San Zaccaria (Fig. 53, page 240) will relegate him to a place of hopeless inferiority. The analysis and portrayal of saintly character was not Carpaccio's gift. Unfortunately it was the requirement of his age, a requirement which John Bellini was able to meet, he and he alone.

Carpaccio's minor religious pictures are numerous and more or less scattered. One at least, the Presentation in the Temple (Fig. 63), a large altarpiece now in the Academy, the visitor to Venice cannot fail to see. The most noticeable thing about it is its obvious imitation of John Bellini, the originator, it will be remembered, of the large group altarpiece. Even the little musicians at the base of the throne, a charming and popular innovation of the older painter, are here copied with scant originality. This innocent but rather frank appropriation is less apparent in his serial pictures. Is it perhaps because their Bellini counterparts have disappeared? One thing about this altarpiece, however, is rather an innovation. It is symmetrical but with no central figure, an unusual and not very happy arrangement which, however, the character of the theme seems to invite.

This altarpiece will serve to emphasize a characteristic which to the writer is everywhere apparent but nowhere so marked as here. Carpaccio's characters are children. They may have the stature of adults but their mentality is that of the child. This is something very different, to the writer's mind, from the beatific guilelessness of Fra Angelico. There is in that a very positive quality perfectly fitted to those who stand "all rapture through and through in God's most holy sight." The Carpaccio childlikeness is not beatific, though to many it seems

Fig. 63, Carpaccio, The Presentation. Venice,
Academy.

gentle and sweet. Even this impression the writer can not wholly share. The Carpaccio character is too negative. Compare the saints in this altarpiece with the Madonna of San Zaccaria. The latter is characterized by a sweetness and gentleness which is ineffable but it is a positive quality, not the mere negation of its opposite. There is a soulfulness in the Madonna, in the Jerome, the Peter, in all the group which does not characterize the work before us. Compared with these souls in which heaven is enthroned forever the saints of Carpaccio's altarpiece suggest at most only a temperamental amiability.

Carpaccio left Venetian painting vastly better than he found it, richer in color, more decided in its medium, and more advanced in its technique. He shared in this advance and in sharing contributed to it. The development of Venetian genre was peculiarly his work. His share in the general advance to which so many contributed is more difficult to determine but considerable. It may be said of him as of Crivelli that he would have been more at home in another country and another age. Among the Dutch genre and interior painters he would have made his mark, perhaps even among the landscape painters of a later day. Fate unfortunately assigned him the role of a Venetian Giotto, a role which was not in the line of his powers.

CHAPTER XIV

Never in the history of art has a single generation witnessed a change so profound yet so logical, so contructive and healthy as that effected by Giorgione and Titian, the great pupils of John Bellini. The nearest counterpart would be the revolution in Florence which followed the advent of Leonardo da Vinci. Leonardo was the greater man, the more universal genius, but in sheer wisdom and insight into the nature of the art which they practised, in creative power and technical mastery within the legitimate laws of art, these men surpass the Florentine.

Giorgione and Titian were both born in or about the year 1477, two years after Michelangelo and twenty-six years after Leonardo. Both were born outside Venice but came early to live in the city. Though of approximately equal age, *Giorgione was the more precocious. As he earlier made a name for himself and throughout his lifetime clearly enjoyed greater recognition, we naturally think of him as the older man, an impression that is strengthened by the fact that he powerfully influenced the early work of Titian without being equally influenced by him in turn. There is no clear evidence, however, that Giorgione had the advantage in age. His leadership rested apparently upon genius, not necessarily greater but earlier manifest.

Both men are said to have died of the plague which so often devastated the city, as the churches built to appease the unseen powers or in gratitude for their supposed intervention so tragically testify, but with this great

---

* Pronounced Jor-jo-nay.

difference. Giorgione died at the age of thirty-three and Titian at the age of ninety-nine, a disparity for which no advantage of genius or opportunity could compensate.

Both men were conventionally religious — for skepticism was almost unknown in Venice — but neither had anything of that deep, personal piety which characterized the Bellini brothers. Both treated religious subjects sincerely enough and with appreciation of their art possibilities, but never as an expression of personal conviction or feeling. Both accepted willingly enough the easy morals for which Venice was noted, but both kept within the limits of conventional decency and good taste. (The rumored "dissipation" of Giorgione is wholly unsupported by all that we know of his life and art). Similarly environed and circumstanced they worked under like conditions, for a time even in collaboration, and their early works form a united whole which it is difficult to separate. Expert opinion is still divided as to the authorship of some of the most important of these works.

Giorgione was born in Castelfranco, a little city on the edge of the Venetian plain just where it halts abruptly before the foothills of the mighty Alps. East and south the plain stretches away unbroken beyond the horizon. North and west rises the mountain barrier which seems to block the way in this direction save where the deep gorge of the Val Zugana opens a narrow way to Trent. Situated on the level and unconstrained by natural features the city is planned like a fortified Roman camp, rectangular, surrounded by walls with corner towers and protected by a wide moat. Fortified gateways give entrance to main streets which traverse the city lengthwise and crosswise. A mere village in extent it seems in comparison with our modern, sprawling, trolley served communities. In its day, however, that is, about seven hundred years ago, Castelfranco was a powerful fortress and flourishing city, and in the later period of Venetian occupation an important outpost of Venetian trade. It boasted its own noble family and provincial court and was altogether an epitome of the great world. Its present quaintness is due to the fact that it went to sleep centuries ago and so remained unchanged in this our changing world.

Rumor, nowhere busier or more irresponsible than in Venice, would have it that Giorgione was the illegitimate son of the lord of Castelfranco and later ages conferred upon him the family name, Barbarelli, a name which occurs in no signature or document of his time. The rumor seems to rest upon another rumor that the local magnate had his body brought back to Castelfranco for interment there, an act not unnatural, it would seem, in honor of a townsman who had attained the zenith of fame. But this rumor in turn seems devoid of foundation in view of the fact that he died of the plague at a time when burials took place by wholesale without ceremony or delay. The likelihood that the body of a plague victim would have been carried seventy miles for solemn sepulture is slight.

Giorgione, therefore, emerges but slightly from that obscurity which envelopes the origin of all the painters whom we have thus far studied. We know the place of his birth and the year; beyond that nothing. It is probable that, as Vasari states, he was of the humblest origin. But he was handsome, fascinating, and gifted, one who made his way as much by his personal charm as by his genius. He is said to have been devoted to music and to have been an exquisite singer, especially of songs of love. With such gifts and in a city most indulgent in these matters the attitude of the fair sex may be imagined. Giorgione's conduct was what might have been expected of one so circumstanced but in the case of a popular idol the myth maker's fancy was sure to be indulged to the limit. Giorgione is the center of a whole love mythology which links his pictures, his life and his death, all with the one absorbing theme. Hence the impression which slowly crystallized into definite tradition that Giorgione was a libertine, that he died of dissipation. Based upon stories, all of them doubtful and some of them disproved, this aspersion may well be disregarded. His art gives evidence of an erotic temperament but we have no reason to believe him a dissipated man.

Giorgione apparently owed his education in painting essentially to John Bellini. His art rests incontestably upon that of Bellini and shows no discernible affinity with any other. The kinship between the two men was as close as could be expected between a finished technician of conservative temperament in the seventies and a supreme and daring genius in the flood tide of youth. The two men differed as much in temperament, in intellectual interests, in art sympathies, as in age, but in a peculiar sense they seem to have differed harmoniously. There was extreme diversity but little conflict, a fact which speaks much for the generosity of both men and especially of the older. Hence it is that while they lived and dreamed in different worlds, on their occasional common ground they attained remarkable similarity. There are no two Madonnas in the world from the hands of different artists which are spiritually so near akin as the Madonna of San Zaccaria and the Madonna of Castelfranco, painted approximately at the same time. We need not assume either immediate association or conscious borrowing either way, but as regards the spiritual essence of Madonna the two men have similar ideals.

Fate has been peculiarly unkind to Giorgione. Not

content with his early death at the very outset of his career she has doomed to destruction most of the few works that he executed. He is said to have been extremely fond of fresco but the climate of Venice is incompatible with fresco and virtually nothing of his work in this medium survives. It was executed chiefly for the decoration of the façades of Venetian palaces, a fashion briefly in vogue in his time, but only meaningless traces remain. Of his numerous easel pieces in oil many of which we have record have been destroyed or lost. Worst of all for critical purposes he early became famous and was assiduously imitated by talented admirers. Dying at the height of his great popularity the rage to possess one of his pictures opened wide the door to fraud. The Venetians were thrifty, their art dealers not least, and with the certainty that a given picture sold as a Giorgione would bring ten times as much as sold under another name, the works of Giorgione continued to multiply after his death. This is still going on. Not only are the owners of alleged works of Giorgione zealous to maintain the precious attribution but writers who cannot resist the magic of his personality are bent upon increasing the number of his works at the expense of Titian and other contemporaries. The tangle thus resulting is one that the experts have not altogether unraveled. Of the numerous pictures that bear or have borne the name of Giorgione only three are entirely unquestioned and less than a score are credited to him by a majority of expert opinion.

A further matter of regret is that these pictures are for the most part so located that they are seen by few even of those travelers who might give them serious attention. Castelfranco, proud possessor of the far famed Madonna, is the easiest of excursions from Padua, but few stop even at incomparable Padua and still fewer make the excursion. The Giovanelli Palace in Venice, possessor of another of the undisputed three, is open to the public but it is remote from the shopping district and seldom competes successfully with its attractions. Vienna, Dresden, and Berlin, each possessor of a single important work, are off the main travel route and especially since the war are little visited. The Uffizi, to be sure, is one of the most visited of galleries and its three authentic works of Giorgione, the Judgment of Solomon, the Trial of Moses, and the Knight of Malta, can be seen by any visitor. Important as these are, however, they are not of a character to attract attention nor would the most ardent of Giorgione's partisans offer them as adequately representative of his art. The Shepherd Boy in Hampton Court is both charming and accessible but it is of all the works usually claimed for Giorgione the one whose authenticity is most doubtful. Similarly, the Concert of the Pitti (Fig. 78, page 311), one of the greatest pictures in Italy, is prominently placed in one of the most popular of galleries, but though the authorities of the Pitti still cling to the coveted attribution there is a growing if reluctant conviction that the masterpiece is from the hand of Titian.

It will be seen that the traveler who is limited to the traditional and, on the whole, wisely chosen route through Europe will have to derive his impression of Giorgione chiefly from a single important and characteristic work the Picnic* (Fête Champêtre) (Fig. 64), of the Louvre. This remarkable picture which, though much repainted, is thoroughly characteristic and still reveals the splendid genius of the painter, occupies a prominent place in the busiest art thoroughfare of the world where, a near

---

*This picture is sometimes called the Concert, an unfortunate term which neither translates the French title nor describes the picture, while it tends to confound it with the very different picture in the Pitti.

neighbor of the Mona Lisa, it is in the vortex of that notoriety cult which Leonardo's enigma continues to inspire. The visitor to the Louvre cannot be too strongly urged to make the fullest use of this, his greatest and perhaps his only opportunity to enter into the spirit

Fig. 64, Giorgione, The Picnic (Fête Champêtre). Paris, Louvre.

of one of the most gifted and inspired of painters. If circumstances permit in addition a visit to Vienna and Dresden and above all to Castelfranco the privileged traveler will have most of the data which the world now possesses for the study of Giorgione.

The works of Giorgione fall into several classes which, however, are so interrelated that the distinctions serve little purpose beyond mere enumeration. There are the religious pictures including the Madonna of Castelfranco (Fig. 65), Christ bearing the Cross (Fig. 66), the Trial of

Fig. 65, Giorgione, Madonna and Saints.   Castelfranco.

Fig. 66, Giorgione, Christ Bearing the Cross. Boston, Fenway Court.

Moses, and a number of similar examples of more or less doubtful authenticity. Of these only the first is seriously to be considered as a religious picture and even there it can hardly be said that the religious interest is the main interest. The second is an ideal study of the Christ and to the writer's mind an unsatisfactory one. The furtive, sidewise glance suggests neither the character of the Christ nor the pathos of the occasion. Whatever its technical merits it suggests what all our knowledge of Giorgione confirms, that he was of all great painters the one least fitted to express pathos and the deeper religious sentiments. The other examples, all minor works, are religious only in the sense that their subjects are Bible stories. The story is always subordinated to the setting, the artist's interest being obviously in the latter. There is little action and nothing of passion or dramatic interpretation. Indistinguishable in spirit from the foregoing are the characteristic landscape and figure scenes by which we know the painter best. These are known by arbitrary names* which are of popular origin and

---

*It has pleased the pedant of a later day to identify these with classical and mythological themes usually of an unfamiliar character. These identifications have been welcomed by those who crave prosaic definiteness and who cannot conceive of a painter indulging in pure fantasies not founded in history or literature. Thus the "Three Philosophers" have been christened Aeneas, Evander and Pallas after Vergil, apparently for the reason that it represents three men out of doors. The "Stormy Landscape with Soldier and Gypsy" has been called Adrastus and Hipsipyle in allusion to one of the least known of ancient stories in which a king discovers the identity of a queen living in disguise as a nurse. Why this plainly dressed youth who stands at a distance from the nursing mother and completely ignores her should be taken for King Adrastus is not clear. In no single case is there anything in the action to justify the proposed identification nor do the characters look their part. We do better frankly to take our stand with Vasari who remarks that for his part he has never been able to understand what Giorgione's pictures mean nor could he ever find anyone who could explain them to him. To which we may add that if he could have consulted the painter himself he would probably have found him equally unable to give him their meaning — at least the kind of meaning that he and others like him desired. All this is merely saying that Giorgione was a poet. His pictures so laboriously labeled with classical names were probably pure fantasies suggested by trivial incidents that came under his own observation. In this book the writer has retained the traditional names which, though arbitrary, are free from misleading implications.

Fig. 67, Giorgione, Portrait of a Man. Berlin.

record a popular impression. They are one and all studies in landscape and genre, the artist's true subject.

Finally the portraits constitute a group which is more or less distinct. Of these there are few of undoubted authenticity but a considerable number that are on debatable ground. Best known of the former are the Young Man (Fig. 67) of the Berlin gallery and the Knight of Malta in the Uffizi. The former is striking in color and sharply defined in contour and detail. Apparently an early work it cannot fail to remind us of Bellini's famous portrait of Doge Loredano to which it bears a certain resemblance. Incidentally we note something of that furtive and not wholly pleasant sidewise glance which we have already seen in the Christ with which it has technically much in common. The Knight of Malta (Fig. 68) is painted in a very different manner, very dark and with hair, beard, and costume merged in the background of dark, obscuring shadow against which the face, the hand, and the shirt front stand out in startling relief. Contours are almost completely obliterated. It is a striking and dramatic style of painting with which Titian has made us familiar. Before raising the question of priority it may be well to recall that again John Bellini has shown the way in his Madonna with Saint Lucy and the Magdalen, one of his most familiar and best beloved pictures, in which this submergence of the figures in their shadow background is carried out with masterly effect. These portraits, priceless as they justly are, do not seem to the writer to be masterpieces of character interpretation. Without disparagement we rest Giorgione's fame on the other works.

The Madonna of Castelfranco was painted as a memorial to a youth of the Costanzo family, a family of sufficient wealth and importance to have its own chapel in the local church. For that chapel this altarpiece was

Fig. 68, Giorgione, Knight of Malta. Florence, Uffizi.

destined. The youth died in 1504. The picture was therefore painted after this date, that is, when Giorgione was nearing the age of thirty. As he had been painting for at least ten years before this time this cannot be called an early picture. Yet from its character it best serves as a starting point for the study of his art. In the first place it is a Madonna, the only one we have from his hand. As a treatment of the traditional theme and the one in which his great teacher had excelled it enables us most easily to see what is old and what is new in his art. A certain kinship with the Madonna of San Zaccaria has already been noted. This kinship is pervasive, a matter of atmosphere, of spiritual mood which pervades the whole, rather than a similarity of facial expression or even of the general character of the Madonna. The similarity may be accidental, superficial, even consciously imitative. It is impossible to feel from all we know of Giorgione that he shared the profound sentiment of reverence and devotion which his master felt for this, his supreme subject. Giorgione was a poet who lived in an atmosphere of joy and song untroubled by conscience or spiritual yearnings. Is it fanciful to suggest that the two men seeking beauty along the lines of their very different temperaments might arrive by different pathways at an identical goal? Might not the lover of pure beauty seeking no religious ends and heedless of all chastening of the spirit find his ideal after all in the vision of John Bellini?

There is of course a further resemblance in the general build and arrangement of the picture. The Madonna sits on a lofty throne with saints below on either side, though the Madonna here sits higher and the attendant saints are fewer. Both arrangement and spirit are monumental and dignified. But this impression of similarity quickly yields to an ever deepening sense of difference.

The throne is here and the marble floor but where is the building, the architecture, which Bellini has so painstakingly, so logically represented? The throne stands, not in a niche, not against a wall, but backed up against a crimson screen, a mere arbitrary band of color which represents nothing in nature and whose excuse for existence is the same as that of a musical accompaniment to words which have slipped the leash of speech and soared into song. This screen is just high enough to serve as a background for the two side figures, Saints Francis and Liberalis (the latter said to be a portrait of the deceased youth here commemorated) and is plainly introduced for that purpose. This introduction of the arbitrary for purely musical or artistic effect is characteristic of the new era, a principle often abused but when controlled by sanity and taste most serviceable to art.

But we must rise above the screen to discover the true Giorgione. As we gaze upon these exquisite landscapes, unapproached up to this time in Italian art, we understand why Giorgione did away with his church and set up the Madonna's throne out of doors. These landscapes do not owe their beauty to the *objects* represented — true landscapes never do — but to their mastery of atmosphere and the transcendental elements in nature. A dreamy light broods over land and sea, softening the outlines, blending the colors, and enduing the whole with a spirit of enchantment which it is the aim of poetic landscape to inspire.

Why do we see in this landscape the real Giorgione? Not because it is better painted than the figures — though on the whole it is, better at least than Saints Francis and Liberalis who bear no comparison to the splendid figures in Bellini's great picture — but because it is the thing he need not have painted, the thing which he strained his theme to get a chance to paint. We

need not ask why Madonna is here or why the saints or
the throne. They were of its essence. We need not
inquire the reason for the arrangement. For that Bellini
furnished the precedent and Leonardo, a recent visitor
to Venice, could be cited as its definite exponent. But
for the landscape as here used there was no such warrant.
Landscape was familiar enough in such scenes as the
Crucifixion, the Agony in the Garden, and others where
it was a natural, not to say a necessary, accessory. But
here it was not necessary, not even natural. Indeed the
painter has noticeably strained his theme to get it in.
Men must have looked with amazement at this throne
set up in a church that was nothing but a floor and against
a screen that was meaningless except as an arbitrary
band of color. Let us hope that there was delight in
their amazement and that they enjoyed and approved.

There is another reason for believing that the painter's
interest was chiefly in the landscape. Landscape is a
prominent feature in his other paintings where it embraces and even submerges the nominal theme. In the
Three Philosophers (Fig. 69) the landscape setting
certainly holds its own with the figures, though the latter
are among the finest of their age. In the Picnic the
balance inclines still farther toward nature and away
from the figures. The latter are no longer painted as
objects of interest in their own right. They are toned,
shadowed, and merged, their faces even shaded to the
point of obliteration, all in the interest of making them
parts of the landscape instead of the landscape being a
setting for them. Finally in the Soldier and Gipsy in a
Stormy Landscape (Fig. 70) the figures are completely
subordinate and that too in spite of the gypsy's unnecessarily challenging nudity. Only the portraits and
the analogous Christ Bearing the Cross are without this
favorite accessary. The conclusion is inevitable that

Giorgione was in essence a landscape painter, potentially
one of the greatest, but born in a time and place which
compelled him to paint other things.   His landscapes
reveal a clear appreciation of two things which are char-

Fig. 69, Giorgione, Three Philosophers. Vienna.

acteristic of modern landscape painting and indeed of
true landscape in every age.

The first is the feeling for mass as contrasted with its
component details.   Foliage is made up of leaves but
you cannot paint foliage by painting leaves.   Dutchmen
like Paul Potter quite demonstrated that.   The reason
is that we do not see foliage as leaves.   We see it as
foliage, that is, as a mass in which the parts, even if
distinguishable, are not in fact distinguished.   A glance
at the landscape pictures above mentioned will show

with what astonishing boldness Giorgione adopts the new principle.

The second principle is even more important and not

Fig. 70, Giorgione, Stormy Landscape with Soldier and Gipsy. Venice, Palazzo Giovanelli.

unrelated, the recognition of atmosphere, over-color, in short, the intangible or transcendental element in nature. This is something of which we do not ordinarily take cognizance in our daily experience. Things that we cannot walk on or take hold of do not enter much into our calculations. Even the color and haze of the atmosphere which modifies the appearance of everything we ignore, looking right through them to the local color beyond. But the painter who would reproduce nature must not ignore them, for little as we heed them consciously, we miss them when they are not there. If we could for a moment strip off this intangible vestment which envelops outer nature it would be a weird and uncanny world that we should look out upon. Moreover we should find to our surprise that it had almost wholly lost its poetical quality, its power to appeal to our feeling. It is the painter, and especially the modern painter, who has discovered this and he naturally shapes his art accordingly. Giorgione must be ranked high among these discoverers. In landscape as in all else, he is supremely a poet.

His treatment of the human figure like that of landscape is always, if somewhat indefinably, poetical. Save possibly in his religious art where convention was more exacting and individual fancy less free Giorgione's characters always come from Arcadia and bring with them the Arcadian simplicity and joy in life. While lacking the eternal childhood of Correggio's characters they are as free as his from that sense of burdened existence which weighs upon the characters of so many an artist from Michelangelo to Millet. The suggestion is not one of frivolity but of joy in living. Happiness rather than gaiety irradiates the scene.

In drawing the nude Giorgione was no anatomy pedant. He is not ignorant; he is not careless. He is simply poetical everywhere, converting prose into poetry by the use, but without the abuse, of the poet's license. The Sleeping Venus (Fig. 71) is the example of this usually cited. By carefully arranged pose and certain unobtrusive deviations from nature the artist has given us a symphony in flowing lines which is largely responsible for an impression of beauty without a rival among nude studies. By means not easily analyzed Giorgione gave to the female nude a freshness and delicacy never surpassed by any other painter. His use of the nude, it must be confessed, was not always in good taste. He

Fig. 71, Giorgione, Sleeping Venus. Dresden.

did not, like Michelangelo, make the nude a vehicle of spiritual expression utterly redeemed from erotic suggestion. Though his nudes are guiltless of anything in act or attitude which is seductive, erotic suggestion is plainly present and almost certainly intended. It would be a mistake, however, to see in his pictures any low pandering to lust. He was a lover of beauty and to him, the artist, there was no forbidden fruit.

Giorgione had an amazing mastery over color. The boldest colors were docile under his hand. Who does not envy the person who can wear the boldest colors in striking combinations and yet not have them seem loud or in bad taste? This in art was Giorgione's gift. John

Bellini, that master of harmony and faultless colorist, secured his harmonies by a cautious conservatism. No crimson screens for him filling half the height of his pictures, but subdued colors mellowed by transparent shadow. Yet Giorgione's crimson screen is so perfectly harmonized with all the rest that the writer, who has seen the picture repeatedly always forgets the screen and is surprised when some allusion recalls it to memory. Not less than in the work of his master there is in Giorgione's art at its best a sense of perfect harmony, a music stranger, richer, and more stirring, but not less harmonious than that which had gone before.

We attribute to Giorgione, possibly with injustice to Titian, the formulation of that true Venetian style which was the glory of fifteenth century Venice. The color is strong and rich but never garish or discordant, toned and mellowed as it is by Bellini's transparent shadows. Modeling becomes less obtrusive and we see figures rather than ornamental details. Outlines become softened and vague thus reconciling figure with environment. There is emancipation from convention but no sacrifice of discipline or order. There is a greater knowledge of nature but freer fancy in dealing with it. The essential theme is moved nearer, shorn of its needless detail, and the superfluous space trimmed away. In short, there is simplification of theme, concentration of attention, a new poetry and a music all its own. No single artist was responsible for this imposing whole. But the world has probably not erred in seeing in the shadowy, almost mythical figure who passes so early and so briefly across the stage the happiest, freest, best beloved of them all.

CHAPTER XV

We approach the greatest name in Venetian painting with the consciousness that no comprehensive survey of his work is possible within the compass of the present work. Titian's life extended over practically a century, the most stimulating and creative, the most glorious century in the history of art. For two-thirds of this period he was the unchallenged leader of art in one of its two most vital centers. Ceaselessly active, he enjoyed the advantages of wealth, recognition, and unlimited opportunity. His patrons were dukes and prelates, kings and emperors. Rarely has great endowment been so favorably circumstanced. The result was an unparalleled series of paintings of which, though hundreds have perished, many hundreds remain. These works reveal a constant progress almost unmarred by decadence, a progress which resumes the whole development of Venetian painting during this, its most progressive period.

The merest enumeration of these works with a minimum statement of fact or conjecture concerning them would fill a volume, while libraries have been written to contain the controversies and discussions to which they give rise. The aim of the present chapter must be limited to the briefest analysis of Titian's art as illustrated by a few representative works.

Titian was born in 1477. He was thus two years younger than Michelangelo and three years older than Raphael, his best known contemporaries. The date of his birth has been disputed, chiefly on the ground that it implies a much later beginning on his part than in the case of his famous contemporaries. The precocious

299

development of Giorgione, Michelangelo, Raphael, Leonardo, and Bernini is well known. While these examples by no means warrant us in assuming a like early development of Titian's methodical and calculating genius it is nevertheless striking that we can identify very little from his hand before the age of thirty. Hence the contention that he was born later than the date traditionally assigned. Against this contention must be set Titian's own statement made to the emperor in 1571 that he was then ninety-five years old — probably to be interpreted that he was in his ninety-fifth year — and the fact that at thirty he was a partner with Giorgione on a commission which would hardly have been given to a beginner and in which he is said to have surpassed Giorgione to the latter's pronounced vexation. The absence of earlier pictures need not surprise us. We know to a certainty that many pictures painted in later years when his work was eagerly sought at unprecedented prices have since disappeared. It is so much the more probable that youthful works unsigned and little prized should have perished or come down to us unrecognized. When it is remembered that the more popular Giorgione is hardly better represented in the same period and that a considerable number of early, undated pictures are in dispute between them there would seem to be no reason to doubt tradition confirmed by Titian's own statement. Titian was therefore the longest lived and the longest active of all artists on record.

He was born in Pieve di Cadore, a small place in the Dolomites, the most romantic region of the Alps. He seems never to have lost his interest in the beautiful scenery of his birthplace which constantly recurs in his paintings. Though living in Venice from early childhood his family remained in Cadore where he retained a foothold throughout his life.

When and how the decision was reached that he should become a painter we do not know but it was evidently with little appreciation of his gifts if we may judge by the humble studios which he first entered. Restlessness or better appreciation sent him later to the studio of Gentile Bellini who was dissatisfied with him because of his too off-hand method of work. The criticism is suggestive. Probably Gentile thought him careless, which he certainly was not as all his later work shows. We may surmise that he was already beginning to show that disregard of unimportant detail, that subordination of accessories to essentials, which distinguished his art from that of the painstaking but prosaic Gentile.

Following this brief relation there was an interval without record and then another and better discipleship under John Bellini. Even this, however, was not happy or long continued which suggests that beside the difference of temperament between the two men, a difference of the profoundest character, Titian was not very tractable. Genius is seldom tractable though intractability is not always a sign of genius. Titian was apparently a poor learner as he later proved himself to be a poor teacher. Though the relation to Bellini was less congenial than in the case of Giorgione it was by no means unfruitful. Titian's indebtedness to this, the greatest of his predecessors, was greater than he realized, though he was perhaps less influenced by Bellini directly than through his great fellow pupil, Giorgione, who seems to have been more receptive to the master's influence than Titian and more influential over his fellow than Bellini. It was apparently in Bellini's studio that the two became acquainted and formed the fellowship which resulted in their brief collaboration.

Tradition would have us believe that this relation in turn was unhappy and that it ended in estrangement.

Possibly, though the fact that Titian was chosen to complete Giorgione's unfinished pictures and that he continued for years to paint in a manner strongly reminiscent of Giorgione's very different temperament does not look like estrangement. Gossip was exceptionally active and malicious in Venice and the well known jealousies of artists furnished abundant pretext. When we remember that Albrecht Dürer was warned not to accept food or drink in Venice from artists lest he be poisoned we need not take too seriously the tale that Giorgione severed his relation with Titian through jealousy and forbade him to enter his house, uttering as his last wish the request that Titian should not be allowed to attend his funeral. Whatever their personal relation, their fellowship in art was an intimate one, their works forming a closely related whole, the dissociation of which is the unending puzzle of the critics.

There were other painters who influenced Titian at this time, one of whom deserves brief mention. Jacopo Palma, known as Palma Vecchio (Palma the Elder) was a full contemporary of Titian and merely as a painter was not unworthy of comparison with him. He, too, was in some sense a product of the Bellini studio as his earliest works clearly attest. He later came in contact with Titian and Giorgione and, like Titian, was much influenced by the latter. The kinship between his own and Titian's works is so close as to leave no doubt that the contact was influential but critics are divided as to which influenced the other. It is reasonable to suppose that the influence was mutual and that the two men worked out their similar style together. It is difficult to believe, however, that Palma contributed anything of value to Titian. He was only a painter and Titian was an artist. By a rare inspiration — or possibly by a happy chance — Palma has given us a single work of

Fig. 72, Palma Vecchio, Santa Barbara. Venice, Santa
Maria Formosa.

true art, the popular Santa Barbara (Fig. 72), a magnificent young woman instinct with life, health, and radiant good nature but quite lacking in spiritual significance. The lines and coloring are superb. But this picture which is the high water mark in Palma's art stands alone. His later works, notably those in the so-

Fig. 73, Titian, The Gipsy Madonna. Vienna.

called blond manner, are quite lacking in inspiration and interpretive and dramatic power. His death at the age of forty-eight was but a moderate loss to Venetian art.

We have no pictures which seem to date from Titian's student days in the studio of Bellini, but there are two, the Gipsy Madonna and the Madonna of the Cherries (Figs. 73 and 74), that must have been painted very soon after. There are superficial resemblances to Bellini in the half length figures (Bellini's specialty) and in the arrangement, the Madonna in the center and the saints, if any, equally distributed on either side. But here the resemblance ends. Bellini's Madonnas have a noble spiritual beauty which is altogether super-earthly and which puts them in a world quite apart. They call forth our reverence, our adoration, but never our sense

Fig. 74, Titian, Madonna of the Cherries. Vienna.

of easy familiarity. To see them in a love scene or on a ballroom floor is inconceivable. Titian's Madonnas would be quite at home in either. They are very beautiful women, not carnal or voluptuous, but still not in the least the embodiment of spiritual ideals or super-earthly interests. Similarly, the Christ child, hitherto called upon to play quite an impossible role, now becomes baby-like and "cute," plays and is played with, all in a manner quite shocking to a true devotional painter.

Quite unconsciously, no doubt, Titian has quietly dropped the great theme of Christian art and under its conventional form has adopted the theme of nature. The Madonna no longer stands for Christianity, for spirituality and chastening of spirit, but for motherhood, for womanhood happy in the enjoyment of its great

Fig. 75, Titian, Madonna with Saints. Dresden.

privilege and the performance of its primary duty. It is the same change as that wrought by Leonardo, the herald of the newer — perhaps the better — day.

Incidentally there is in these two pictures a somewhat strained effort to secure the triangular group so dear to Leonardo. The great Florentine had visited Venice when Titian was twenty-three. It is hardly to be imagined that his visit was without influence upon the youth who, even in his extreme old age, was consciously or unconsciously influenced by Leonardo's wonderful compositions.

Soon even this formal resemblance to Bellini disappears. Titian abandons the centered group, apparently deeming it too formal, sets the Madonna and child on one side, and loosely arranges his figures in a balanced but no longer in a symmetrical group. Such are the Madonna with Saints in Dresden (Fig. 75) and the

Fig. 76, Titian, Madonna with Saint Bridget.   Madrid, Prado.

magnificent Madonna with Saint Bridget in Madrid (Fig. 76), works that vie with the noblest of the artist's creations but almost completely neglected because unfortunately located. If these works do not attain the highest level of spirituality they are splendidly dignified and glorious in their human beauty. They rise far above the level of mere prettiness. There is never anything about them that is sentimental or weak. Indeed it is just here where they are at their best that Titian's Madonnas are most open to criticism. Those who are looking for sentiment will, with Mr. Ruskin, find them cold. They are of quite too large and dignified a type to cuddle their baby in public and provide those pretty scenes that move with their superficial appeal. They are never lachrymose or pathetic or ethereal or heavenly. Call them mundane if we will — as Michelangelo did, not unjustly but less sympathetically than is their due — but in such an application the word loses all its reproach. This splendid type, perhaps best embodied in the Madonna of Dresden, is undoubtedly of this world rather than of the other, but she reconciles us to a world that can claim a creature so magnificent. In her strength without grossness and her beauty without seductiveness Titian has arrived at a subtle balance which, whatever its spiritual value, is utterly above reproach. To appreciate how skilfully Titian has steered between the Scylla and Charybdis of grossness and sex appeal we have but to recall the familiar type of Rubens and the Danaë of Correggio, nay, even the familiar works of Giorgione.

It is just here that, to the writer's mind, the work of Titian differentiates itself most markedly from that of Giorgione even at the time when he is most under the latter's influence. Whatever Titian's habits may have been, his art is not erotic. No man appreciated better than he the beauty of the flesh and the delight of the eye, but beauty to him is not inseparably bound up with sex suggestion. Giorgione could paint — did paint — a more spiritual Madonna, one to incite more to devotion, than Titian, but the moment that woman lays aside the immunity of that high rôle she becomes for him little more than the beautiful embodiment of sex suggestion. To Titian she is, both in that rôle and out of it, simply magnificently human. There are exceptions but the wonder is that in sixteenth century Venice they were so few.

This broadly human appreciation of beauty is confirmed by a study of the male figures included in these groups. Splendid as is the physical beauty of Titian's women as seen in these early Madonna groups, it is perhaps surpassed by that of the male figures that accompany them. Titian was throughout his career primarily a painter of men. Taine was undoubtedly right in pronouncing him the greatest interpreter of masculine character that ever lived. While his preference for the sex increases with the years and becomes especially marked in his later portraits it is clearly apparent in these early works. It would be difficult to find in all art a nobler masculine type than the Saint George who stands guardian over the Madonna and Saint Bridget. Even the glorious concept of Donatello must take second place. The Madonna with the Cherries, the Madonna with Saint Anthony, and the Madonna with the Three Saints furnish examples hardly less admirable. These figures combine with masculine strength a wonderful calm and poise tempered with an unobtrusive kindliness that attracts and reassures. Once again these figures are mundane. They are not dreamers or seers. They feel no ecstasies. They do not stand consciously in the presence of the eternal. They are at home in our world, albeit of a kind too rare.

From these and other pictures we pass by the easiest of transitions to portrait, always a chief interest of our artist from his earliest to his latest years. At a comparatively early date Titian adopted for his male portraits a dark style with sharp contrasts of light and dark somewhat after the manner of Giorgione's Knight of Malta. These particular portraits of which there are several are best known through the Man with the Glove (Fig. 77) which has obtained a surprising though not undeserved popularity. Almost wholly lacking in bright color, the man's black garment and hair are outlined against an almost equally dark background. The face, hand, glove, shirt front, and ruffs at neck and sleeves are

Fig. 77, Titian, Man with a Glove. Paris, Louvre.

sharply contrasted in their several degrees. The moustache, a mere down on his upper lip, betrays his adolescence. There is a subtlety about this portrait that defies analysis and which is peculiar to Titian. The youth is at once alert yet quiescent and calm. There

is no action, scarce a suggestion of assertion even, yet
the figure is unmistakably dynamic. The suggestion is
that of power perfectly in hand.

Technically akin to this wonderful portrait yet in
essence widely different from it is the Concert (Fig. 78)

Fig. 78, Titian (or Giorgione?), The Concert. Florence, Pitti.

of the Pitti Gallery, a work already mentioned as in
dispute between Giorgione and Titian. Critics are
sharply divided and rather unusually positive in their
divergent judgments. The present writer claims no
authority in the difficult science of attributions but he
cannot resist the conviction that the picture is intensely
characteristic of Titian at this stage of his development
and that like the Man with the Glove it conveys a

suggestion of profound significance by means of the subtlest and most elusive character. The figure of the man at the organ has fascinated more beholders than almost any other in Venetian art. It is doubtful if any other figure produces a more certain and uniform impression or one more baffling and incapable of analysis. While utterly free from dramatic pose or expression it is marvelously idealized and suffused with emotion. It is the most successful attempt in art to express the emotional effect of music.

Doubly significant in this series is Titian's portrait of himself (Fig. 79) now in Berlin (not to be confounded with the weak copy in Florence). The virility, urbanity, and quiet power of this splendid portrait not only give it a high place among portraits but reveal a personality which explains these qualities in Titian's art.

More intensely dynamic than the portraits thus far considered is that generally known as Parma, Titian's physician. The portrait is painted upon a lighter background and in a lighter key, perhaps in deference to the subject's gray hair.

Two portraits in the Pitti may serve to complete this part of our study. One is the portrait of an unknown man long called Howard, Duke of Norfolk. (Fig. 80). This again is a dark portrait upon a dark ground, though rich, sober color takes the place of the seeming black used earlier and the contrasts are less extreme. There is a vitality about the eyes and a sense of power in this determined but self restrained figure that has always won for it the highest praise. Competent judges have placed it at the head of Titian's portraits and even of all human portrait art, a pardonable if not a wholly defensible judgment.

The other portrait is that of Pietro Aretino (Fig. 81) which would be accorded quite as high a place if it were not prejudiced by its subject. An infinitely showy and seemingly conscienceless man, a parasite and embodiment of all the vices, he was a man of rare intellectual

Fig. 79, Titian, Portrait of Himself. Berlin.

gifts which he prostituted to the most unworthy purposes. His hospitality was so constant and so open that strangers mistook his house for an inn. Yet the money thus spent was other people's money secured by the unworthiest expedients. A habitual slanderer and cynic, he was a master of fawning flattery as well, choosing his talent as befitted the case. He was a prince of good fellows at

a banquet and no great occasion was complete without
him. At a banquet quite appropriately he met his

Fig. 80, Titian, Portrait ("Howard Duke of Norfolk"). Florence,
Pitti.

death, having thrown his head suddenly back in a guffaw
of laughter at a funny story and dislocated his neck.

For inscrutable reasons there was the closest intimacy
between this man and Titian, a man who shared none of his
objectionable characteristics. It is difficult to attribute

Fig. 81, Titian, Portrait of Aretino. Florence, Pitti.

disinterestedness or affection to a man like Aretino but if he ever felt such sentiments it was toward Titian. Reciprocally Titian seems really to have cared for him. Aretino was a born advertiser and he was never tired of extolling Titian's art, usually by means of sonnets which he wrote in honor of one work after another as they appeared. That he aided greatly in securing commissions for Titian is doubtless true and he was no wise reticent or over modest in asserting his merits in this connection.

If we can briefly forget our detestation for a personality so unworthy and look upon this portrait simply as a character interpretation it will appear as a masterpiece of the highest order. If it were possible for art to find its culmination in the representation of the repellent this portrait might well carry off the palm.

Titian's portraits of women are very different. They are always masterpieces of painting but rarely of character interpretation. The solitary exception is that of his beautiful daughter, Lavinia, whom he dearly loved and portrayed with love in the brush. It is difficult to draw the line between avowed portraits and fanciful subjects like the Flora which are plainly portraits but thinly disguised. The famous portrait known as La Bella (Fig. 82) may serve as example for both. She is undoubtedly a beautiful woman but almost wholly expressionless. We can divine neither her character nor her passing mood. She is a lay figure for the display of the most beautiful costume, head dress, beads, and jewels that can well be imagined. Her flesh tint, according perfectly with her amber beads, is of course as beautiful as the rest and, we may add, is of the same order of importance. But this is not said in disparagement. Though utterly commonplace in photographic reproduction, it is the most glorious piece of color that ever came

Fig. 82, Titian, La Bella. Florence, Pitti.

from Titian's hand, perhaps from any hand. It infinitely transcends in beauty anything that any woman or any costume can in nature offer. Let the observer who stands in the presence of this wonderful picture ask himself such questions as these: Would a string of amber beads on any woman's bosom produce a harmony so subtle as this? Would that costume with its incredible but exquisite combinations of blues and purples, if reproduced and seen in whatsoever light make such music as it does here? In both cases the answer must be instantly, no. The painting surpasses any possible reality which we may imagine as its counterpart. We could reproduce the colors but not the harmonies. These are due, not to the color alone but to their modulation and blending by transparent shadow which the painter can dispose as nature is powerless to do. No picture better reveals the art of Venetian coloring, an art which, unlike that of more recent painters, depends not upon color alone but upon color and shadow with an ever increasing emphasis upon the latter as we pass to the maturer Titian and to Tintoretto.

The Flora, a picture much overrated because of fanciful and groundless stories about the subject and her relation to the artist, has the character vacuity of La Bella with a color scheme which, if equally harmonious, is less rich and attractive. The gorgeous Laura Dianti, gratuitously known as Titian's mistress, is another example of magnificent painting and splendid beauty divorced from personality and mood.

We are forced to the conclusion that Titian was not greatly interested in women. He was doubtless sensible to certain of their charms but no Delilah clipped his locks. In whatever connection we meet him he gives the impression of one who has himself perfectly in hand. A man of the world in the fullest sense, one who used the world as not abusing it, Titian was certainly no puritan, but it is noteworthy that the charge of licentiousness which was brought against Giorgione was never whispered against him. For this their different attitude toward women was undoubtedly responsible. Titian was interested in women as objects of physical beauty, as wearers of fine costumes and jewels, as the chief color notes in the pageant of Venetian life. He could on occasion make them the vehicles of some tremendous emotion in the great dramas which were his supreme creation. But Titian's intimates were men. He had no Vittoria Colonna.

We have still to consider the works upon which his fame popularly rests and which on the whole display his highest powers, the great altarpieces. These begin with the famous Assumption of the Virgin (Fig. 83) which Titian finished in 1518 at the age of forty-one. If the paucity of earlier works makes this age seem too old the character of this almost makes it seem too young. Judge it as we may, no one will see in it signs of immaturity. It has been accorded, almost by spontaneous acclaim, the rank of Titian's masterpiece. Without hastening to accept this judgment we must admit that it is among the best of popular judgments. It is probably to be accounted the world's greatest dramatic picture. Others are more startling, more momentary, more intense, and for just that reason inferior. For the dramatic has its limitations in painting. Dealing, as from its nature it must, with the transient, the momentary, its place in the static arts which perpetuate and eternalize these transient and even unbearable moments is necessarily circumscribed. The scene thus unnaturally perpetuated should be a bearable situation and withal one not too instantaneous. Titian perfectly understands these limits which Tintoretto and others have so often overstepped.

Fig. 83, Titian, The Assumption. Venice, Church of the
Frari.

The theme is one congenial to the mediaeval imagination and by that same token almost unintelligible to our own. The heaven with its streets of gold and gates of massy pearl, the waiting throne beside that of the Eternal, the assembled throng, ten thousand times ten thousand, who await the glad event, and now a mortal woman who has suffered as never woman suffered before, is borne heavenward to take her place as Queen of Heaven beside the throne of God. What vistas of unearthly splendor! What peans of welcome that roll out to the very confines of space!

The theme has been treated often enough before — once even by Titian — in the familiar, conventional way. In this conventional rendering the Madonna, a pretty lady, rises, unmoving and unmoved, and gazes back with smiling complacency upon those left behind. There is no consciousness of the glorious goal on her part or on theirs and therefore no suggestion of it to us.

Only Titian in this supreme creation focuses the theme on heaven. Upward rises the magnificent Madonna, the same we knew long since in her splendid beauty and strength, but now grown soulful through suffering. With an expression of ineffable relief she gazes upward toward God the Father who comes to meet her on the way. A radiance that anticipates that of the blessed city encompasses her splendid form whose outline quivers against this background of golden light. A joyous angel throng surrounds this central radiance. Most impressive of all, the earthbound group of apostles, half lighted in a terrestrial twilight, stand gazing self-forgetting as though their very souls would slip their mortal leash. Heavenly and earthly are merged in one all-embracing passion.

In no picture of the writer's acquaintance is the focusing of attention so complete, so intense, so reinforced by distinct but concurrent factors. Most obvious is the distribution of light, intensest about the head of Madonna where it seems to quiver about the outline as the heat quivers over the landscape on a hot summer day, then lessening outward and downward where it passes insensibly into the somber half light of earth. No one can resist the leading of light graduated and focussed like this.

Not less effective is the psychic focus to which the artist devotes an even rarer skill. Every figure is drawn toward a single apparition and dominated by a single overwhelming passion. The almost universal stage consciousness of such pictures is here lacking. Both Raphael and Correggio would have detailed at least one of the apostles to look around and see if we were looking and act as showman for the occasion. Not so Titian. His apostles do not know we exist, scarce know that they themselves exist. Their eyes, their thoughts, are turned toward her, toward that opening heaven where God is all in all.

Even so the picture might have fallen short of the present perfect achievement if the central figure had been unworthy of the attention thus focussed upon her. Recall once more that dazzling splendor and that waiting throng. What kind of a woman is it for whom that throne, that throng, are waiting? Raphael's Madonna would faint upon the first stair. Correggio's is even more inadequate. Over the whole range of art we look in vain for one worthy. We turn at last to the great, impassive, splendid creature of Titian's youth. Cold, they call her, lacking in feeling. Lacking, yes, in the little feelings of little folk, unresponsive to the little stimuli of petty occasions. But now supreme occasion stirs the hitherto unsounded depths of her larger soul and she reveals herself the Queen of Heaven.

It is difficult to know which to admire most, the

masterly psychology of this grandest of dramatic interpretations or the perfect mastery of color and shadow by which this interpretation is effectively expressed. Let us repeat, it is the greatest dramatic painting. Can we venture a broader, a more hazardous inquiry? It may seem gratuitous in the presence of such a masterpiece to question its fundamental principle, but here if anywhere the principle should justify itself. It is impossible, however, to blink the fact that the picture slowly loses its power over the frequent beholder. It is not that prolonged acquaintance reveals defects in either its psychology or its technique. Both will bear the closest and the most prolonged scrutiny. The weakened impression is simply the penalty which art pays for congealing the fluid and perpetuating the momentary. The demand of the age was for the dramatic in art of every kind. It was a demand that well nigh ruined Raphael and Correggio. To Titian it was congenial and consonant with his unrivaled powers. In dramatic painting Titian knew how to conceive and to execute. Above all he knew where to stop.

In the same Church of the Frari and not far from the Assumption hangs the Madonna of the Pesaro Family (Fig. 84) which must be accounted Titian's greatest altarpiece, perhaps his greatest painting of whatsoever kind. It has been justly said that "in this Pesaro Madonna he wrought as mighty a revolution as had ever been experienced in the history of the altar picture." Revolution is not the measure of excellence in art even when far reaching in its effects but in this case the two coincide. The revolution in this case was wholly in the direction of progress. It gave to art a liberty undreamed before, a liberty susceptible to abuse as all liberty is but one which the genius of Titian used with masterly wisdom and skill.

To get the full meaning of Titian's achievement the visitor should begin by observing carefully the famous altarpiece by John Bellini (see page 237) which hangs, as if for this very purpose, in the sacristy of this same church. The great master is here represented perfectly in character if not at his best as some would claim. It is a triptych, that is, a picture in three parts which are separated by pilasters or members of the architectural frame. In the central space which is treated as an architectural niche sits Madonna enthroned with the child in her arms and two little musicians, Bellini's quaint conceit, in earnest performance on the steps of the throne. In each of the side spaces are two saints facing toward Madonna. We will not concern ourselves here with the perfection of the painting or the beautiful spirit which pervades the work. We are concerned for the moment to note the conception of composition or picture construction here represented. The arrangement is entirely symmetrical. Madonna sits in the center, facing the spectator. Two saints on either side, the one in the foreground and the other in the background, match each other perfectly. This arrangement, we have seen, is entirely mediaeval. Bellini has accepted in essence the mediaeval altarpiece merely introducing the third dimension with all its implications of perspective and modeling, and of course with a profound transformation of its spirit. The significant thing is that he was satisfied to work within the limits of the mediaeval scheme.

Titian was not. He saw as plainly as Bellini that a picture must not be lopsided or unbalanced, but this prim, symmetrical arrangement which suited the serenity and peace of Bellini's saints was wholly unsatisfactory to one who sought to represent the mobility, the spontaneity, and the passion of human life. At all costs art must rid itself of this straightjacket. Yet the need of balance remained. How could these conflicting interests be reconciled?

Titian always approached the problems of art in a scientific and reasoning spirit. Though the greatest of all portrayers of passion he was not impulsive or passionate as an artist but coolly analytical. He seems therefore to have asked why this balance was necessary and in what its essence consisted. The earlier assumption had been simple and naïve. If you have a man on one side, balance requires a man on the other side, a woman a woman, and so on down the list. But does it? What is a picture anyway? A group of men and women? No, only a surface covered with color which is interesting in its own right and which is interesting further because of the persons, things, and sentiments which it suggests. The essential of balance, therefore, is that interest should balance interest and basically that color should balance color.

If we have grasped this thought we may well settle back for a moment and reflect on the immeasurable reach of this discovery, perhaps the greatest in the whole history of art. It is no longer a question of man for man, woman for woman, but of object for object, interest for interest. The objects need not be alike, the interests need not be similar, need not indeed have anything in common except the mere fact of interest. The artist now has a thousand motives at his disposal where he had one before. To be sure, the new liberty has brought new dangers, as always. So long as it was a question of man for man it was tolerably easy for an artist to secure a balance of interest, color, and all else. But when balance is secured by objects from different categories and by interests from different spheres, miscalculation becomes dangerously easy as the history of modern art abundantly proves.

Fig. 84, Titian, Madonna of the Pesaro Family.　Venice,
Church of the Frari.

Whatever the pitfalls of the new pathway Titian treads it with consummate success. The Pesaro Madonna represents no scene of tense emotion like the Assumption and it has therefore received less plaudits from that Baroque age whose judgments we have inherited, but it is a greater picture. Painted some five years later it represents a similar but more advanced technique. Applying the new principle not timidly but with the boldness of one who saw the end from the beginning, the Madonna is seated high up on the right-hand side of the picture. A flag, one of the most splendid representations in color in all art, occupies a corresponding position on the left. In the center considerably lower sits Peter, perhaps the finest representation in art of this chief of the apostles. Not even Bellini has given him a greater sense of spiritual calm and power. Below on either side are the two groups of the family made famous by this their gift, the civil members on the right and the ecclesiastical on the left.

The resulting composition takes the form of the letter X in complete disregard both of the symmetrical group of Bellini and the triangular group which Leonardo had bequeathed to Florence and which had influenced both Giorgione and Titian during the Giorgione period. It would be interesting to know what Leonardo and Bellini would have thought of this seemingly decentralized and yet amazingly unified composition which henceforth is more or less traceable in Titian's work. It was one of art's greatest innovations.

Turning to the characters and the sentiment expressed — always and legitimately the chief interest of the lay observer — the picture is worthy but not preëminent. The Madonna is the strong and somewhat unmoved creature with which the artist's earlier pictures have made us familiar. She is splendid but does not touch our hearts. Peter, as we should expect, appeals far more to this painter of men. Hardly less admirable are the two family groups, so admirable indeed that we are tempted to forget the intrinsic impertinence of their presence. Michelangelo would never have painted them in such a company. Even the great Julius had to forego that honor. Titian, like Raphael, was more pliant. But he knows as well as anyone that they imperil the integrity and the dignity of his theme. What interests us is to see with what skill he guards against that peril. Painted with the consummate art of this greatest of portrait painters these portraits, simply as portraits, must be counted among his best. But they are not simply portraits. There is nothing of that individual detachment and separate appeal which disintegrates so many otherwise admirable groups. In sincere but unstrained devotion they merge themselves in the whole with unobtrusive humility.

Here as always the artist conjures with color and shadow. Throughout the entire picture the same gamut of color prevails but with wide variations of brilliancy, now clear and challenging, then subdued to pianissimo by the transparent shadows which he handles with the skill of a Rembrandt. The picture is not deeply emotional but it is dignified, noble, and sincere. Like so many of Titian's pictures it tempts us to say "magnificent," "splendid," and that not alone as regards the flesh but also the spirit.

A striking feature of the picture is the introduction of the two columns whose capitals are beyond the field of vision and whose soaring shafts carry the mind into the very empyrean. Other painters, including the younger Titian, had sought to draw attention away from the frame and concentrate it within the limited field of vision. The great innovator here boldly reverses this traditional policy and asks us to pass beyond the frame and in imagination explore the illimitable. An amazing picture!

The visitor to the Academy in Venice will find another large picture of this period, the Presentation of the Virgin (Fig. 85), in the place for which it was originally painted. It occupies the entire end wall of a room

Fig. 85, Titian, Presentation of the Virgin. Venice, Academy.

lighted from one side and is therefore lighted unequally, the brightest light being somewhat to the left of the center. Of all this Titian has taken the fullest account. As an example of his mastery of color and shadow it is equal to the great picture just considered. In seriousness and integrity of theme it is inferior. The background is splendid, with noble architecture and the mountain scenery of Cadore. A staircase with midway platform approaches the temple entrance on the right where stand the priest and his assistant to welcome the Virgin as she ascends the stairs. At the foot of the

staircase and occupying the luminous spot already
referred to stand a group of the most magnificent women
of the Titian type that the artist ever painted.   Behind
these and occupying the extreme left of the picture is a
group of grave and reverend signors, quite obviously
contemporary portraits.

Again we say, splendid, magnificent, but this time of
the parts rather than of the whole.   The background is
unrivaled in all Titian's pictures.   The priest is above all
praise as the embodiment of that dignity and benignity
that fits the part.   The little Virgin, if not greatly impressive, is at least unconscious and her attention is
properly directed.   The women at the foot of the stairs
are gorgeous beyond anything we have yet seen in their
costumes of lemon yellow, cerulean blue, and the sober,
rich red that Titian loved so well.   But these women
who are devoid of personality and quite irrelevant to the
theme are quite too splendid and quite too prominent,
occupying as they do the luminous center of the wall
and costumed to make the most of it.   This picture
represents the zenith of Titian's interest in bright, clear
color and the undue length of his wall tempted him to
try an experiment with color which, despite its dazzling
success, mars the picture.   It is not great art but it is
very great painting.

The series of great altarpieces continued.   The Death
of St. Peter Martyr painted a few years after the
Pesaro Family was perhaps Titian's extremest venture
into the violently dramatic.   The picture perished some
years since in a conflagration and is imperfectly known
to us through a copy.   Its power is beyond question
but to the writer's mind the violence of the moment
represented is unsuitable for pictorial representation
and the exigencies of such a theme force the artist to
certain artificialities from which he has hitherto been free.

One more remains to be considered, last but not least. Titian had chosen as his burial place a spot in front of a certain altar in the Frari and for this altar he began in extreme old age an altarpiece, the Pietà (Fig. 86) or mourning over the body of Christ. Though still

Fig. 86, Titian, The Pietà. Venice, Academy.

sturdy his sight was grievously impaired and he saw men as trees walking. That he should have painted at all under such circumstances is suggesstive of his extreme eagerness to leave a personal memorial to himself. That he should have executed a masterpiece both in composition and color is a marvel. It was unfinished at his death and was reverently completed by his pupil, Palma the Younger.

The background is an architectural niche with a statue on either side. Across this niche in powerful diagonal are arranged the chief figures of the composition, the climax being reached in the Magdalen who gives dramatic expression to her violent grief. An angel bearing a torch combines with minor elements in the opposite corner to form a broken counter diagonal thus giving the familiar X. The whole is painted in the loose and suggestive style of Titian's later years in contrast with the highly finished style of the Presentation and the Pesaro Family. Bright color, too, has given place to soberer hues with chief reliance upon subtle contrasts of light and shade. Yet Titian was never more of a colorist than in these relatively hueless works of his old age.

But there are other elements of power unknown to his earlier art. The two statues, the stern Moses representing the old dispensation and the smiling female figure representing the new, are significantly contrasted with each other. They are still more significantly contrasted in their stony coldness with the agonizing group between them. In the presence of the great tragedy at the sight of which the heavens were darkened and the graves gave up their dead these stony figures stand unsympathetic and unparticipating. Having eyes they see not and ears they hear not. This is not Titian's first use of the dramatic foil. In the Crowning with Thorns the bust of Tiberius gazes out cold and supercilious over the suffering Saviour. The dramatic foil is a powerful psychological factor added to his already ample dramatic resources. Titian was dramatic to the last.

Nor can it fail to strike the thoughtful observer that the great mundane, as the shadows gathered round him and the end drew visibly near, should have chosen as his memorial and his last message the same theme as his great Florentine contemporary. While this powerful, dramatic creation of Titian can not compare in unutterable pathos with the last, half uttered message of Michelangelo, it is not without significance that prophet and mundane alike seek remembrance in commemorating the great sacrifice through which they hope redemption.

Great numbers of Titian's works and even whole phases of his art have of necessity been excluded from this brief chapter. Among these are works of the first importance such as the mythological series painted for Duke Alphonso d'Este and the numerous portraits and other works painted for Charles V and Philip II, his most distinguished but not his most judicious patrons. Biographical details, too, have necessarily been excluded and with them many a side light upon Titian's art. Even landscape which Titian developed with scarcely less enthusiasm than Giorgione but recast in his distinctive and more dramatic mould has been the subject of but casual allusion. For these omissions there is hardly need of apology. The life that filled a century with ceaseless industry guided by supreme genius cannot be disposed of in a chapter. It is enough if the chapter give incentive to the further study of the world's greatest painter.

CHAPTER XVI

THE LAST OF THE GIANTS

Venetian art is dominated in each of its three phases by two men. In the first or ascendant phase the Bellini are supreme. In the second phase, commonly accounted the greatest, Giorgione and Titian hold unchallenged the first place. A third phase, less easily characterized, remains, a phase dominated by the titanic figures of Tintoretto and *Veronese. Alongside these mighty leaders troop the lesser figures of imitators and would-be rivals, few at first and relatively individual, then more numerous but more dominated by the growing tradition and the overshadowing influence of their great contemporaries. Increasingly interest centers in the leaders. We cannot ignore Carpaccio even in the presence of John Bellini but Paris Bordone need not detain us though as a painter he could at times surpass Carpaccio. We have time only for the giants.

Giants they certainly were, these successors of Titian. The genius of Venetian painting reflecting the character of Venetian life tended naturally toward the grandiose, the magnificent, the gigantic, rather than toward the subtlety and the finesse of the Florentines. This tendency was accentuated greatly by the temperament of these its chief exponents. One wonders what they would have been if they had been reared in Florence and had studied under Botticelli. Different, no doubt, and yet not in essence. They would still have been Tintoretto and Veronese.

Tintoretto is the *enfant terrible* of Venetian art. On the background of Venetian history his figure looms

---

* Pronounced Vay-ro-nay-zay.

more gigantic than that of Titian but more undisciplined and more uncouth. No artist has been the subject of more superlatives or more controversy. There is as little prospect now as ever of agreement as to his place in art. To some he is the culmination of Venetian art; to others its decadence. Yet curiously enough there has always been substantial agreement as to the facts in the case. The difference lies in the evaluation of these facts. Everybody recognizes his exuberant imagination and creative spontaneity and everybody concedes his lack of discipline and his reckless improvisation. But what is the relative value of spontaneity and discipline? On this point we differ, whole ages differ, and the pendulum swings to and fro. We will not prejudge the issue but we do well to recognize it.

Jacopo Robusti, as he was accustomed to sign himself, was born in 1512 or, as some say, in 1518, this latter, by the way, the date when Titian at the age of forty-one finished the Assumption. The son of a dyer (tintore) and employed as a boy in his father's establishment, he was known as the "Little Dyer" (il Tintoretto) a name by which he has ever continued to be known. Having decorated the walls of his father's establishment in childish fashion with his father's dyes, a fond parent thought to detect in these youthful essais the evidence of artistic genius which he proceeded to cultivate. In due time the youth obtained the most coveted of all privileges, a place in the studio of Titian, where he succeeded in remaining for just ten days. Later rumor has it that he excited the jealousy of Titian by his evidence of genius and that this was the reason of his dismissal. The explanation is unplausible and unnecessary. The least acquaintance with the work of the two men is sufficient to demonstrate their incompatibility. Titian was the soul of discipline, of scientific inquiry and steady, unremitting industry. Tintoretto was slapdash and temperamental, impatient of delay and restraint, and restive under discipline. Withal, Titian was a poor teacher who grudged time spent upon pupils and Tintoretto was a poor pupil who grudged the time spent upon tasks set by a teacher. In addition Tintoretto came with a good deal of self-taught proficiency, the value of which he doubtless rated somewhat higher than did his teacher. That all this should have become manifest in the space of ten days is nowise remarkable. Nor is it strange that with this discovery Titian should have dismissed the intractable pupil, not through jealousy but from the conviction that he was not worth bothering with. That this should have been construed as jealousy in later years when the two men had become rivals and were not on friendly terms is again nowise strange. The story is merely retroactive.

Dismissed from Titian's studio the youth seems to have continued his course of self education, a course in which the works of Titian, if not the master, played an important part. If he lacked discipline he certainly did not lack industry. These early years were crowded with feverish activity, most of it of the humblest sort, for serious commissions were long withheld, the lack of studio credentials and the known disparagement of Titian doubtless contributing to this result. In these humble and hurried tasks the young painter developed that marvelous facility which ever characterized him and too often betrayed him in the day of more serious things. The usual procedure of making a preliminary sketch, carefully calculating the space, and studying the effect of the proposed arrangement was necessarily dispensed with and the habit thus formed was continued when changed circumstances should have dictated a more careful procedure. That is what is meant by saying that Tintoretto was an improviser. He often began painting one end of a picture without having any idea what he was going to put in the other end, obviously a most hazardous thing to do. He would add one figure after another as he went along, occasionally working in an extra one in some place where he thought it would be an addition. Such a method, of course, rendered quite impossible the studied compositions of Bellini and Titian. Good compositions are not unknown in the work of Tintoretto but they are exceptional and apparently the result of chance. In such a picture as his Crucifixion, often regarded as his masterpiece, there is virtually no composition, merely a random distribution of figures over the large space as chance would will.

Of course there are people who like this. They are the people who dislike the orderly arrangement of a room and who place the chairs, perhaps with much study, in a way to simulate accident and chance. They delight to start on a journey without knowing where they are going or how long they are going to stay. To a person or an age so minded there is merit in such a procedure especially if one has a talent for improvisation. Not so to a Titian who saw freedom only in calculation and order.

A more questionable characteristic of Tintoretto was his hasty execution. Here again he stood in sharpest contrast with Titian whose procedure was characterized by extreme patience and deliberation. Titian was accustomed to carry a number of pictures along together leaving each untouched for weeks and even months at a time and allowing each coat of paint to harden all the way through before another was added. This, of course, was possible only to a man whose work was perfectly planned from the beginning and who worked by calculation rather than by mood. Tintoretto was not and never could have been such a person. Nothing is more characteristic of him than the way in which his artistic impulses seem to storm at the gate for liberation. When obsessed with an inspiration he was under the imperious necessity of getting it out of his system. He could seldom wait through the tedious process of competing for a commission. When his bid was in and the decision did not come at once he would reduce his bid, possibly reduce it again, and at last even offer to paint for nothing if they would furnish the materials. This of course exasperated his fellow artists who naturally saw in it "unfair competition." It is said that his patrons, and especially the Venetian government, learned to speculate on his impatience and to withhold the decision till he cut his price. On one occasion when asked to present a competitive sketch for a picture in the Scuola di San Rocco he appeared with the others at the appointed time, not with the sketch but with the finished picture which he had contrived to install in place. The committee was offended at this attempt to force its judgment and asked for the sketch, whereupon the artist replied with perfect truthfulness "This is my way of sketching." Seeing that they were not disposed to accept the picture he presented it to the Scuola taking advantage of a rule which forbade the Scuola to refuse a gift. There the picture remained to be followed later, when good feeling returned, by a series of more than sixty pictures which makes of the Scuola his monument.

When at last the opportunity to paint came, Tintoretto went at the work like one possessed. No alteration of subject, no waiting for paint to harden, often no real completion of the picture at all, but a bold sketch in vain attempt of the hand to keep pace with his tempestuous thought. The great majority of his pictures as we see them now seem sadly suggestive of this breathless technique. When he does take pains he is a great colorist, but mostly he doesn't and the color is sometimes atrocious. It was Mr. Ruskin, the most extravagant of all his champions, who characterized certain of his pictures as "mere daubs redounding to the painter's everlasting shame." It was a comtemporary painter who cleverly said of him that "at his best he is the equal of Titian; at his worst he is inferior to Tintoretto." There is an unaccountable blackness in many of his pictures, a blackness which on the faces of his portraits often appears as a smuttiness or discoloration. The explanation usually given is that "the backing has come through," the artist having painted his picture before the heavy coat of backing had hardened save for a thin film on the surface. This sounds plausible but if true it must have happened early for Vasari who saw the paintings when they were new criticised them much as we do now. Some seem to assume that they are even now much as the artist left them and that they express his intention.

Here again there are not wanting admirers of what to others seems a defect. In every department of art there is in progress a cult of the uncouth, a revolt against finish, refinement, and the traditional conceptions of beauty. The followers of this cult loathe the finish of Praxiteles and Tennyson. They prefer the work of certain of our contemporaries whom it were best not to name. And for identical reasons they prefer Tintoretto to Titian. An age which stakes everything on spontaneity and untutored initiative is irked by Titian's "infinite capacity for taking pains." To such Tintoretto is the greater genius.

A genius he certainly was. In intensity of emotion and sheer power of imagination Michelangelo is his only rival. But despite this rivalry there is little kinship between the two men. Tintoretto is utterly Venetian.

He differs from his predecessors merely in degree. Broadly speaking he takes Titian's art where the latter left it and carries it farther along lines already determined. Like Titian he is a colorist but he learned early what Titian had spent half a lifetime in learning, that in the partnership between color and shadow the latter is the more suggestive, the more spiritually impressive. Titian's symphonies in bright color are slowly transformed by a simple shift of emphasis into a conjuring with light and shadow barely relieved by hints of subdued color. Without prejudice to the color harmonies which he loved, Titian's dramatic instincts were not slow to perceive the dramatic power of light and shadow in effective combination. Where Titian's progress ends Tintoretto's begins and strides forward with seven league boots. No painter before Rembrandt has understood so well as Tintoretto the power of light and shadow nor has anyone used it with such boldness, such stunning effect. Few things could be more impressive than to compare the Last Supper of Tintoretto (Fig. 87) with that of Leonardo. In Leonardo's picture the pathos of the theme is expressed through figure and facial expression. Environment counts for little. In subtlety of composition as of psychological analysis this is perhaps the world's greatest picture. Of all this Tintoretto gives us nothing. His composition is a fortuitous and meaningless mass in which no figure or line has special significance. Faces are scarcely visible and are without significant expression. The Christ, subordinated and scarcely distinguishable, is without spiritual dominance or significance of any kind. Not an act or an attitude is suggestive of the pathos of the occasion. Withal there is the vulgar intrusion of the dog and the prominence of the servants, so characteristic of this period and so inconceivable to a Leonardo. Everything that makes Leonardo's picture great is here lacking.

But this picture is great none the less, great by virtue of elements of which Leonardo knew nothing and which only Rembrandt would have understood. In a stately apartment filled with massive shadows, great shafts of light entering through unseen windows and broad, open door, fall athwart the floor and rest as powerful high

Fig. 87, Tintoretto, The Last Supper.   Venice, Scuola di San Rocco

lights upon the figures grouped as chance has willed. The emotional values of the picture are not in faces, forms, attitudes, not in the human element at all. They are in the place, in the lights and shadows, in the mood which these impart unconsciously but irresistibly to the spectator. The psychologist will find here no such theme for study in his line as in the work of Leonardo but the normal individual will get from it a more certain and unconscious emotional reaction. Without disparagement to the Florentine, an incomparably greater man, it

may be admitted that the Venetian has chosen a medium
of spiritual expression more appropriate for painting.

In this conjuring with light and shadow Tintoretto is
simply carrying the procedure of Titian a step farther.
In his later dramatic works like the Crowning with
Thorns and the Pietà, Titian depends very much for his

Fig. 88, Tintoretto, Marriage at Cana. Venice, Santa Maria della
Salute.

emotional appeal upon this environment of light and
shadow. But with Titian this is always an accessory.
He never reduces his figures to meaninglessness or makes
them mere objects for the play of light and shadow.
Remove this shadow environment from the Pietà and
the picture would suffer immensely but remove or obscure the figures and it would suffer more. Not so with
Tintoretto. From his figures we may imagine much —
assuredly a point to his credit — but in many of his
works, and among them the greatest, they tell us nothing.

Everything is in the stage setting, nothing in the play. This is equally true of Rembrandt, an artist of far greater mastery than Tintoretto but one whose chosen medium is the same.

Fig. 89, Tintoretto, Finding of the Body of Saint Mark. Milan, Brera.

These powerful effects of light and shade are conspicuous in most of the tarist's work, notably in the Finding of the Body of St. Mark (Fig. 89), Christ before Pilate (Fig. 90) the Deposition, the Presentation of the Virgin, and in the Annunciation (Fig. 92) in San Rocco as well as in the entire series in that famous hall where Tintoretto is to be seen in all his power as also in all his weakness.

The hall is a feebly lighted interior and the artist instead of countering with bright colors and clear light has accepted this half light as the key to his painting. There is something of the nocturne about these representations, a mood that in certain of them like the Flight into Egypt is exceedingly impressive. In the familiar metaphorical sense of the word this may be described as a dramatic use of shadow. It is here, too, that Tintoretto approaches nearest to true decoration in his decorative treatment of foliage represented in silhouette against the faintly luminous sky. These decorative effects are apparently accidental. Tintoretto had little of the instinct of the decorator.

Tintoretto's mastery of light and shadow is best illustrated in his Marriage of Cana (Fig. 88), to the mind of the present writer the finest of Tintoretto's paintings and apparently his favorite. Here is nothing crude or hurried, nothing vulgar or irrelevant. Painted for one of the scuole the picture reproduces with admirable effect the stately apartment in which it was to be placed, constituting thus in accordance with the custom of the time an apparent extension of the hall. The figures are neither neglected nor obliterated — they are worthy of Titian himself — but they are skilfully subordinated to the whole. You see a room and a banquet, not individuals, which is as it should be. We may demur that the guest of honor is relegated to insignificance but the objection will not be based on grounds of art. The picture is characterized by complete harmony, absolute consistency. Tintoretto's interest is as usual in the lighting. The theme is not dramatic and the artist with admirable restraint has avoided any sensational play of light and shadow such as he uses and often abuses in the treatment of other themes. It is one of the earliest serious studies in side lighting and one of the best. The artist has aimed not to exaggerate but to interpret nature in one of her subtlest and most spiritual aspects. Art has other ways of being great but this is one of her most legitimate ways and one of her most indubitable successes.

In his treatment of the human element which is by no means always subordinated as above, Tintoretto again starts with Titian but goes farther. Like Titian he was dramatic but unlike him he was often extravagant and sensational. He has been called the greatest dramatic painter, apparently because he indulged in the extremest manifestations of passion. This title we have reserved for Titian, who never forgot that dramatic intensity must be tempered by the restraint that is essential to the static arts. Of this restraint the impetuous Tintoretto knew nothing. The Pietà is the limit of the dramatic in Titian's art. To Tintoretto it apparently seemed tame. The group at the foot of the cross in his Crucifixion (Fig. 94) is unquestionably more intense than anything Titian ever painted, perhaps more intense than anything else in painting. Whether this is a merit each will decide according to his sympathies. It is upon the momentary power of this group, a power which the writer once felt to the full, that this otherwise indifferent picture bases its claim to be Tintoretto's masterpiece.

Unfortunately Tintoretto's dramatic powers are not always so appropriately employed. Here the theme justified his effort in nature if not in degree. Often it did not, but no matter how undramatic the theme, Tintoretto's figures seem unable to stand quietly and in a dignified manner. They strike an attitude and pose in theatrical fashion without the slightest plausibility or need. An example is the Finding of the Body of Saint Mark (Fig. 89), a scene worthy of the cheapest of cheap theatres in which the pose of the figures and the

Fig. 90, Tintoretto, Christ before Pilate. Venice, Scuola di San Rocco.

sensational play of light and shadow are alike extravagant and inexplicable.

Tintoretto was fond of producing dramatic effect by having a figure come plunging headlong through the air. A goddess or a saint or an angel furnished the necessary pretext. In this way he sometimes got pretty com-

Fig. 91, Tintoretto, A Miracle of Saint Mark. Venice, Academy.

binations of lines and attractive if unplausible compositions but his figures, always robust and nowise ethereal, are ill suited to this hazardous employment. The sensationalism of these irruptive figures is usually heightened by equally sensational contrasts of light and shadow as in the Miracle of Saint Mark (Fig. 91) and the Bacchus and Ariadne (Fig. 93) the latter one of the most elegant and poetical of the artist's works.

One of the most remarkable and to the writer one of the most inexcusable of Tintoretto's dramatic extravagances is the Annunciation in San Rocco (Fig. 92). Into

the realistically ruinous apartment of the Virgin plunge
the angel and his cherub escort with the violence of a
projectile.   Broken walls and battered brickwork enhance the impression of a bombardment.   The startled
Virgin looks up at the intruder with undisguised terror

Fig. 92, Tintoretto, The Annunciation.   Venice, Scuola di San Rocco.

and throws up her hands in helpless gesture.   There is
the usual powerful side lighting with its dramatic contrasts of light and shadow.   There is nothing in the
theme and nothing in the tradition of Christian art to
justify this vulgar sensationalism.   Clever and powerful
it undoubtedly is but inappropriate and inadmissible,
a plain prostitution of the artist's powers.   Titian's
Annunciation in the same building and hanging only a
few yards away should have suggested a better ideal.

Unfortunately that may have been the very thing that

prompted his revolt and led to his extravagance. The soberer taste had had its day and had scored its utmost triumphs. What was the use of a Tintoretto painting another Annunciation like Titian's? "What can the man do that cometh after the king? Even that which

Fig. 93, Tintoretto, Bacchus and Ariadne. Venice, Doge's Palace.

the king hath already done." Here lies the real meaning of decadence. Not decaying powers or declining technique but restiveness under a sense of completed achievement. The concepts suited to art expression are slowly accumulated as the result of social experience. Art in its intermittent activities struggles with these concepts and finally exhausts their possibilities within its normal and legitimate limits. What next? Shall the artist go on repeating what has been adequately, perfectly done?

Who wants to do that? Shall he turn to new themes? Men must live some more before the new themes are matured for his purpose. What remains? Simply to treat the old themes in new ways, in more sensational, more striking ways, ways more hazardous and less conformable to the nature of the art in question. Artist

Fig. 94, Tintoretto, the Crucifixion (detail). Venice, San Rocco.

and public alike tire of the old perfection. There is a demand for ginger and pep, and the lamp of art flares up in a lurid, smoky gleam that heralds its temporary extinction.

As thus understood decadence does not imply weakness or lack of skill. On the contrary it is a time of redundant technique and artists of the decadence are often giants as were Tintoretto, Bernini, Rodin. Decadence is simply a phase through which art passes periodically and inevitably in its evolution, a phase as normal

and to the student as interesting as any other. But it is
decadence all the same, the descending rather than the
ascending curve, the phase least loved of all when once
its day is past.

Like his contemporaries of the decadence Tintoretto
in his search for new ways of treating old themes
occasionally descends to sheer vulgarity as when, in
Washing the Disciples' Feet (Fig. 95) he represents an
apostle tugging at the high hip boot of another who lies

Fig. 95, Tintoretto, Christ Washing the Disciples' Feet. Spain,
Escorial.

on the floor and raises his leg for the purpose. This
treatment of the theme is certainly not trite but its
spiritual significance is doubtful.

Tintoretto's peculiarities became more pronounced
as his years increased, possibly because his later and
greater commissions were such as to give them larger
scope. His colossal Paradise executed for the Hall of
the Great Council following the conflagration of 1577
is the largest canvas ever painted. To the writer's
mind it has little other claim to distinction. The number
of figures is stupendous and there is method in their
arrangement although it is not immediately apparent.
But neither figures nor arrangement have beauty or

Fig. 96, Tintoretto, Portrait of a Procurator.   Florence, Uffizi.

serious significance while the dominant black tone of the whole, whether intended or not, is repellent.

Tintoretto's fondness for the gigantesque influenced his drawing of the human figure unfortunately. His figures are powerful, sometimes quite inappropriately so, but heavy with an inevitable tendency to coarseness. As a portrait painter of men he at times rivals Titian (as in Fig. 96) but the impression is usually one of strength rather than of refinement or subtlety. He could never have painted the Man with the Glove. Occasionally but not often his pictures are marred by vulgar irrelevancies. The dog in the Last Supper and the boot episode in the Washing of the Disciples' Feet have been mentioned. But in general such grossness and vulgarity as can be laid to his charge — not a very great deal — inheres rather in the spirit of his work than in its adjuncts.

Tintoretto outlived his younger contemporary, Veronese, dying in 1594 thus adding one more, and this the last, to the list of long lived Venetian painters. With him the race of giants passed.

CHAPTER XVII

The great change which took place in the fortunes of Venice during the sixteenth century is not reflected in the art of Titian. It is true that the fateful discovery of the sea route to India which was her undoing was made while Titian was still a child climbing over the hills of Cadore. But the effects of this discovery were not at once apparent and the Venice that Titian knew in the years of his greatest achievements was still a busy and powerful city, as yet unconscious that she was stricken with mortal decay. Titian's art reflects this consciousness of health, this balance of vital forces. His art is "mundane" for he loves the life about him and rejoices in its sanity and magnificence. Whatever his theme it is in no spirit of other-worldliness that he treats it. Even the Madonna ascending in glory is a magnificent, human creature who faces her glorious exaltation with perfectly intelligible human emotions. Never a Madonna or a saint in Titian's long series that would not be at home in well bred society.

But if Titian is mundane he is not objective. Though splendid in his rendering of form and color, these are never the essence of his theme. Life is interpreted in terms of its impulses and emotions. These are never celestial or beatific but intensely and sanely human. These emotions are the true subject of his greater pictures, form and action, though splendid in their own right, being but their outward expression. It is this perfect balance between objective and subjective corresponding to his like balance between color and shadow that makes Titian the supreme painter. It is his interpretation of life in terms of emotion that makes him the dramatic painter of all time. Emotion is never wasted, never misapplied, but economized and kept not only within the limits of good breeding but within the narrower limits imposed by the static arts. He is the incarnation of sanity in art.

Such was the legacy which Titian left to his successors. We have seen the use which Tintoretto, the true successor of Titian made of his inheritance. The change which he introduced may be summed up in a single word, exaggeration. The frequent claim that he is greater than Titian is based upon the obvious fact that in everything he goes a step further. The shadows with which Titian softens his colors and suffuses his pictures with emotional susceptibility in Tintoretto's art become weird and charged with magic. The virile becomes gigantesque, the dramatic becomes spectacular and theatrical, and emotion passes into uncontrollable passion. Tintoretto has been justly credited with the intensest expression of human emotion known to art, a doubtful compliment.

As the years went on conditions in Venice visibly changed. Territories were lost and commerce declined. Life became less strenuous and more self indulgent. The retrenchment that wisdom would have dictated was farthest from Venetian thought. The city had vast accumulated wealth, profitable industries, and mainland possessions. Time won from business was devoted to pleasure and the center of interest gradually shifted from work to play, the sure precursor of decadence.

Art inevitably reflects the change. The painter depicts what the Venetians love, their pageant, their sumptuous entertainments, their magnificent materialism. It is a theme well suited to painting, this objective and colorful life, a theme far less exacting than those psychological enigmas that taxed the genius of Leonardo, but a theme unsatisfying to a humanity whose quest of pleasure is forever interrupted by moods of introspection and spiritual striving. For even the most frivolous soon tire of carnival and men crave viands that are not served on the table of Aretino. The criticism is often heard that Leonardo in his subtle, subjective studies went beyond the legitimate limits of painting. Yes, but in an effort to meet the legitimate demands of humanity. The new art of Venice contented itself with the easier and less satisfying task.

The apostle of the new age is Paolo Caliari, better known as il Veronese, the man from Verona, the city where he was born in 1528. He was thus younger than Tintoretto by ten years (according to other records by sixteen years) enough to align him with a younger generation and to make him its exponent. This parting of the ways was emphasized by the circumstances of his birth and training. Tintoretto was born in Venice and grew up under the shadow of Titian and in that shadow he lived and wrought to the end. Unsympathetic as were their personal relations, Tintoretto was influenced by Titian, by way either of attraction or of repulsion, in all that he did.

Veronese was not born in Venice and did not go there until he was twenty-seven years old. By that time he was a developed painter and had executed important works in both Verona and Mantua. Though undoubtedly influenced by Titian as were all painters at this time he was not under his spell and was in no sense his disciple.

Veronese received his early instruction in his native city and from masters of no great distinction, though probably competent instructors in the highly developed technique of the time. Coming to Venice in 1555 at a

time when Titian and Tintoretto were at the height of
their influence and creative activity, he seems always to
have worked in friendly relation with both but quite
independently. Since neither Titian nor Tintoretto were
noted for their amiability the friendly relations established by the newcomer and rival are much to his credit.

Veronese was fortunate in the time of his arrival.
The panoramic picture, always a favorite in Venice, was
developing new possibilities. It will be remembered
that Venetian art began with the execution of great
historic pictures in the Doge's Palace by foreign masters.
These were followed by others, both for the Doge's Palace
and for the *scuole grandi*, painted by the Bellini, father
and sons. Carpaccio spent most of his life upon similar
pictures for the lesser *scuole*. Giorgione and Titian had
made their contributions to the series. So far, however,
these pictures had been essentially secular in their use
and measurably so in their character. Both *scuole* and
state, of course, were deeply religious and miracles and
other religious elements entered into the subject matter
of their art which is to say that the difference between
secular and religious art was merely one of degree. But
after all there was a difference. These secular panoram-
ics do not deal with the scenes of the passion or with the
more sacred themes of Christianity generally. These
were reserved for the church.

But the church did not at first employ the large panoramic picture. In the church proper there was seldom a
place for it. The various altars, centers of devotion,
called for an object of devotion rather than for a story.
This was supplied at first by the small altarpiece, then
by the group altarpiece of John Bellini, and finally by
the vast creations of Titian such as the Assumption and
the Madonna of the Pesaro Family. Imposing as
these altarpieces became they were still quite unlike the
panoramic picture.

Gradually, however, the church and especially the monasteries adopted the prevailing fashion. If there was no room for a panoramic picture above the altar there was room in the ceiling, room in the sacristy, room especially in the refectory or dining room where appropriate incidents from the sacred story might be represented unto edification. The altarpiece of course came first but with the increase of luxury and the spirit of display it was only a question of time when art would fill these vacant spaces. That time had now come and in the enlarged program of art Tintoretto, Veronese, and many others found their opportunity.

Veronese was first employed to decorate the sacristy of the church of San Sebastiano, a commission which he fulfilled so acceptably that he was commissioned to decorate the church itself. This commission which was extended from time to time, occupied him intermittently for more than a decade and made the church his monument as it was later to become his burial place. His work here attracted attention and won the approval of the all potent Titian who recommended the painter to the service of the state, a service in which he was engaged at intervals until his death.

Veronese's work in San Sebastiano reveals him as both a developed and a highly creative painter. It is especially memorable for his great innovation in ceiling painting which revolutionized that branch of the art and was largely responsible for the popularity of painted ceilings in Venice in the period immediately following. The Renaissance was quite too realistic to be willing to use wall paintings upon a ceiling as the mediaeval artist had naïvely done. To represent standing figures in a horizontal position was obviously unnatural. It was Melozzo da Forli who first attempted to set his ceiling figures right by foreshortening them, a practice followed by Michelangelo on the lower slopes of the vault of the Sistine. On these lower slopes of vault and dome this was feasible since the wall inclined but moderately from the perpendicular and by skilful foreshortening figures could here be made to appear upright. But in the middle where the surface was essentially horizontal it was different. Here Michelangelo refused to attempt foreshortening, preferring the unnaturalness of the horizontal figure to the grotesqueness of the fully foreshortened figure. Correggio made the opposite choice in his celebrated dome of Parma. All are familiar with the remark of the bishop when he gazed upon the dangling legs of these fully foreshortened figures that they reminded him of a fricassee of frogs, a pleasantry from the sting of which the painter never recovered.

It was this problem that confronted Veronese as he was called upon to paint the ceilings of San Sebastiano and the Doge's Palace. The problem presented itself in its most difficult form, for the Venetian ceilings which the painter was called upon to decorate were not vaults or domes but perfectly horizontal surfaces. Veronese's solution of the problem is unique and, though open to the objections which hold against every scheme of overhead foreshortening it is the best that had yet been devised and must be recognized as stunningly effective. We are supposed to be standing in a lower or basement story and to be looking up, not at a flat ceiling, but at a large opening through which we get a view of an upper story much more splendid architecturally than our own. A balustrade surrounds the opening with people standing behind or leaning upon it while splendid columns and noble architecture rise around it. Assuming that we are standing at one end of the room we obtain a fairly extensive view of this splendid upper story and of the great event which is represented as there taking place.

The artist has only to assume a raised platform for his main characters to give the spectator a comparatively normal view of this upper story scene. The foreshortening required is moderate and the necessity for dangling

Fig. 97, Veronese, The Coronation of Esther. Venice, San Sebastiano.

legs is eliminated. Artificial and in some ways unplausible as this scheme undoubtedly was, it was so much superior to any other that it at once became the norm for Venetian ceiling painting. The whole idea of picture ceilings is questionable but if we are to have them this should perhaps be our choice.

The Coronation of Esther (Fig. 96) in San Sebastiano

is one of the earliest of Veronese's attempts in this line. Seen in reproduction the heavy foreshortening is unpleasant and inexplicable. But when we recall that the picture is to be seen over our heads it at once becomes intelligible. A similar foreshortening is seen in the numerous ceiling panels in the Sala del Collegio in the Doge's Palace and above all in the huge central panel in the ceiling of the Hall of the Great Council representing the Triumph of Venice (Fig. 97). The last may be taken as representing in the highest degree the artist's cleverness and the inherent difficulty and inadequacy of the whole Renaissance scheme of ceiling painting.

Aside from this special problem of location and its resulting adaptations these pictures do not differ essentially from the great wall paintings with which the painter's name is chiefly associated. It is remarkable, indeed, that these early works so nearly attain the standard of his fully developed art. So far as the works of his Venetian period are concerned the question of date is of little importance. The painter maintained throughout a high standard of technical excellence and a comparatively uniform style. We shall find it more profitable to consider his works in groups according to their character and function.

First may be mentioned the great altarpieces the tradition of which, based on Titian's epoch making creations, was still in force. Of these Veronese executed a number including the Marriage of Saint Catherine in the Venetian Church of that name, the Holy Family in the Venetian Academy, and the great triptych now in the Brera in Milan, not to mention examples from his earlier period. These altarpieces seem to have been too little considered in estimates of Veronese's art. If they are less characteristic of the painter than his great banquet scenes it is simply because they are free from his

Fig. 98, Veronese, The Triumph of Venice.   Venice, Doge's Palace.

Fig. 99, Veronese, Saints Gregory and
Jerome (detail of altarpiece). Milan, Brera.

more conspicuous faults. Though never spiritual, the artist in these altarpieces is at least dignified. The first two mentioned above are obviously reminiscent in their composition and structure of Titian's Madonna of the Pesaro Family, though not to be compared with it, we must admit, in spiritual nobility or even in the sensuous elements of art. The great triptych, however, a strange reversion to an obsolete and abandoned type, is unique among altarpieces of the period. With a central picture and two doors the artist has felt himself constrained to restore in essence the symmetrical composition which Titian, working under no such constraint, had been free to discard. In the center Saint Anthony Abbot sits upon a high throne with Saints Cornelius and Cyprian on either side something as Bellini would have arranged them. Like and yet wholly unlike as a moment's comparison with Bellini's triptych in the Frari will make clear. There is no sense here of a constrained or formal composition. A spirit of complete liberty dominates the whole and the grouping is merely a happy accident like any other. These central figures and even more the figures of Saint Gregory and Saint Jerome (Fig. 99) on the door to the left are without a rival in the art of Veronese, almost in the art of Titian himself. Rarely has the strength and dignity of noble manhood been so impressively expressed. When we add to this the artist's mastery of color here present at its best, we cannot withhold from this great work the title of masterpiece, possibly the masterpiece of all Veronese's work.

The transition from altarpiece to other religious pictures is a gradual one with numerous intermediate terms not easy to classify. Themes like the Finding of Moses and the Coronation of Esther have been mentioned. Essentially panoramic in character they differ

but little from such incident altarpieces as the Marriage
of Saint Catherine mentioned above. They were congenial themes to Veronese and illustrate perfectly those
characteristics which it will be our purpose later to note.
Less congenial and fortunately less common in his art
are the deeply emotional and tragic themes which form

Fig. 100, Veronese, Christ at Emmaus.   Paris, Louvre.

so large a part of Christian art.   His Calvary and Christ
at Emmaus (Fig. 100) both in the Louvre, are familiar
examples.   Most famous of all, however, and in a class
quite by themselves are his banquet scenes, ostensibly
religious subjects like the Marriage of Cana (Fig. 103)
and the Feast in the House of Levi, but in reality
scenes from contemporary Venetian life.   It is upon
these that he lavished his powers and by these that he
will always be known.

Ostensibly in a different class but essentially like the
above are his mythological pictures, especially those
in the Anticollegio of the Doge's Palace, one of which,
the Rape of Europa (Fig. 101), has acquired wide fame.

Here too we may mention his one great historical picture,
Alexander meeting the Family of Darius (Fig. 102),
now in London. A few portraits and miscellaneous
works of secondary importance must be added to make
this list complete.

Fig. 101, Veronese, Rape of Europa. Venice, Doge's Palace.

What are the general characteristics which these
numerous but closely related works reveal?

First of all, Veronese is a colorist. As a Venetian
painter of high rank this might be taken for granted but
it is true in quite an individual sense. Titian, as we have
seen, employed color always in subtle association with
shadow, holding the two in unfailing balance. Much of
the effect that we attribute to color in Titian's painting
is in fact due to shadow through whose aid he effects
his harmonies.

This association of color and shadow was largely dissolved by his successors. Tintoretto, we have seen, emphasized the shadow and exploited its possibilities, not to the disregard but certainly to the subordination of color, bright color being pretty much eliminated. His pictures impress us as somber.

Veronese made the opposite choice. He is fond of bright and clear color which he handles with masterly skill. Experts declare that his colors are studied not only individually but in their relation to one another as regards location, size, intensity, etc., precisely as Beethoven organizes sounds into a symphony. They confess their inability to analyse his compositions and we are left, as in so many other cases, to take it on faith. But the result seems to justify the theory for as a matter of pure color his compositions are certainly music.

But Veronese reduced shadow to its lowest terms. He of course understands the necessity of shadow for modeling and for the proper representation of objects in space and for this basic requirement he uses it with skill. But shadow as an element in itself, a thing that has moods and creates moods, a solvent and a temperer of color, of this he knows nothing. It follows inevitably that he can not render the more emotional themes. The mood, the sentiment of a Gray's Elegy cannot be invoked in noonday light. The proof lies not with Rembrandt and Tintoretto but with the twilight experiences of every one of us.

This is not saying that there are no art possibilities in pure color. Quite the contrary. What is meant is that color apart from shadow is ill suited to certain subjects, subjects very prominent in the Christian repertory, subjects which Veronese made no attempt to avoid. Compare his Calvary where bright colors and clear skies dominate a scene of which the more appreciative evangelist tells us that "there was darkness over the whole land." Compare his Christ at Emmaus in the Louvre with Titian's treatment of the same subject now hanging in the same room, or with Rembrandt's incomparable picture also in the Louvre. To Veronese's neglect of shadow as a medium of emotional expression is due in no small part his inadequacy as an interpreter of the spiritual. Or was it his inability to interpret the spiritual which led to his neglect of shadow?

Fig. 102, Veronese, Alexander Meeting the Family of Darius. London, National Gallery.

A second element of uniform excellence in Veronese's art is his splendid setting. It has been aptly pointed out that Veronese was the only great Venetian painter who was city born and bred. His landscape backgrounds, therefore, are always city landscapes, architecture and sky, to which we must add, however, an occasional decorative use of trees which is admirable and in its definite decorative purpose unique. In general, however, the background is of architecture and sky, each above all praise. No artist has suggested the illimitable range of space like Veronese. His architecture, too, is superb. It would be difficult to point out a building in Venice built in Veronese's time which is as fine as the architecture in his great pictures. It is practicable, too, and would seem to be quite worthy of the builder's consideration. This architecture is admirably disposed as a stage for his representations, a shallow stage for the performers, galleries and terraces for the lookers-on, and soaring colonnades to frame and bound it all. Neither Tintoretto nor Titian have anything to compare with this palatial setting. These backgrounds also furnished in their ivory tinted columns, their fleecy clouds and pale blue skies that pale, silvery tone which Veronese, following the tradition of his native city, sought as a foil to the clear colors of his central composition. This, it will be noted, was a distinct departure from Venetian tradition which in general preferred a dark background for its stronger notes of color. These pale, clear backgrounds are largely responsible for the cheerful appearance of Veronese's pictures. They of course excluded by their very nature the use of shadow environment.

The foregoing suggests another quality generally recognized in Veronese's art. In defiance of the usual rules his pictures must be accounted admirably decorative. They have not the flatness usually prescribed for decoration nor is there any of the line assimilation which is so marked a feature of mediaeval decoration. His modeling is high and attitudes are wholly spontaneous. But his figures are arranged in planes parallel to the wall and figures and setting alike seem to furnish a fitting termination of the room in which they are placed. Different, yet dictated by the same instinct is his treatment of foliage, not in masses as in the work of Titian and Giorgione, but in leafy patterns silhouetted against the sky. This was not quite his monopoly for Tintoretto gives us similar effects in some of his pictures in San Rocco and the leafy silhouette can be traced even in the work of Bellini. But Veronese seems more conscious of what he is doing and of his reason for doing it, his impulse toward decoration being less hindered than theirs owing to his subordination of shadow and use of pure color.

We must further recognize in Veronese a unique power to handle large groups with ease and with freedom alike from formality and disorder. His arrangements are unconventional but not confused. Everybody is comfortable. Nobody gets in anybody's way or makes an effort to get out of anybody's way. Nobody tries to be "proper" or yet to be "shocking." Yet it must be confessed that this ease tends constantly to become indecorus and betrays the artist into vulgar irrelevancy. Unconventionality becomes vulgar when in the Feast in the House of Levi one of the guests sits at the table wearing a slouch hat and another peers between two pillars picking his teeth with a fork. Conscious of his gift at handling crowds, he crowds the stage unnecessarily. Not only irrelevant personages but dogs, cats, and monkeys are conspicuously present. In the Feast in the House of Levi a dwarf in the foreground plays with a falcon and a large dog watches a cat under the table. Imagine a dog and cat incident in the Last Supper of Leonardo.

Peculiarly instructive in this connection is the comparison already suggested between Veronese's Christ at Emmaus and Rembrandt's incomparable treatment of the same theme. In Rembrandt's picture the mood of dropping day, the Saviour dimly outlined against the deepening shadows, the two disciples dumb and motionless in their amazement, the unconscious servant busy with his humble task, these unite to form a spiritual whole which is without a rival in its emotional appeal.

In contrast with this simple and consistent group Veronese introduces twenty-three figures not to mention dogs and other irrelevant objects. A meaningless group said to represent the artist's family, alike non-participant and uninteresting, occupy the right of the stage. Two little girls seated in front of the table in the center foreground play with a large dog, not forgetting meanwhile, that they are the center of attraction and careful of the spectator's attention. The Saviour — Veronese's finest study of the Christ — strikes an attitude and the two brawny disciples stretch out their arms in a wholly meaningless gesture. And full daylight, a seeming necessity of the artist's color scheme, is over it all.

A mere inventory like this is sufficient to show that the artist has not entered in the least into the spirit of his theme. To intrude a group of family portraits into a scene representing one of the most moving incidents in the life of our Lord is to say the least egregious bad taste. The objection is not urged in the name of religion. It would hold equally of a dignified secular subject. It holds of the monkey that burlesques the pathos of the meeting of Alexander with the Family of Darius. It is a question not of conventional sanctities but of fundamental integrity of theme.

There are those, to be sure, who set little store by this consideration. It is enough if figures are well grouped, drawing correct, and colors well chosen and harmonious. Similarly there are those to whom literature is only style and oratory a question of rhetoric. And there are times when art and literature are governed by these ideals. But the art which men have accounted great has not been born of these times or these ideals. Great themes greatly and sincerely expressed are its essence. When theme becomes pretext and art degenerates into form we have the decadence.

For the creation of ideal types Veronese was singularly lacking in creative imagination. Ideal figures are few in his pictures and lacking in both character and beauty. The Madonna with Saint Catherine, the Europa, the women in the Family of Darius, all are expressionless and characterless, mere lay figures for the display of the splendid costumes with which he so inappropriately adorns them. Failing the wonderful flesh tint of Titian they are lacking not only in sentiment but (to the writer's mind) in sensuous beauty as well. Peculiarly infelicitous are his ideal creations conceived for purposes of spiritual suggestion. The Annunciation, for example, conceived in the sensational manner with which Tintoretto has made us familiar, illustrates this infelicity. Fra Angelico and Carpaccio and even Titian may represent the angel as standing or kneeling, but for these moderns this is too tame. The celestial visitant must arrive by air and as unannounced and startlingly as possible. For no painter was this motive so unfortunate as for Veronese. Not only is he entirely lacking in dramatic faculty, but the excessive corporeality of his figures and their sensuous and unspiritual character completely unfits them for this delicate role. The massively built angel descends heavily into the presence of the buxom Madonna who greets his amazing announcement with the familiar signs of coquetry. No beauty of background or excellence of technique can redeem this travesty of a hallowed theme. Even more unsatisfactory is his conception of the Christ, perhaps the most meaningless and unspiritual in the whole range of Christian art. His practice of subordinating this figure, perhaps assigning him a place in the background of the picture, is quite pardonable in view of the total inadequacy of his conception.

In contrast with this feebleness of creative imagination Veronese had a rare gift for portraiture of a sort. He rarely painted individual portraits and his few ventures in this line were not notably successful. He had little ability to depict moods or to interpret personality, things requisite for individual portrait and for dramatic art. But he could paint a crowd and make each figure a portrait of great lifelikeness. This is a very different talent. Men in a crowd leave their subtleties, their moods, and in large measure their personalities at home. The writer is familiar with the looks of an audience from a lecture platform. They all look natural, quite like themselves in form and feature, but of that which they reveal in individual relations there is nothing. Paint them as they appear and you will have a satisfactory group portrait but not a group of satisfactory portraits.

It is thus that Veronese paints them. His canvases are crowded with the notables of his time, Venetian and foreign. In the Marriage of Cana the Venetian painters compose the orchestra, Titian playing the bass viol and Veronese himself, conspicuous in his light costume, playing the cello, while the guests at the table include all the reigning monarchs of Europe, even the Sultan of Turkey. In the Feast in the House of Levi, on the whole the finest of these great canvases, the artists are advanced to the position of guests. Michelangelo and Titian are given exactly equivalent positions near the two ends of the table while Veronese himself, now in the role of host, finds occasion to outline his splendid figure against one of the marble pillars of the hall. This portrait and the portrait of Titian — the latter worthy of the highest praise — are the high water mark of Veronese's art. Such pictures are historic documents of the highest interest, in the contemplation of which we are tempted to forget their inherent absurdities and vulgar irrelevancies.

These irrelevancies and vulgarities, however, did not pass unchallenged in the artist's own time. As Veronese painted one after another his great banquet

scenes these peculiarities steadily increased. The Feast
in the House of Levi as originally painted was much more
audacious than at present. In addition to the page, the
dwarf with his falcon, the cat and dog, and the man
picking his teeth there was a man bleeding at the nose and
a pair of soldiers in German costume half drunk and in

Fig. 103, Veronese, Marriage at Cana. Paris, Louvre.

most questionable attitudes. The picture was a plain
piece of bravado and the serious and the devout were
outraged by the liberties taken. The Inquisition, guardian of the sanctities, condemned the picture in 1573 and
haled the painter before its tribunal. They demanded
his reasons for these affronts to sacred tradition and to
the decencies of life. Why the dwarf, the drunken
soldiers, the man with the bleeding nose? Why the
dog in this sacred scene? Would not a figure of the
Magdalen have been more appropriate? The questions
as recorded in the church archives are interesting and in
spite of our difference of viewpoint it is difficult to deny

their validity. The painter's answers are more interesting than convincing. He seemed unable to get the point of his critics. These offensive persons and objects were parts of his composition and gave him the kind and amount of color that he wanted. The Magdalen would have been too large for the place and would not have fitted into his composition. But when the objections which he had nowise met were further urged he confessed frankly that he had never thought about those considerations, that he had intended no irreverence toward religion but had simply permitted himself, perhaps wrongfully, a certain amount of license such as is accorded to poets and fools. All this was probably true but it was a lame defense and was rightly so adjudged. The Inquisition, having regard to the contrite attitude of the painter and also, perhaps, to the very limited authority which it enjoyed in Venice, contented itself with the requirement that the painter should paint out some of the more objectionable features. The bleeding nose disappeared and the drunken soldiers became more sober and assumed a more seemly attitude. In view of the items that remain the Inquisition can hardly be said to have been intolerant. The changes required were not in the interest of dogma but of common decency. A nosebleed does not make art, no matter how well painted.

Veronese was a great painter but he lacked the high-mindedness that goes to the making of great art. His figures are splendid but they are lacking in thought and emotion, often even in good taste. His art, as we have already noted, is objective. The outward aspect of Venetian life he saw as few men have seen it and painted it as no other has painted it. But after all it was the outside and we want something more than the outside.

In contrast with all works here shown and in contradiction with all conclusions here reached stands one great

Fig. 104, Veronese, Vision of Saint Helena. London, National
Gallery.

picture, the Vision of Saint Helena (Fig. 104). Here is no banquet, no crowd, no dog, no monkey, no superfluity of splendor, no vacuity of mind or soul. A single figure exquisite in repose and mood, wholly free from self consciousness or dramatic pose, with a countenance suggestive of the things of the spirit, she calls us away from these days of sensationalism and display back to the sincere and soulful days. Here is all the facility and freedom of Titian and his followers with the simplicity and sincerity of Bellini. We like to believe that every artist at least once rises above himself and "puts on the glory." For Veronese this was that supreme occasion — unless, as some aver, the work is not his but another's. We fain would know to whom homage is due.

Veronese died in 1588 at the age of sixty, leaving the venerable Tintoretto, representative in a sense of an earlier generation, to carry on for a brief six years the great Venetian tradition. Neither had any immediate successors who demand our serious attention, though their influence is easily traceable in the century of mediocrity that followed. Gradually that influence is dissipated and in the mildly interesting pictures of Canaletto and Guardi, pictures of the city itself, its canals and landmarks, there is little to remind us that the painters are Venetian. And then, after the lapse of more than a century, the lamp of art flamed up again, clear and strong and utterly Venetian.

Giovanni Battista *Tiepolo was born in 1696. The name was one of the most distinguished in Venetian history but it is not clear that the painter was descended from the distinguished members of the family. If so, they were in fallen estate. There is much dispute as to the name of his teacher but the question is of little interest. He drew his inspiration and his real instruction

---

* Pronounced Tee-ay-po-lo.

Fig. 105, Tiepolo, Institution of the Rosary. Venice, Gesuati.

from the great painters, especially from Veronese, of whom he was an avowed follower. The kinship is very obvious in spite of the fact that Tiepolo is by no means a mere imitator and that in some respects he surpasses his model, particularly in ceiling painting which, it will be remembered, was a specialty of Veronese. His first great work in this line, following a desultory series of youthful works now difficult to trace, was begun in 1738, just a century and a half after the death of Veronese. This was a great ceiling decoration, the Institution of the Rosary (Fig. 105), in the Dominican Church of the Gesuati in Venice. It is based on the principle of Veronese's decorations, an apparent opening through the ceiling with soaring architecture around but with blue sky and clouds occupying much of the pictured space. Other ceiling commissions followed fast and the artist departed farther from the scheme of Veronese, depending less on architecture and giving more space to the pale blue sky with its flecks of cloud and a cherub or two birdlike and far away. There is an extraordinary cheerfulness and sense of light and space in these beautiful creations, unquestionably the most beautiful of all pictured ceilings that we possess. An Austrian bomb unfortunately destroyed one of the finest of these during the recent war and others are now in museums, on side walls, removed from their intended place and intelligible only by the aid of an informed imagination.

In the Church of the Gesuati, too, is one of the first of the considerable series of altarpieces in which Tiepolo's genius is not less distinctively displayed (Fig. 106). These altarpieces and indeed all his figure paintings, were profoundly influenced by a magnificent model, Christina, the daughter of a gondolier but a woman whose magnificent beauty and haughty bearing suggested the lineage of kings. She is described as of "a rare

Fig. 106, Tiepolo, Madonna with Saints. Venice, Gesuati.

perfection, large and svelte, with a queenly carriage, an exquisitely outlined profile, oval face, eyes of a Circassian — piquant, one could say, the neck of a swan, the hands of a patrician, form supple and full." How far Christina influenced the ideal of the painter and determined the character of his art it is difficult to say. It is probable that she merely embodied his ideal and helped him to express it, in itself a potent influence. Christina in the pictures in which she appears is not spiritual or gentle or lovable or sweet. She is simply stunning. She appears in many roles and with a certain amount of appropriate adaptation, but she is always Christina under the thinnest of disguises. Whatever her influence upon Tiepolo's art her co-operation became indispensable and constant. She followed him everywhere, even to Germany where he was occupied for some time, and to Spain where the last eight years of the artist's life were spent.

Though an avowed follower of Veronese, Tiepolo was an independent spirit and an original genius. In some important particulars he not only differs from Veronese but quite surpasses him. He has a vaster sweep, a more imposing conception. His architectural setting is less voluminous than that of Veronese but it is even more grandiose and splendid. He has none of Veronese's fondness for crowds, still less his inclination to form them of contemporary and irrelevant personages. His ideal, however formed, dominates his composition which is never vulgarized by portrait intrusions. Even his banquet scenes like that of Antony and Cleopatra are constructed with less than a dozen figures, attention being the better concentrated upon the two with whom we are concerned. But he shares with Veronese the love of brilliant costumes and splendid fabrics and his interpretation of the world in terms of color. His color is peculiarly bright and cheerful, a friend of the sunlight. No Venetian was more absolutely a painter than Tiepolo. It is not simply that he sees nature and discerns her artistic possibilities. He sees always her paintability, discarding all other possibilities. With him the painter's difficult art has become an instinct, compelling and unerring.

But Tiepolo's painting like Veronese's is objective. He is concerned with outward appearance far more than with inner spirit. Like all the artists of the period, too, his art is self conscious and theatrical. In this respect he is inferior to his great model. Veronese's art is objective but it is not theatrical. With rare exceptions his characters do not pose or act a conscious part to be seen of men. The same cannot be said of Tiepolo. His transcripts of nature are wholly delightful even if somewhat imaginative. His color harmonies are gorgeous bursts of music and the stamp of royalty is upon all he creates. But it is an age of pose, of stunning, theatrical effect, an age whose spirit we know so well in its many and diverse manifestations. It was a stunning climax upon which destiny rang down the curtain.